LEGENDS
of the
ALL
BLACKS

LEGENDS of the ALL BLACKS

with KEITH QUINN
edited by JOSEPH ROMANOS

the book of the series

Hodder Moa Beckett

FOR THE...
Football News
of the District, read the
KENTISH MERCURY.

Certified Weekly Sale 23,500.
Chief Offices, Greenwich, S.E.
Established 1832
Every Friday Morning—ONE PENNY.

Blackheath Fixture List.
FIRST FIFTEEN.

Date. 1905.	Club.	Ground.
Nov. 4	New Zealanders	Blackheath
" 11	Cambridge	Cambridge
" 18	Bristol	Bristol
" 25	Richmond	Blackheath
Dec. 2	Oxford	Oxford
" 2	England v New Zealand	London
" 9	Cardiff	Cardiff
" 16	Harlequins	Wandsworth
" 16	North v South	...
" 30	Marlboro' Nomads	Blackheath

GEORGE LEWIN,
ESTABLISHED 1869.
8, Crooked Lane, Cannon Street,
London Bridge, E.C.
Athletic Clothing Manufacturer and Club Color Specialist.

Outfitter by special appointment to the Anglo-Australian and South African Rugby Teams, also all the principal Rugby Clubs throughout the world. WRITE FOR ESTIMATES & SAMPLES.
G. LEWIN personally attends club meetings and gives estimates.
Telegraphic Address: LEOTADE, LONDON. Lieber's Code used.

RUGBY FOOTBALL UNION.
Blackheath Football Club,
RECTORY FIELD, BLACKHEATH.

BLACKHEATH v. NEW ZEALAND.
Saturday, November 4th, 1905.   Kick-off 3 p.m.

BLACKHEATH.

Back
H. Lee

Three-quarter-backs
W. H. Newton   B. Maclear   H. J. Anderson   S. F. Coopper

Half-backs
J. C. Joughin   C. G. Robson

B. C. Hartley   B. A. Hill   W. L. Rogers   C. J. Newbold
W. T. Cave   W. S. D. Craven   J. E. C. Partridge   C. G. Liddell

NEW ZEALAND.

D. Gallaher (Wing)   W. Johnston   C. Seeling   F. Glasgow
W. Cunningham   J. O'Sullivan   G. Tyler   S. Casey

Half-back
F. Roberts

Five-eighths
J. Hunter   W. Stead

Three-quarter-backs
D. McGregor   G. W. Smith   W. J. Wallace

Back
G. Gillett

Referee: Mr. P. COLES.   Touch Judges:

	Goals.	Tries.	Points.		Goals.	Tries.	Points.
BLACKHEATH—				NEW ZEALAND—			

RESULT—Won by New Zealanders 32 = Blackheath

JOHN PIGGOTT, Ltd. Football Outfitters, see advertisement inside.

ELLIMAN'S
ELIMINATING trials reduce the number of really safe and useful MASSAGE lubricants to one,
For the Relief of Aches and Pains as Rheumatism, Lumbago, Sprains, Bruises, Sore Throat from Cold, Cold at the Chest, Chronic Bronchitis, Neuralgia from Cold, Chilblains before broken, Cramp, Stiffness, Soreness of the Limbs after Cycling, Football, Rowing, Golf, etc.

MASSAGE with ELLIMAN'S Universal Embrocation is known to give best results. TO MASSAGE IN AN EFFICIENT way can easily be learned by obtaining a copy of the ELLIMAN R.E.P. BOOK (Rubbing eases pain Handbook). 36 Pages, Cloth Board Covers. Illustrated. FOUR WAYS of obtaining the Elliman R.E.P. Book:—1. Order of Elliman, Sons & Co., 1s. post free to all parts of the world (Foreign stamps accepted). 2. Upon terms to be found upon a label affixed to cartons containing 1s. 1½d., 2s. 9d., 4s. ELLIMAN'S UNIVERSAL EMBROCATION; 3. Order at the Railway Bookstalls, 1s. net. 4. Order of your Chemist, 1s. net.

ELLIMAN, SONS & CO., SLOUGH, ENGLAND.

Blackheath Fixture List.
"A" FIFTEEN.

Date. 1905.	Club.	Ground.
Nov. 4	R.M.C.	Sandhurst
" 11	R.M.A.	Blackheath
" 18	Rosslyn Park "A"	Blackheath
" 25	Richmond "A"	Richmond
Dec. 2	Haileybury College	Haileybury
" 9	Haileybury Wanderers	Blackheath
" 16	Royal Naval College	Blackheath
" 23	Rosslyn Park "A"	Blackheath
" 30	Harlequins "A"	Wandsworth
1906.		
Jan. 6	London Scottish "A"	Blackheath

WELCOME ALWAYS. KEEP IT HANDY
Grant's MORELLA Cherry Brandy.

In cold weather—invigorating and comforting.
In muggy weather—a perfect pick-me-up.
In hot weather—refreshing when mixed with aerated waters.

ALSO
Grant's Cherry Whisky.

ASK FOR GRANT'S AND DON'T BE PUT OFF WITH INFERIOR MAKES.

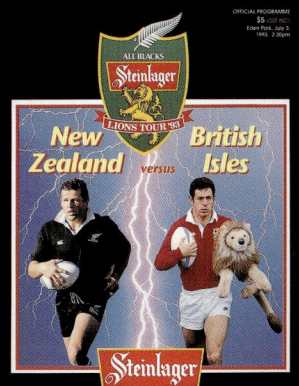

Acknowledgements

The photographs in this book came from several sources. Special thanks to Peter Bush, the doyen of New Zealand sports photographers, for the use of his superb images. "Bushy" trawled his vast collection of rugby pictures and came up with some absolute gems. The publisher also acknowledges the invaluable assistance of News Media (Auckland) and the New Zealand Rugby Museum (Palmerston North). Both organisations provided access to their extensive libraries and were always happy to co-operate. Thanks also to Photosport (Auckland), *The Sydney Morning Herald*, Keith Quinn and TV One.

ISBN 1–86958–777–4

© 1999 – Original text Television New Zealand Ltd
The moral rights of the author have been asserted

© 1999 – Design and format Hodder Moa Beckett Publishers Ltd

Published in 1999 by Hodder Moa Beckett Publishers Limited
[a member of the Hodder Headline Group]
4 Whetu Place, Mairangi Bay, Auckland, New Zealand

Designed and produced by Hodder Moa Beckett Publishers Limited

Printed by Toppan Printing Co. Ltd, Hong Kong
Film: Microdot, Auckland

All rights reserved. No part of this publication may be reproduced or transmitted in any form or by any means, electronic or mechanical, including photocopying, recording, or any information storage and retrieval system, without permission in writing from the publisher.

Contents

Introduction 9

South Africa
The Enduring Rivalry 13

The Captains
Taking the Lead 61

British Isles
Battling the Brits 87

The Coaches
Makers of Legends 123

Australia
Bledisloe Battles 153

Pro Rugby
Money, Money, Money 177

The Players
In Their Own Words 207

World Cup
Going for Gold 223

Editor's note

During his research for *Legends of the All Blacks*, Keith Quinn interviewed nearly 100 rugby players, coaches, officials, supporters and followers. The interviews often stretched for well over an hour. When they were transcribed, they comprised more than two million words. It was these transcripts which have formed the basis of this book. Naturally it was not practical to include each interview in its entirety, so an editing process was required. I have culled the transcripts for what I regard as fresh material, whether it is humorous, critical, praising, provocative, historical or analytical. Great care has been taken during the editing of the transcripts to ensure that quotes, while they may have been cut in length, remain accurate and in context.

Joseph Romanos
June, 1999

Introduction

This book is a spin-off from the TV One documentary series of the same name, which was filmed during the first six months of 1999. The idea came from TV One, which asked prominent Auckland documentary-maker Colin McRae to assemble a crew to film, edit and compile a six-part series that reflected the huge significance of All Black rugby to New Zealand this century. The wide brief of the series was to search out the many moments of the great and glorious in the history of All Black rugby and to assemble those stories in an order that would be appropriate as a build-up to the 1999 Rugby World Cup and the approaching millennium.

I was delighted to be asked to be the reporter-presenter for the series.

In January-February, 1999, I journeyed around the world for five weeks with Colin McRae, directors Chas Toogood and John Keir, and camera crew Dave Caldwell and Leighton Clapham, to talk to offshore All Blacks such as Don Clarke, now a resident of Johannesburg, and a large number of their most significant opponents. We then did a similar journey from north to south within New Zealand, eventually interviewing nearly 100 famous current and former All Blacks and their rivals, plus other important figures in the history of All Black rugby.

I was overwhelmed by the assignment, which has proven to be one of the most significant, enjoyable and stimulating of the 30-plus years I have had as a professional rugby writer and broadcaster.

The response of the people we interviewed was truly amazing. No-one turned us down, no-one asked for money in return for their recollections. I found the openness and frankness that you will read in these pages quite staggering. At the end of all the filming a possible conclusion to be drawn was that many of the former players chose our series as a place to get their best rugby memories "off their chests" as the millennium (and perhaps advancing age) approached. It goes without saying we are very grateful to them all.

It must also be said that space constraints prevented many eminently usable memories and stories from being aired in these pages (and in the television series). Only a fraction of the two million-plus words of transcripts of the interviews could be used in this book, which explains why some of the great rugby identities interviewed are not represented here.

For the off-shore part of the series, our crew went first to South Africa, then north through France, Belgium, Scotland, Ireland, Wales, England, Japan and Australia before returning home.

Legends of the All Blacks

Belgium, I hear you say? What role could that small country have played in the New Zealand rugby story? Well, on a personal note, it provided one of the two most moving moments of the tour. For me, to stand in the graveyard at a First World War cemetery at Poperinghe in Belgium and film at the graveside of Dave Gallaher, the man who captained the first team to be known as the All Blacks, was the rugby equivalent of worshipping at the holiest of sporting shrines. And to stand at the graveside of the great George Nepia in the remote East Coast area of New Zealand's North Island to commune with George's family and whanau was the other. Those were truly memorable days.

We met and talked with a myriad of test players – some of them all-time greats – Eric Tindill, Gareth Edwards, Robbie Deans, Colin Meads, Andy Irvine, Billy Bush, Sir Brian Lochore, Cliff Morgan, Sir Wilson Whineray, Wayne Shelford, Bryan Williams, Blair Furlong, Gavin Hastings, Neil Thimbleby, Sid Going, Mark Ella, Waka Nathan, Bruce Robertson, Okey Geffin, Wynand Claassen, Grahame Thorne, Fergie McCormick, John Eales, Jeff Wilson, Louis Babrow, Jonah Lomu, Nick Farr-Jones, Graham Williams, Andy Dalton, Will Carling, Josh Kronfeld, Andy Leslie, David Campese, Ross Brown, Tiny White, Ray Gravell, Kevin Skinner, Andrew McCormick, Pierre Albaladejo, Ian Kirkpatrick (both the New Zealand and South African players of that name), Naas Botha, Graham Mourie, Jaap Bekker, Ken Catchpole, Gary Whetton, George Gregan, Sean Fitzpatrick, Phil Kearns, David Kirk, John Gainsford, Taine Randell, Des Connor and Grant Fox. What a privilege it was to be in their company.

Equally helpful were a vast number of coaches, selectors, referees, administrators and historians, some of whom have also been fine test players. I thank most sincerely John Hart, John Connolly, Laurie Mains, Bob Templeton, Alex Wyllie, Alan Jones, Fred Allen, Bob Dwyer, Earle Kirton, Ian McIntosh, Eddie Tonks, Graham Henry, Clive Norling, Warren Gatland, Stephen Baines, John Mitchell and JJ Stewart. What a lot of wisdom and wit they provided us with.

Within the hundreds of hours of videotape we collected were many stories I for one had never heard before. To learn that members of the 1956 Springboks plotted before a test to "get" a famous All Black, no matter what, was a total shock, as was the assertion by the 1976 All Black Kit Fawcett that he had been seriously misquoted in the newspapers over his infamous "We'll score more off the field than on" story. Welshman Gareth Edwards delighted us when he told of the time an All Black, in the middle of a test, invited him to shelter "out of harm's way" under the New Zealander's body at the bottom of a ruck. When the All Black concerned, Graham Williams, laughingly confirmed that yarn, the true spirit of rugby in the "old days" emerged.

Before we began our interviews, we pinpointed particular stories we wanted to highlight. The tragic incident involving Danny Hearn and Ian MacRae, in which Hearn was paralysed for life after tackling MacRae,

Introduction

Keith Quinn at the cemetery where Dave Gallaher is buried, Poperinghe, Belgium.

proved to be a poignant story, but one which also exemplified the camaraderie that exists in international rugby.

We dealt with Newport's upset victory over the 1963 All Blacks and Stuart Watkins, Brian Price, Dai Watkins, Alan Thomas and Dick Uzzell, the man who drop-kicked the famous match-winning goal, were more than willing to relive that great day. Similar stories were told when some of the Munster team of 1978 gathered to tell us about the time their unfancied side upset Graham Mourie's All Blacks. Moss Keane, Brendan Foley and Tom Kiernan obviously retain vivid memories of the greatest day in Munster rugby history.

Brian Muller, better known in New Zealand by his nickname of Jazz, has, as he says, lived a fairly reclusive life since he closed his All Black career in 1971. He was not really very keen to be interviewed or filmed, but eventually consented, and he gave us a valuable insight into what being an All Black can mean to a person.

Some of the leading figures in the rugby media around the world also offered their assistance and I would like to thank Peter Bush, John Reason, Bill McLaren, Paul Dobson, Tony Lee, Pierre Salviac, Peter FitzSimons and Spiro Zavos.

One thing which astounded me, and which I have to say is different in the game today, was the jocular way past All Blacks now refer to the violence which existed on the rugby field in their days, and which they apparently took part in.

On a more serious note, you will find in these pages fresh details which have emerged over matters like the rebel Cavaliers tour of 1986 and the 1995 attempt by the World Rugby Corporation to take the game from its traditional amateur structure and make it a professional sport. I believe we have finally unearthed the true reason that the ambitious WRC plan did not proceed in 1995, and it is a startling revelation, as I'm sure you'll agree when you read that section in these pages.

From both sides of the principals of that "rugby war", we spoke to men like Jock Hobbs, Richie Guy, Andy Haden, Ross Turnbull, Geoff Levy, Louis Luyt and Francois Pienaar. Their summaries of various events proved crucial to the full story of the All Blacks this century.

In this wonderful experience at attempting to capture the images of the television series and the words of this book, there are a number of people who worked tirelessly behind the scenes. The aforementioned TV One crew

Legends of the All Blacks

travelled amicably together around the globe and made the whole project a great deal of fun, as well as professionally fulfilling. Also to be thanked are the television production crew at home in Auckland. They include TV One General Manager Shaun Brown, who gave us the overall production approval, and the people who laid the ground for their crew's arrangements – Margot McRae, Jill Bailey, Diane Revell and Anthony Muru.

Leon Hagen, with his assistant Leslie Geza, provided the excellent camerawork in South Africa, and Tim Mason did similar outstanding work in Australia. Others giving us assistance at particular times included Alan Trotter in Durban, Robyn Murray and Muff Scobbie in Scotland and Dave Priestman in Dublin.

I would also like to acknowledge Kiwi Rowlands (George Nepia's daughter), Brian and Doug Clarke of the Waikato, Australian poet Peter Fenton and Ian MacRae's wife Marilyn. Like so many people around the world, they could not have been more helpful.

Concerning the production of this book, Joseph Romanos of Wellington has done a superb job in breaking down the mountain of words from the transcripts into the most readable and significant quotes. This he achieved in an absolute minimal time in his usual highly-professional manner. His ability to spot the most interesting quotes and new developments in stories is a major reason why this book is such compelling reading. The transcripts were proved for him by Jan Young and Fay Roozendaal, who, if they had just a passing interest in rugby at the start of the project, must surely now have an in-depth knowledge of many aspects of New Zealand rugby this century.

Several of New Zealand's leading sports journalists wrote substantial introductions to the chapters in this book. Any book which includes the writing of Ron Palenski, Phil Gifford, Lindsay Knight, Bob Howitt and Joseph Romanos cannot but be considerably enhanced. Thanks also go to Warren Adler of Hodder Moa Beckett, who was the overall book producer and who was also responsible for picture research.

Keith Quinn
June, 1999

South Africa

The Enduring Rivalry

By Bob Howitt

Winning the World Cup at Eden Park in 1987 might, on a planetary scale, rank as New Zealand rugby's greatest achievement. But for New Zealand's true rugby aficionados, the greatest satisfaction has unquestionably come from the series victories over the Springboks, 40 years apart, in New Zealand in 1956 and in South Africa in 1996.

The reason is obvious: throughout the 20th century New Zealand and South Africa have consistently been the two strongest and best rugby nations in the world. Nothing stirs sports followers in the two separated lands quite like a contest between the All Blacks and the Springboks. No wonder esteemed South African writer Paul Dobson chose the title *Rugby's Greatest Rivalry* when in 1995 he chronicled a history of contests between the two nations. He quotes Boy Louw, one of the toughest and best Springboks, as saying in the dressing room before the 1949 test series kicked off: "When South Africa plays New Zealand, consider your country at war."

The rivalry certainly approximated war when the Springboks came to New Zealand in 1956 to defend a cherished record. Not only had the mighty men of the veldt not lost a series in their entire history, but more pertinently they had delivered a humiliating 4-0 whitewash to Fred Allen's New Zealand team in 1949. They'd also claimed the series in New Zealand in 1937. No other nation had so belittled the All Blacks. New Zealanders wanted revenge.

In his book *Winters of Revenge*, Spiro Zavos describes the mood in New Zealand in 1956: "A type of crusading fever swept the country as the Springboks made their triumphant way through Australia, edging ever closer to New Zealand. Old-timers emerged to give warnings about how tough, rough, nasty, shrewd and overpowering the South Africans were likely to be. The atmosphere when the team finally landed in New Zealand resembled that of France when the first German troops stepped foot on its soil in 1940. There was fear, loathing for past humiliations, anxiety, awe, a fierce desire for revenge and, above all, a determination to win at all costs."

South African Fred Labuschagne, in *Goodbye Newlands, Farewell Eden Park*, says the South Africans discovered upon their arrival in 1956 that "behind the smiling faces, the back-slapping and the open-handed hospitality there lurked a fanatical resolve to beat the Springboks which,

Legends of the All Blacks

as events proved, bordered on hatred".

There has never been a series quite like 1956. For New Zealand, the stakes were so high. Rugby's Goliath had to be felled. Some of the All Blacks who participated in the series recall almost with awe the intensity of the build-up. Tiny White, the great Poverty Bay lock, remembers the earth-shattering team talk before the first test. "I thought, 'Wow, what's the game coming to?' We were virtually told that New Zealand would be struck off the map if we lost to the Boks."

Ross Brown, who played three of the tests at centre and one at first-five, says he wouldn't have wanted to go through that series again. "It went beyond sport — we were playing for national prestige. It honestly took me three months to recover. I didn't sleep properly for three months, those tests had upset me so much."

History shows that the Springboks of 1956 were captained by Basie Viviers. What is little known, however, is that Viviers owed his selection, and the leadership, to a punch thrown in anger in a hotel in Cape Town by the man who should have captained the team, Salty du Randt.

Du Randt, who had been the vice-captain against the British Isles in 1955 and who was an uncompromising forward, was the natural successor following Stephen Fry's retirement as the great tour of New Zealand approached. But after du Randt's team was defeated by Jan Pickard's unfancied fifteen in a trial match at Cape Town, there ensued a sensational incident at a hotel that evening. Du Randt, obviously piqued that his side had lost, got into an argument with Pickard and knocked him down with a hefty punch. Retribution was swift — not from Pickard, but from South Africa's rugby president Danie Craven, who was to manage the team to New Zealand. Du Randt was made to apologise the next day — to all 120 trialists and even to the media.

With du Randt suddenly unacceptable as a captain, the South African selectors did an unbelievable thing — they decided to drop one of the fullbacks already selected to tour and bring in Basie Viviers in his place. And they made him captain. Viviers, a Springbok last in 1952, had never played in a test and, until then, had never seriously challenged for a place in the touring party. When the side was announced with Viviers as skipper, South Africa was stunned. No player in the touring party ever found out what the true story was behind Viviers' selection. It was years later before the truth came out.

Similar drama was to unfold in New Zealand after the All Blacks lost the second test in wintry conditions at Athletic Park. The New Zealanders, captained from halfback by Pat Vincent, had delighted the nation by winning the opening test of the series at Carisbrook, thanks to a sensational intercept try by Ron Jarden.

But when the Springboks levelled the series with an 8-3 victory at Wellington, the nation was stunned. Serious deficiencies in the All Black

South Africa

front row had been exposed by the Springbok iron men, Jaap Bekker, in particular, and Chris Koch. They had forced Mark Irwin to retire injured at Dunedin and had also effectively destroyed his replacement Frank McAtamney in Wellington. Forward supremacy was imperative if the All Blacks were to finally overcome the Springbok juggernaut. But how to achieve this?

Tom Pearce, an outspoken national administrator from Auckland, knew what was required. He'd seen the impact the big-booting young fullback Don Clarke had made as Waikato brought down the Springboks in the tour opener. And Pearce, a fair sort of pugilist himself, knew that only a front rower of the stature of Kevin Skinner, a former New Zealand amateur heavyweight boxing champion, could sort out the awesome Springbok front row.

Pearce called an emergency meeting of the NZRFU council in Wellington, in the wake of the test defeat. Never before, and certainly not since, has the ruling rugby body been brought together to issue instructions to the selectors. But, then again, there's never been an administrator like Tom Pearce. He could be fearsomely persuasive.

Given the message by the council, and having already inquired of Skinner whether he would be available to play in the series, the selectors made four significant changes in the pack, bringing in three of the most ruthless forwards of their time – Skinner (now 28, who had been persuaded to come out of retirement), Peter Jones and Tiny Hill – along with hooker Ron Hemi. At fullback was the player who would become known as "The Boot" and who would rewrite the record books, Don Clarke. And at halfback, replacing the captain, was Ponty Reid, another hero of Waikato's win. At 5ft 3in and 9st 7lb, he rates as perhaps the smallest individual to pull on the All Black jersey.

If there's one match which has etched itself into New Zealand rugby folklore, it's the third test of that 1956 series, played in front of more than 50,000 frenzied fans at Lancaster Park. Two players wielded a massive influence on proceedings, one with his boot, the other with his fist. Within three minutes of kick-off Don Clarke landed a massive penalty goal, the first of the 781 points he would accumulate for the All Blacks. He would go on to achieve legendary status.

Clarke's achievements were there for all to see. Not so obvious to

Athletic Park, 1956 – not a spare seat in the house.

the masses was the sorting out that was going on among the front-rowers. Even before Clarke had slotted his first goal, the first (telling) punch had been landed, by Skinner on Koch's nose. After halftime, Skinner swapped sides to deal with Bekker. South Africans later claimed it was pure intimidation. Fred Labuschagne wrote: "Long after the kicking exploits of Don Clarke and the rhino-like charges of Peter Jones are forgotten, South Africans will recall the flying fists of the former heavyweight boxing champion, Kevin Skinner."

Who better to put the record straight than Skinner himself? He objects to the phrase "flying fists" and says much of what happened that day has been exaggerated.

Skinner, ostensibly retired, had got caught up in the rugby fever that surrounded the Springbok tour and had resumed training, so when the selectors approached him about playing at Christchurch, he was down to 14st, the lightest he'd ever been. He says that when the All Blacks assembled in Christchurch, he couldn't believe the atmosphere. "I likened it later to a training camp for kamikaze pilots. We were told we had to win for the sake of New Zealand rugby. There seemed to exist a feeling that if the All Blacks lost the third test, the world would collapse."

He found the Springbok front-rowers had been built up as larger than life. "I talked to Bob Duff and Tiny White and asked what had been going on. They said they were being intimidated. 'Come on,' I asked. 'Guys like you intimidated?' These were the same guys I had opposed in South Africa in 1949. They were big and strong, but no better than us. However, they were resorting to gamesmanship in a big way. So we would call their bluff. It was in the lineouts they were unsettling the All Blacks by coming through and kicking the ball away from the halfback. I determined if the referee wasn't going to stop them, I would."

At the first lineout at Lancaster Park, Koch advanced on to the New Zealand side. "That'll be the last time you do that, Chris," said Skinner. Second lineout, Koch came through again. Wallop – Skinner hit him.

"I'd have been a mug to have missed," says Skinner. "These guys were bigger and stronger than me. My attitude was that if there's a donnybrook, let's sort it out here in front of the referee. The Boks didn't come through the lineout again!"

At halftime, Ian Clarke, assigned to mark Bekker, asked Skinner if he would mind swapping sides. "It was an understandable request," says Skinner, "because Bekker was the sort of guy who liked to throw his weight around and work on you. It could get tiring after forty minutes. So we swapped." Immediately play resumed, Bekker started trying to "pop" Skinner, dropping his shoulder and generally making a nuisance of himself. So Skinner hit him.

"It led to a scuffle which was soon sorted out," says Skinner, "and that was that. We had found in 1949 that the Boks would always try you on. If you

South Africa

didn't back away, they settled down and played rugby. Those were the only two incidents in that third test, but from what has been written since, you would have thought the fighting lasted the entire 80 minutes!"

The All Blacks won that third test in 1956 17-10, then clinched the series at Eden Park through a mix of goals by Don Clarke and a wonderful, stampeding try by Peter Jones, a happening that sent the crowd of 61,240 (many of whom had slept out all night to secure vantage points) into raptures. The invincibility of the Springboks had finally been shattered.

Two succinct comments made to the admiring crowd that gathered in front of the main grandstand after the final whistle are well remembered.

Referee Bill Fright sorts out an altercation between Kevin Skinner (13) and Jaap Bekker.

Said Springbok manager Danie Craven: "It's all yours New Zealand."

Said try-scoring hero Peter Jones: "I don't know about you, but I'm absolutely buggered."

Sean Fitzpatrick didn't use Peter Jones' words, but that's exactly how he felt 40 years on, after his All Black team had held on under the severest pressure to defeat the Springboks at Loftus Versfeld in Pretoria in 1996 to secure a famous first series win on South African soil.

Fitzpatrick had briefly contemplated retirement 14 months earlier when the disappointment of losing the World Cup final to South Africa at Ellis Park had threatened to overwhelm the New Zealanders. "Everyone was shattered at the final whistle," recalls Fitzpatrick, after the Springboks had claimed victory in extra time through a dropped goal by Joel Stransky. "It was horrible – you just didn't know what to do."

But when he was making his speech at the dinner in Johannesburg that evening, Fitzpatrick knew within himself that there was unfinished business in South Africa. He told the gathering that, despite the loss in the World Cup final, this All Black team would go on to become one of the great New Zealand teams. He would make the observation later that, in hindsight, the players would feel that losing the final was the best thing for them, that they weren't yet ready to take on the mantle of world champions.

The 1996 season, when John Hart supplanted Laurie Mains as All Black coach, was remarkable for the fact that the All Blacks and the Springboks played each other five times. The newly-instituted Tri-Nations championship pitted them against each other at Christchurch and Cape Town. Then there followed a three-test series in South Africa.

New Zealand had journeyed to the republic full of optimism on five previous occasions for full series – in 1928, 1949, 1960, 1970 and 1976, only to return home every time demoralised. There always seemed to be valid excuses for the All Blacks not winning, South African referees and the altitude prominent among them.

This time the referees were neutral, the touring party numbered 36 – freeing the test players from midweek commitments – and with experience, through the Super 10 and Super 12 competitions, of regularly playing at stadiums like Ellis Park and Loftus Versfeld, altitude was no longer considered such a handicap for New Zealanders.

On those five previous tours New Zealand had never won a first test. So a victory at King's Park in Durban was imperative if the men in black were to create history. Psychologically, they were primed, having won at Christchurch (owing to Andrew Mehrtens' golden boot) and at Cape Town (where they came storming back from a 12-point deficit).

Fitzpatrick created a remarkable record at Durban, becoming rugby's most capped forward. It was his 81st appearance, one better than the mark set by the great Irish and Lions lock Willie John McBride.

If Fitzpatrick, the player South Africans loved to hate, was the sentimental star at Durban, Zinzan Brooke was unquestionably the player of the game as the All Blacks carved out a 23-19 victory. Brooke executed countless thumping tackles, provided a deft flick-on pass that created a try for Christian Cullen and, fittingly, scored the cruncher himself. The Springboks had been beaten on one of their luckiest grounds. They had lost only once in 15 tests in Durban – to Australia, way back in 1933.

The All Blacks were within sight of glory, but the greatest challenge lay a week away at Pretoria. The All Blacks, who were starting to feel the effects of a long, demanding season, didn't want to go on to Ellis Park with the series still alive.

New Zealand made the running at Pretoria and opened up a 24-11 advantage, the result of three brilliantly-taken tries, two of them to Jeff Wilson. Those who thought the series was in the bag reckoned without the fighting qualities of the South Africans and underestimated the debilitating effect altitude and heat – it was 25 degrees Celsius in the stadium – can have on touring teams.

The All Blacks were playing almost by remote control in the third quarter when the Springboks launched their telling counter-offensive. In the space of three minutes the Springboks stunned the All Blacks with two tries. Two conversions and the Boks would have been in front, but Joel Stransky, the Rainbow Nation's superstar at the World Cup, was enduring kicking woes and struck the upright with the second kick, leaving the All Blacks ahead, 24-23.

Come in two heroes, one predictable, the other unlikely – Zinzan Brooke and Jon Preston. Preston joined the action when Simon Culhane broke his wrist and in double-quick time landed two crucial penalty goals,

South Africa

Zinzan Brooke – bloodied warrior.

one of them from halfway. But still the Springboks stayed in touch. Zinny, ever the man for the moment, then drop-kicked a goal to restore New Zealand's seven-point advantage.

Three minutes remained. For Fitzpatrick and his troops, knowing a converted try by the South Africans would keep the series alive, those three minutes seemed an eternity. Not wanting to become the first South African team to concede a series defeat at home to their traditional rivals, the Springboks threw everything into those final hectic moments. They drove at the New Zealanders from lineouts, from scrums, from tap penalties. The defence was resolute, but how long could it last?

Fitzpatrick describes the last, desperate assault upon the New Zealand line. "When I saw the Springboks readying for one last tap penalty," he says, "I wondered if collectively we had enough energy left to stop them. It was the most physically sapping game in which I have ever been involved."

Stop them they did, and then came the sweetest sound in the world, French referee Didier Mene blowing for full time.

Brooke was one of the few All Black forwards with enough energy to stand, let alone throw his arms in the air. Most of the others were strewn on the turf, near exhaustion, their energies entirely spent. Fitzpatrick took almost a minute to get to his feet. He had played himself to a standstill. In the grandstand the reserves, in their elation, broke into a haka. John Hart hugged his players. They had achieved a great and famous victory, not only for themselves but for all the All Blacks who had toured South Africa before.

There has always existed a special bond between New Zealand and South Africa. The truth is that matches between the two nations are the real tests of rugby, nerve, sinew and skill. How appropriate then that after 67 years of the most intense rivalry the record should stand at 24 victories each with three tests drawn.

While the record books will show New Zealand-South African rugby rivalry began at Carisbrook in August 1921, rugby contact between the two countries stretches back a lot further than that, to the Boer War at the turn of the century.

In the first war that New Zealanders fought abroad, they went to South Africa. Among the Kiwi soldiers were Dave Gallaher, who would captain the 1905 Originals to Britain, and Bunny Abbott, who would also tour with that team. Another was William Hardham, the only New Zealander to be awarded the Victoria Cross in the Boer War. Hardham played 53 games for Wellington, his name being perpetuated by the Hardham Cup, which is still played for in the Wellington senior club competition. It is claimed that Bunny Abbott learned to play rugby during the Boer War.

During the war there was almost a truce for a rugby match. The Boers and the British actually agreed to a cease-fire on April 29, 1902, near Okiep, but there was a skirmish on the 28th and the match did not happen. But that year Corporal Dave Gallaher led a team of New Zealand soldiers against a South African team in Johannesburg, the New Zealand soldiers winning. That was the first real match between teams representing New Zealand and South Africa.

At the conclusion of the war, while peace terms and demobilisation were being sorted out, three clubs of New Zealanders were established. The one in Durban was hugely successful and was instrumental in the foundation of the Durban Rugby Sub-Union. Its players, not surprisingly, wore black jerseys with a silver fern on the breast, their patron being none less than Richard Seddon, the Prime Minister of New Zealand.

That it was almost 20 years before New Zealand and South Africa played their first test wasn't for want of endeavour. The South African Board invited New Zealand to play matches on their way to Great Britain for the great tour of 1905-06, but it wasn't possible because the All Blacks were sailing around Cape Horn not the Cape of Good Hope and were returning via New York.

New Zealand, in turn, invited the Springboks to undertake a tour of 10 or 12 matches in 1907, but the South African board declined and also flagged away a further invitation in 1912. South African officials regarded the invitation as a compliment but said it would take too long to organise finances and the tour would interfere with the planned Currie Cup tournament. Yet another invitation was declined for 1914, for the same reasons, with the South African board adding that there was a danger of over-doing tours. What would they make of events in the 1990s!

It took the First World War to get the New Zealanders and South Africans operating together again.

Immediately following the war there was an inter-services tournament in England (in March, 1919) with the King's Cup at stake, in essence the first World Cup. Taking part were the Mother Country, the Royal Air Force, the Australian Imperial Forces, the Canadian Expeditionary Force, New Zealand Services and South African Forces. New Zealand was the strongest side, beating South Africa 14-5 at Twickenham and losing only to Australia. The decider was between the Mother Country and New Zealand, which New Zealand won 9-3.

Putting the chance of a rugby tour above an immediate return home, the New Zealanders went on an odyssey through South Africa, upping the ranks of the tourists so there were no privates in the touring party. The initiative for the tour had come from the Transvaal Rugby Union. The New Zealand servicemen played 15 matches, winning 11, drawing one and losing to Western Province Universities, Griqualand West and Western Province. Although the tour was a huge success and produced a surplus of one thousand pounds for the South African Rugby Union, the New Zealanders battled to pay their way. They were saved when an ex-New Zealander, making his living in South Africa as a jockey, gave them useful tips at the races!

Seventeen of the tourists had played for or would represent the All Blacks, including the captain Charles Brown. Several played tests against the 1921 Springboks – Percy Storey, Moke Belliss, Jim Moffitt, Dick Fogarty, Alf West and Bill Fea.

The stage was set in 1919 for the real rugby tests. By that time, South Africa and New Zealand were clearly the top rugby nations of the world, both having swept successfully through Great Britain.

And so, finally, in 1921 the great rivalry commenced with the Springboks touring New Zealand. In those far-off days before air flights revolutionised international travel, a journey from South Africa to New Zealand was a monumental event. Those first Springboks left Cape Town early in May on the steam ship *Aeneas*, stopping off in Australia to play five matches, and did not return home until November – six months later!

The most notorious match of the 1921 tour was the South Africa v New Zealand Maoris clash at Napier. Some of the South Africans, and accompanying journalist Charles Blackett, resented the visitors being matched with dark-skinned players and became annoyed when spectators supported the Maori team.

The trailblazing South African side featured no fewer than five players named Morkel and was captained by Theo Pienaar. Remarkably, Pienaar did not feature in the test series and, in fact, never did win an international cap. In the tests, the tourists were captained from No 8 by Boy Morkel, aged 35.

Although the All Blacks had proven themselves masters of rugby, particularly on the famous 1905 tour of the UK, the Boks were regarded with awe and billed as specimens of incredible physical proportions. We can

Legends of the All Blacks

laugh at New Zealand's apprehension now because that Springbok team was the smallest to represent South Africa anywhere. The forwards averaged only 5ft 11in and 85kg. They would be dwarfed by both countries' colts teams today.

Prop Frank Mellish was unique. Having stayed on in Britain after the war, he played for England, then hot-footed it back to South Africa to qualify for the tour. He ranks as the only individual to play international rugby for two major nations in the same year. Later he became chairman of selectors and managed the great 1951-52 Springboks to Britain.

Internal travel was arduous in 1921. The team travelled overnight by train from Auckland to Wanganui, arriving mid-morning to play that afternoon against the Wanganui representative team. They won their opener 11-6, but quickly appreciated that there would be no easy contests in New Zealand.

To get from Wellington to Greymouth, they sailed overnight in the inter-island steamer *Maori*. It was an eventful voyage as a storm raged through Cook Strait. There was a great deal of seasickness and Royal Morkel's desperate cries earned him the nickname of Mama! The queasy set of Springboks then journeyed west by train to Arthur's Pass before transferring to a horse bus to cross the Alps and back into another train for the final leg. It took them from Saturday night to Tuesday morning to get to Greymouth!

New Zealand opponents of the South Africans were intrigued that the captain Pienaar dispensed his instructions in Afrikaans, or Dutch, as the press referred to it at the time. It inspired a cartoonist to produce a drawing showing an All Black leaning disconsolately against the goal posts, scratching his head. The caption read: "The rules will have to be amended to allow the All Blacks to take a Dutch dictionary on to the field."

Carisbrook was the venue for the first test. Because of the war, the All Blacks hadn't played a test since 1914 although they had undertaken a tour of Australia in 1920.

In the front row for the All Blacks was Ned Hughes of Wellington, aged 40 and playing his first test in 13 years. He remains the oldest player to represent New Zealand. Captaining the side from centre in his test debut was George Aitken, a surprise as he did not captain Wellington. The other quirky feature about the All Blacks as they ran on to Carisbrook on 13 August was that they carried letters of the alphabet on their backs, not numbers. This was to thwart pirate programme-sellers.

Although the honour of scoring the first try in clashes between the two countries went to Springbok winger Attie van Heerden, the All Blacks, to the delight of the 25,000 spectators who packed Carisbrook to capacity, scored three tries and won 13-5. One of New Zealand's tries was an astonishing effort by winger Jack Steel. Thrown a hasty pass, he trapped the ball with his left hand behind his back. This didn't stop him beating his marker or the fullback. As he sprinted away to the goal line, he finally managed to manoeuvre the ball forward to his arms so he could force it behind the posts!

South Africa

The Springboks hit back to win the second test, in front of 40,000 spectators at Eden Park, creating a winner-take-all setting for the finale at Athletic Park. Unfortunately, after weeks of fine weather, it began raining in the capital on the Friday night and poured throughout Saturday. The field became a quagmire and despite the best intentions of both sides, the game finished in a 0-0 draw. The battle for world rugby supremacy remained unresolved.

There was still not be a clear-cut champion after the next series – in South Africa in 1928. This time the great rivals would square the tests 2-2.

After the stunning success of the Invincibles in Britain, Ireland and France in 1924-25, New Zealanders anticipated further triumphs. But, as with all New Zealand touring teams to South Africa, they found test success damnably hard to come by.

There were, of course, extenuating circumstances. Maoris were not acceptable to the South African authorities, which didn't cause any great outrage then. But in despatching a sanitised team, the All Blacks were without two of their outstanding Invincibles, fullback George Nepia and halfback Jimmy Mill. They were also missing the mercurial midfielder Bert Cooke, whose late withdrawal, for business reasons, came as a huge shock.

Maurice Brownlie, the great Hawke's Bay loose forward, captained the touring party, but it was one of the great mysteries why the vice-captain Mark Nicholls, a proven tactician, was omitted from the top line-up until the fourth and final test when his clever play helped New Zealand achieve a famous victory and square the series. Nicholls himself later claimed he was the victim of a South Island clique.

Maurice Brownlie

The South Africans didn't hesitate to select at flyhalf Bennie Osler, whose cultured boot wielded a major influence on the series. In the first test at Durban, when the All Blacks suffered a humbling 17-0 defeat, Osler landed two dropped goals (in those days worth four points each) and two penalty goals. Mark Nicholls wrote in his book *The All Blacks in Springbokland* that Osler was the hero of the day, "his kicking being magnificent and his tactics correct. To my mind, he was justified in kicking for the line right throughout the game.

Legends of the All Blacks

Never have I seen one pack of forwards so dominate the other in scrum work as the Springboks did".

In the circumstances, it was a mighty achievement by the All Blacks to come back and win the second test, at Ellis Park. A goal from a mark counted three points in 1928. Thus the goal which front rower Phil Mostert landed gave the Springboks a 6-3 advantage. Archie Strang's pot 10 minutes from time allowed the All Blacks to steal the game by 7-6. The Springboks were back in charge at Port Elizabeth, winning 11-6, before the All Blacks levelled things again with an outstanding 13-5 victory on a heavy surface at Newlands.

Considering the challenges confronting the tourists – arduous travel, the altitude factor and the strength of South African rugby – the 1928 team did phenomenally well to square the series. It would be 68 years before an All Black team would do better. The 1928 team sailed from Auckland on board the *Marama* on April 13 and returned on the *Ceramic* on October 9, a venture extending over six months.

A question that used to be asked was, "What is the greatest rugby team to leave New Zealand?" The answer was the 1937 Springboks. That question was popular before the marvellous Lions team of 1971 came Down Under and created history by winning a series on New Zealand soil. Notwithstanding that feat and the performances of such legendary players as Barry John, Gareth Edwards, Mike Gibson, JPR Williams and Willie John McBride, there are still astute rugby people around who argue for the 1937 Springboks as the greatest team to visit these shores.

Those Springboks were a mighty lot indeed, many of them still household names in South African rugby. According to Danie Craven, who was probably their brightest star, they should never have lost a match. That

Ron King (left) and Danie Craven lead out the teams for the first test of the 1937 series.

they did, the first test at Athletic Park, was entirely attributable to over-confidence, Craven always claimed. It irked him that the players were laughing and joking in the dressing room before they ran on to the field. The other 16 matches were won, most of them handsomely.

That 1937 series featured two individuals who were to become outstanding administrators in their respective countries, Jack Sullivan and Craven. Sullivan appeared for New Zealand at centre, from where he scored two tries in the second test, and at wing, while Craven, who

South Africa

revolutionised halfback play with his dive pass, surprisingly appeared in the first test at first-five. Even more remarkable, in a test in Australia, en route to New Zealand, he packed down at No 8 when injuries depleted the touring party.

New Zealanders had little doubt the All Blacks would be crowned world champions after the three-test series and considered their rugged provincial sides would be too strong for the visitors. But optimism swiftly changed to pessimism as the Springbok forwards ground the opposition to a standstill before bringing their talented backs into action with devastating effect. If they weren't scoring tries, fullback Gerry Brand was booming over goals. The 100 points he scored on tour created a record which stood until Barry John arrived 34 years later.

Auckland, Wellington and Taranaki crumbled before the South African onslaught and although New Zealand ground out a 13-7 win in Wellington, the series thereafter belonged to South Africa, the deciding test at Eden Park being won by a resounding five tries to none (far more decisive than the 17-6 scoreline would indicate).

So great an impression did the tourists make that three of the Springboks, captain and lock Philip Nel, centre Louis Babrow and fullback Gerry Brand, were duly named players of the year by the *New Zealand Rugby Almanack*. Also in contention for such recognition must have been flyhalf Tony Harris and the dive-passing Danie Craven.

Finally, after 10 tests between New Zealand and South Africa, the stalemate had been broken: the Springboks were the true champions of the rugby world.

The 1949 tour is the one New Zealanders prefer to forget – the one that went horribly wrong. No one was more devastated by the Springbok whitewash than the captain Fred Allen. "I was bitterly disappointed," he says. "It took me a long time to recover." The test results were close – 15-11, 12-6, 9-3 and 11-8 – but they were all lost. Fred Allen, still hale and hearty and living on the Whangaparaoa Peninsula north of Auckland, says there are several reasons why the forty-niners failed.

They had a coach who couldn't coach, they weren't properly fit, they lacked an international class halfback (having been forced to leave Vince Bevan, a Maori, behind), the referees caned them and they had problems scrummaging against the South Africans' new formations. Allen makes the point that his team conceded only eight tries in 24 matches, yet suffered seven losses. In the tests, they scored more tries than the Springboks.

Allen says the New Zealand union made a calamitous mistake in sending the 66-year-old Wellingtonian Alex McDonald away as coach instead of the outstanding coach of the time, Otago's Vic Cavanagh. McDonald, too old to start with, became a sick man on tour and Allen effectively took over the coaching of the team. Those experiences would help Allen, a decade and a half on, become one of New Zealand's most successful coaches.

Legends of the All Blacks

The 1960, 1970 and 1976 tours by New Zealand to South Africa followed almost identical patterns with the tourists losing the all-important opening test before winning the second, but always losing the fourth test.

The only variation in the theme came in 1960 when Wilson Whineray's team dramatically salvaged a draw in the third test at Bloemfontein to keep the series alive. The man who made that possible was giant fullback Don Clarke, who continually amazed South Africans with his prodigious kicking. At Bloemfontein, Whineray's men appeared to be down when they trailed 11-3 inside the final 10 minutes. But when you had Don Clarke in your side, anything was possible. First, he slammed over a massive penalty goal from his own 10-metre line, then with time up, he coolly slotted a sideline conversion to a try scored by Frank McMullen. If the nation back home was in a state of frenzy as Clarke prepared for that final kick, the man himself was supremely confident. "After you've played a lot of rugby, you know when you can kick a goal," he declared later. "That day I was confident. Putting the ball down the middle was a simple matter."

Unfortunately, the All Blacks couldn't produce that little bit extra in the final test, going down 8-3 at windswept Port Elizabeth. The game wasn't without controversy, the All Blacks convinced McMullen scored a try the referee didn't award.

The intensity of 1956 was absent when the Springboks toured New Zealand in 1965. This was a happy tour under a good-natured manager, Kobus Louw, whose favourite phrase was that well-worn cliché, "Rugby is the winner."

It wasn't a vintage year for the South Africans. They had lost five matches out of five on a tour of Ireland and Scotland, then dropped both tests to Australia en route to New Zealand. A 23-6 hammering by Wellington in the second tour match did not bode well. But, as always, the Springboks proved extremely competitive. They dropped only one other provincial game, to Auckland, in a demanding 24-match schedule and pulled off a remarkable comeback victory in the third test at Lancaster Park. Two tests down and trailing 5-16 at halftime in Christchurch, the Springboks appeared headed for oblivion. Revenge for New Zealand's 1949 whitewash was being talked about. But Louw's team displayed enormous courage in the second half. Led by centre John Gainsford, one of the great Springboks, they stormed back to level at 16-16 before giant lock Tiny Naude kicked a magnificent penalty goal out of the mud to secure a famous victory.

Although the result brought the series dramatically alive, the Springboks' celebrations were shattered by President Hendrik Verwoerd's statement from South Africa that there would be no Maoris in the All Black team when it toured in South Africa in 1967. That decision would lead to the cancellation of the tour. In the tour finale at Eden Park, the All Blacks achieved their largest winning margin against South Africa, scoring five tries (two of them to Spooky Smith, one of the few All Blacks to come out

South Africa

of North Otago) as they romped to a 20-3 victory. The Springboks had been largely outplayed throughout the series by a potent All Black pack that included such celebrated players as Colin and Stan Meads, Wilson Whineray, Brian Lochore, Kel Tremain and Ken Gray.

The All Blacks should have toured South Africa next in 1967 but this time, with Maoris still unacceptable, the New Zealand Government put its foot down. Its stance paid dividends. The 1970 tour, while it produced another bitterly disappointing series defeat for New Zealand, did unearth a brilliant talent in Bryan Williams. Beegee did more than just rewrite history as a non-white in a white man's domain. He absolutely wowed the South African audiences with the quality of his play. Only 19, he produced the finest rugby of his career.

Unfortunately, it wasn't enough to ensure success for the All Blacks, who were sensationally successful in the provincial matches but only mediocre in the games that mattered most, the tests.

There is a massive sand hill at East London, where the 1970 team opened its tour. It survives as a memorial to the coach Ivan Vodanovich. One of nature's gentlemen, Vodanovich stood accused of over-training his players and he found that sand hill irresistible. Prop Jazz Muller made the classic comment midway through the tour that he was going to have to play more matches to get fit for Vodanovich's training sessions.

Losing Colin Meads with a broken arm in the sixth tour game at Springs didn't help. Nor did the fact the touring selectors used 27 players in the four tests. But although the All Blacks, captained by Brian Lochore and boasting powerful forwards and two great halfbacks in Chris Laidlaw and Sid Going, arrived in South Africa favoured to succeed, they were hugely disappointing in the tests.

Ivan Vodanovich

One of the gutsiest performances by the tourists came from Keith Murdoch. He played the fourth test at Ellis Park with a rumbling appendix. Back at the hotel that night he collapsed, was rushed to hospital and operated on. He flew home four days after the rest of the team. The Springboks possessed dynamic loose forwards Jan Ellis and Piet Greyling, a speedy try-hungry winger Gert Muller, a crash-tackling centre Joggie Jansen and, as always, an accurate goal-kicker, Ian McCallum, who later said of the test series: "The underdogs had pretty sharp teeth."

When the All Blacks toured again in 1976, it meant two successive visits without a Springbok return visit in between. That was because New Zealand's Prime Minister, Norman Kirk, had asked the New Zealand union

Legends of the All Blacks

to postpone the 1973 Bok tour until South Africa ran mixed trials. Jack Sullivan, rugby chairman at the time, saw the Prime Minister's request as "a requirement and a direction". The tour was canned.

JJ Stewart's team of 1976 lacked a quality fullback, a reliable goal-kicker and power scrummagers. In the opinion of the coach and the players, they also lacked fair referees. The New Zealanders protested to no effect that they were robbed of a victory in the final international at Ellis Park because referee Gert Bezuidenhout refused to award a penalty try for blatant obstruction against Bruce Robertson.

It was the last time the All Blacks had to operate in South Africa without neutral referees. Is it purely coincidental that on the next two visits (in 1992 and 1996), they were sensationally successful?

There were few highlights, sadly, from the tour of 1976. Not only did the side captained by Andy Leslie lose three of the four tests, they were also defeated by Western Province, Northern Transvaal and Orange Free State. Grant Batty, a potential star, battled through the tour with a cumbersome brace on his seriously damaged knee.

The 1981 Springbok tour is remembered more for the protests and the violent clashes between protesters and police than for the rugby – a sad commentary on a nation which has traditionally been bonded by sport, particularly rugby. In 1981, though, New Zealand was in turmoil, a nation rent asunder. Even families were split. And the feelings were expressed with increasing violence.

Ironically, the Springboks were touring with a mixed team for the first time, the touring party including one Coloured player (Errol Tobias) and a Coloured assistant manager (Abe Williams). But it was the apartheid system still in place in South Africa that provoked the protesters. Initially, they tried to stop the tour. When that failed, they targeted individual matches. They had one notable success, in Hamilton, their invasion of the Rugby Park pitch causing the Waikato game to be abandoned. To give the police a rest, the match against the Hanan Shield Districts team at Timaru was cancelled. Otherwise, in often bizarre circumstances, the show went on, the Springboks completing 14 matches.

For the three tests, the Springboks were accommodated in heavily guarded fortresses, at the Linwood squash courts in Christchurch and in the grandstands at Athletic Park and Eden Park. Many of the fields they played on were ringed with barbed wire, and often violent clashes between police and protesters raged outside the stadiums. A Cessna buzzed Eden Park incessantly while the third test was being played out.

Notwithstanding all the distractions, the Springboks, captained by genial Wynand Claassen, won all their provincial games, though they were held to a 12-12 draw by the New Zealand Maoris in Napier.

In the matches that mattered most, the tests, they were dead square with the All Blacks, but with about two minutes of injury time remaining at Eden

South Africa

Some of the anti-tour protesters who forced the cancellation of the Waikato match in 1981.

Legends of the All Blacks

Park Allan Hewson calmly slotted a 40-metre penalty goal that wrenched the series away from them. After all they'd been through, it was a heartbreaking final act for the Springboks.

The Springboks had dropped the first test in Christchurch, largely because they had been embarrassed in the scrums, but they had struck back to claim the second test at windswept Athletic Park.

Six minutes into injury time at Eden Park the scores were locked at 22-22. Referee Clive Norling of Wales had asked the two captains, Claassen and Andy Dalton, if they wanted him to compensate for the stoppages caused through flour bombs being dropped from the Cessna, flares going off etc. They said yes. That explained how long the rugby raged on after the scoreboard clock had hit full time.

Finally came the penalty for an early strike by Bok hooker Robert Cockrell. The mark was advanced 10 metres when the Springboks failed to retire the required 10 metres. Up stepped Hewson. He kept saying to himself, "It has to go over, it has to go over." And it did. New Zealand 25, South Africa 22. And there ended one of the most amazing test matches ever played.

After the dramas of 1981, the All Blacks and the Springboks would not meet again for 11 years. There should have been a tour to the republic in 1985 but a High Court injunction scuttled that. What eventuated instead was a masterpiece of covert planning that became the Cavaliers tour. Most New Zealanders had no concept of what was happening until the players assembled in South Africa. Missing only David Kirk and John Kirwan of the originally selected 1985 side, the Cavaliers undertook a 12-match tour. All too predictably, the tour followed the pattern of the three previous All Black tours. Captained in the tests by Andy Haden and Jock Hobbs (after Andy Dalton had his jaw shattered against Northern Transvaal), the Cavaliers dropped the first test, won the second, but lost the series 3-1.

Thereafter, the Springboks – in fact, South African sport in general – was thrust into the international wilderness. It meant the Springboks were significantly absent from the first and second Rugby World Cups. Not until the dismantling of apartheid in the early nineties would the All Blacks tangle with their great rivals again.

Contact was resumed on a modest scale, with Laurie Mains' All Blacks having five matches in the republic tacked on to their tour of Australia. They won them all, which was a mini-triumph. The South Africans, out of international play for so long, found the pace of the game beyond them. With players like Inga Tuigamala, John Kirwan and Frank Bunce in explosive form, the All Blacks built up a commanding 27-10 advantage in the test and held on to win 27-24.

There were no protesters, no barbed wire, no animosity when the Springboks returned in 1994 for a 14-match tour. Sadly for the South

South Africa

Africans, coached by Ian McIntosh, there were no test victories either. They were defeated at Carisbrook and Athletic Park and although they scored the only tries at Eden Park, six penalty goals by Shane Howarth allowed the All Blacks to force an 18-18 draw. It was the first occasion in the 73-history of contests between the two great rugby powers, that the Springboks had failed to win a test. Furthermore, they lost to Otago and on their return home, McIntosh was sacked.

Under Kitch Christie and Francois Pienaar, South Africa rebounded in double-quick time. They had to, as hosts of the third World Cup, in 1995. Once the Springboks defeated the Wallabies in the tournament opener, there was an air of inevitability about rugby's greatest rivals clashing in the final. The All Blacks were raging hot favourites after smashing England into oblivion in Cape Town while the Springboks only just survived against France in soggy Durban.

Francois Pienaar

But with the entire Rainbow Nation behind them, with their president Nelson Mandela bedecked in a Springbok jersey and with their players operating like men possessed, the Springboks cut down the All Black juggernaut. After 80 minutes it was 9-9. After a further 15 minutes it was 12-12. And then Ellis Park erupted when Joel Stransky slotted a difficult dropped goal. The world crown was South Africa's. The All Blacks were devastated.

Rugby is about accepting defeats, regrouping and coming back stronger than ever. The All Blacks did that and 14 months after their World Cup disappointment they were rejoicing at a famous series victory over their greatest rivals on South African soil.

Because of the Tri-Nations competition, the All Blacks and the Springboks now clash annually on a home-and-away basis. If there was a fear the familiarity would lessen the importance and potency of these contacts, it hasn't been apparent yet. While the All Blacks were supreme in 1997, the Springboks under new coach Nick Mallett dominated in 1998.

Legends of the All Blacks

Whitewashed in '49

Fred Allen
captained the All Blacks to South Africa in 1949.

The All Black team that toured South Africa in 1949 was actually picked during the 1948 season, a ludicrous situation. Christmas was coming up and these fellows were naturally going to enjoy their lot. We did some training on the beach in Auckland for a few days, but some of our players had put on weight. Then we went to South Africa by boat, so that was another 26 days. There was about a six-month gap between the selection of the team and playing. The boat had no training facilities. All you could do was jog around the deck. In the sea air these fellows worked up big appetites. Three or four of them put on three stone and it was very difficult to get it off when we arrived in South Africa because cunning old Danie Craven had sent us to a place called Hermanus, which was the Riviera of South Africa, about 90 miles from Cape Town. They had no real fields there and it was all socialising. Trying to stop it was difficult.

Kevin Skinner
made his test debut in South Africa in 1949.

Throughout the 1948 season, we had trials up and down the country. The South Island trials started in Invercargill and finished up in Dunedin, Timaru and Christchurch. They did the same in the North Island. The side was announced in September and we didn't leave until the following Easter. The boat over to South Africa was another disaster because there wasn't enough training space on board. When we finally got there, we'd had a full summer at home, plus a trip across the Indian Ocean, so we were pretty much out of condition and had to put in a lot of work before we got into any sort of form.

Fred Allen

The refereeing hurt us a lot in South Africa in 1949. We played 24 games and had our line crossed only eight times. We scored more tries than South Africa in the test series, but it was hard to cope with the refereeing, especially in a low-scoring series. On the way home, I called the team together in the lounge and said it would be no use complaining about the referees when we got home. I said it would be no use blaming Alex [McDonald, the coach] or Jim [Parker, the manager] and that if they wanted to blame somebody, they should blame me. We had

Alex McDonald

1937: 'The Greatest Team'
Paul Dobson
South African journalist.

The 1937 Springbok team to New Zealand was full of legendary players – the Louw brothers, Jan Lotz, Gerry Brand, Pierre de Villiers, Ferdie Bergh, Dai Williams, Tony Harris, Freddy Turner, Louis Babrow, Phil Nel and many others. It was a golden period for South African rugby. Craven said the only time they lost [in the first test] was their own fault. He said they were over-confident and got lazy. To South Africans that 1937 team that won the series in New Zealand was the greatest team to leave South Africa.

Louis Babrow
was one of the Springboks' outstanding backs in 1937.

We thought we would win the first test very easily, but we were over-confident and chose the team badly. We dropped Philip Nel, our captain, who was a fine player.

South Africa – The Quinn Tapes

other sports teams that would go to South Africa and other All Black teams so it wouldn't be a good idea to come back and blame the referees. And they didn't. It was about fifteen or eighteen years before anything much came out about their referees on that tour. But it's no use denying it. They did us no favours.

Hennie Muller used to stand off the end of the lineout and there was no 10-yard rule in those days. The referee never worried about looking at him, and he would come straight at either me or Jim Kearney at centre. As the ball was arriving he'd be hitting you.

I stood down after the second test. I thought I couldn't do any more than I had. I was trying to coach them and it's absolutely impossible, even now, for a captain to try to coach as well.

Besides the South African referees, two other factors really hurt us in 1949. Not being able to take Maori players to South Africa had a tremendous effect on our chances of winning. If we'd have been able to take players like Vince Bevan and Johnny Smith – and there were others, too, who would have helped – we might still have won the series. And if Vic Cavanagh had been coaching us, I'm sure our test results would have been much better.

Louis Babrow

It was a terrible thing that we wouldn't allow Maori players to be selected in New Zealand teams touring South Africa. Our board should never have requested it, and the New Zealanders should not have sent their team. It meant that New Zealand came with not a second-rate team, but a poor side. Looking back, New Zealanders should have insisted that their best team leave New Zealand and the South African rugby public should have insisted that the best team came to play. It was a grave injustice to the Maori people.

Fred Allen

We had a weakness at halfback in 1949. The two halfbacks we had over there – Bill Conrad and Larry Savage – were great fellows, but a player like Percy Tetzlaff would have been ideal. We'd really love to have had Vince Bevan. He was an extra good halfback, but he was ruled out after Winston McCarthy blew his cover in Newcastle, New South Wales, in 1947. Winston mentioned several times during his broadcast that day that we were fielding an all-Maori backline for the first time. Most people didn't know until then that Vince was a Maori because he didn't look like a Maori. But after that there was a big hue and cry in South Africa and he was barred from being selected for South Africa. In those days they wouldn't allow us to take over any dark-skinned players. It was a real tragedy for us because with Vince we might have won, despite the referees. The irony was that Maori people didn't feel Vince had enough Maori blood in him to play for the New Zealand Maori team.

Kevin Skinner

We didn't really know Okey Geffin was a goal-kicker before the first test in South Africa. It was my first test and I was marking Okey in the lineouts. Johnny

Okey Geffin and Kevin Skinner in 1980.

Legends of the All Blacks

Whitewashed in '49

Simpson said to Okey at one point, "C'mon, lay off it, you Afrikaaner bastard." We had another lineout about half a minute later and Geffin turned to me and said, "Kevin, tell Johnny I'm not an Afrikaaner. I'm a Jew boy." He had a great sense of humour and I've been friends with him ever since.

Okey Geffin
Springbok prop and champion goal-kicker in 1949.

Danie Craven decided before the first test that I would be fourth kicker. He picked Jack van der Schyff as the No 1 kicker, Floris Duvenage as the second kicker, Hannes Brewis next and me as a last resort fourth. During the game, van der Schyff missed two, then the ball bounced at my feet when we were awarded another penalty. By then we were losing 11-0. I looked around and nobody came forward, so I had a go, and it went over: 11-3. Then I had another kick: 11-6. The rest is history. I kicked five goals and that made me the South African place-kicker.

•

Bob Scott's kicking form was too shocking for words. As we were walking off the field after the fourth test, I said to Bob that I thought he was hooking the ball at the last moment. He said, "This is a nice time to tell me!" Yet he wasn't a bad kicker, and he was a fantastic guy. Many years later when I was invited to New Zealand, he said to me we were going to have a kicking duel. I said to Bob that was crazy, because I was dressed in ordinary civvies and he was togged up. We found five thousand spectators there. They had come to watch these two stupid blokes having a kick. Thirty yards was my limit, but Bob asked if we could go back to halfway. I said I couldn't even see the posts from there. Then he took off his boots and kicked with bare feet and the ball went right through the poles. He was an uncanny kicker, and had just had a bad run in 1949.

•

Before the first test the great Boy Louw gave us a team talk while everyone was putting on their Springbok jerseys. He said, "For the benefit of my English-speaking friends, we're at war. I want you to remember that I played against their grandfathers and if you can't bite, punch and kick, don't go on the field, because they'll murder you. I want you to play hard and clean, but always remember that it's easier to play against fourteen than it is against fifteen.

John Gainsford
was a Springbok centre from 1960-67.

In 1949, when I was nine years old, the All Blacks toured South Africa. The vision we had of the All Blacks, the image, was that they didn't mind biting, trampling, pushing or jumping on people. In my young mind, they were tough, tough men. That was the impression we had of them.

Bob Scott

South Africa – The Quinn Tapes

The Battle for the Rugby Crown

Ian Kirkpatrick
was a centre for the Springboks on their 1956 tour of New Zealand.

We got Waikato first up and Don Clarke was their young fullback. We had never experienced a person who could kick a ball like he did. At one stage he kicked for touch and it went out of the stadium. That's how magnificent the man was.

Jaap Bekker
Springbok prop in the 1956 series.

During the second test at Wellington a scrum collapsed and I was kicked from the lock side of the scrum. I don't remember anything else until I woke up in hospital at three o'clock on Sunday morning, though I apparently finished the test match. I felt Bob Duff was the man who was guilty. Afterwards I suggested to Danie Craven that we should retaliate – do exactly the same back – but he said we must not.

Ian Kirkpatrick

The third test was a battle of front row versus front row. Skinner was brought in to destroy our front row, which he definitely did, whether he did it legally or illegally. I didn't like the way he did it, but it was a good selection by New Zealand because they won the series when he came in.

Jaap Bekker

Kevin Skinner came in [to the All Black team] for the third test. During that test, Chris Koch said Skinner hit him. Then he was apparently hitting one or two other guys. He was clever because he knew who he wanted. He would stand next to or near that player. Then when Chris marked Kevin at the front of a lineout, I saw Chris fall and he had cuts from his teeth right through his lips to the outside of his mouth. Later as we broke out of the scrum came a short punch in my ribs. He was not only demoralising some of our guys, but he was interfering with the game in so much as we had our minds on Kevin and not the game.

The night before the fourth test, Butch Lochner, James Starke and myself were talking and planned that we must get Skinner, really get him. He had disorganised our test side and we must get hold of him good and solid. Now Kevin Skinner had a knee guard on his right leg and Tiny White had a knee guard on his left leg. There was a lineout and I thought I saw Skinner come down on his back and I kicked him. But it wasn't Kevin, it was Tiny White. I was sorry about it, but Tiny White went off and Kevin didn't.

I have never spoken about this incident before. I have carried it inside me. I never met Tiny White again after that game but if I did, I would apologise to him.

Tiny White
was New Zealand's outstanding lock during the 1956 series.

Two important things happened to the All Blacks during the 1956 series – the selection of Kevin Skinner and Don Clarke for the third test. There was an immediate uplift within the team. They were both playing good rugby and were picked by the public in the team right from the start. We scraped through the first test, then lost the second fairly decisively. We had our problems. The front row wasn't going well and the backline was still changing around. I felt sorry for Pat Walsh because he went from first-five to fullback, so the selectors hadn't really settled on what they wanted.

Then they made the bold decision to bring Skinner into the front row and Clarke at fullback. We were suddenly transformed from an international team to a very good international team. They fitted in exceptionally well and you could see the lift in our training before the third test. There was nobody more experienced than Kevin Skinner, and Don Clarke ▶

Legends of the All Blacks

The Battle for the Rugby Crown

had been in the winning Waikato side.

When Don put over that first penalty from about 45 metres [in the opening minutes of the third test], that took us up another notch. I don't think any side would have beaten us on that day. The Springboks, who had been dominating the front row battles, were beaten by sheer power, strength and scrummaging ability. It was the first time they'd met a front row that was better, that they couldn't break, and that they couldn't undo. They tried to meet us man for man in weight and strength and they were beaten. Ian Clarke and Kevin Skinner were probably two of the strongest front row props that New Zealand ever bred. They never ever buckled. They were exceptional: they could take the strain and the pain and out-perform their opposition.

Of course, if you're being beaten by strength and power you're going to try to do something to disrupt it. The easiest way to disrupt somebody is to talk and grizzle. I always tried to take no notice, because that used to annoy the opposition more. The more annoyed they got the worse their rugby became. It's been said there was a lot of fighting in the third test. That's the legend. But of all the tapes I've seen of that series, how many fists do you actually see flying around? There was all the talk of Skinner going from one side of the front row to the other to knuckle somebody. I don't know anybody who actually saw it happen. Okay, he might have done a little bit of niggling along the line, but that was all part of the game. It wasn't open punching.

KQ: *Tiny, you were involved in an infamous incident near the end of the fourth test at Auckland. What happened to you?*

There were two incidents, actually. The really serious one occurred during a lineout. I took the ball with two hands. I had two of South Africa's strongest men opposing me and to make sure they didn't take the ball off me, I went straight to the ground with the ball, facing them. Within seconds I felt a shot of pain go up my spine. I didn't know who did it, but apparently 64,000 people on the bank thought they knew. Various names have been mentioned since, but I haven't got eyes in the back of my head, so I had no idea who kicked me in the tail. I've never endeavoured to find out who kicked me because what was I going to do about it?

It was the second injury I'd received that day. The first was early in the game when I got a belt in the kidneys. I said to Bob Duff, our captain, that I didn't feel too good. He said to take some deep breaths and keep going. There were no replacements in those days. So I nodded and did the best I could to carry on and forget about the injury.

With the second incident, the pain made me stretch right out. My legs went straight out and I just lay there. The first thing I did was wiggle my big toe. When you're hurt that badly, you want to know what limbs work. I was pleased my toes moved because that meant my spine wasn't broken. But for the first few seconds the pain was something I'd never felt before. I was always told that if I got in that position not to try to get up and I stayed prone on the ground until the St John people came out. The first person I saw was either Skinner or Duff standing above me making sure nobody else could get near. It was uncanny — almost as if everybody knew it was going to happen. As soon as I hit the ground I made a bit of noise and the game stopped before the whistle even blew. There was a couple of seconds of dead silence right around the ground. All the crowd heard was me letting out a yell to try to quash the pain. Then the public and police appeared out of nowhere and you could almost feel the pressure around the ground, with not a sound. There were 64,000 people squashed into Eden Park that day.

I wanted to play on. What player wants to be taken off? But when the doctor came out, he told me I was not staying on the paddock. I actually walked off, because by that time the pain had abated. But when I went to sit down in the changing room I couldn't. It felt too uncomfortable. By the evening I had no pain and

South Africa – The Quinn Tapes

Tiny White is assisted from the field at Eden Park.

outstanding rugby players, but they lowered their dignity and faith in the game even considering such action. It's probably one of the reasons we won the series. If you can sit down and plan something completely unethical and outside the morals of amateur sport… no true sportsmen would do that. If that happened, it would take a lot of the glint off my impressions of the 1956 South Africans.

KQ: Jaap Bekker says he has held the secret in his heart for 43 years, that he never mentioned it even to his wife. He told us with a tear on his cheek that he'd like to come to Gisborne to apologise to you.

Well, that would be something I would respect. I think it would be tremendously manly of him, although it is more than 40 years later. If he ever came, if the opportunity ever arose, it would be a unique occasion for both of us. It would help to eliminate the fact that they had a pre-match pact. If he's prepared now to sincerely admit an action which was unsportsmanlike, I'd accept the apology. It can't be easy for a person of his standing, as one of South Africa's great front row forwards, to know he's been party to a completely unethical action. It has obviously affected him a lot more than it has affected me and I think it would take a lot of courage for him to make the admission now and offer an apology. It speaks well of the person. I would be very happy to host him if he came to Gisborne.

I've never had any since. It must have been something which either my strength or physical ability absorbed. I was lucky not to have any after-effects.

KQ: Jaap Bekker has told us that the Springbok forwards met the night before the game and decided they were going to get Skinner any way they could. He said that he made a mistake during the test, that he meant to kick Skinner and kicked you instead.

Well, that disappoints me. They were such

Legends of the All Blacks

The Battle for the Rugby Crown

Peter Jones scores his famous try at Eden Park.

Don Clarke
was one of New Zealand's special heroes during the 1956 series.

The fourth test [of the 1956 Springbok series] was dramatic in many ways. We'd set ourselves to win the series. Peter Jones had a phenomenal game. They said that Peter Jones side-stepped Basie Viviers, but I think Basie Viviers side-stepped Peter. When Peter took that ball, I don't think many players would have stood in his way. He was a man possessed.

Kevin Skinner
proved to be New Zealand's saviour when he returned to test rugby in 1956.

In the 1950s, I was running my own business and every time I toured, I had to pay someone to do the job for me, and that wasn't really working. I'd married and had a family. So I retired and played just club rugby in 1955. Then I moved north to Waiuku and played a bit of club rugby there and got into the Counties side. Next thing, Jack Sullivan approached me before the second test, wanting to know my thoughts about having a go against the Boks. I told him it was a bit early, that I'd need to get my body a bit fitter. So they waited, and selected me for the third test.

The All Blacks needed some steadying down. Some fantastic stories had been written about the Boks — Bekker and Co snapping goal posts in half by pushing against them and this sort of thing. Some of our fellows were shattered before the South Africans arrived in New Zealand, although it helped when Waikato beat them first up. That showed they were human after all! But this feeling sneaked back into the test side later — these fellows were so big and rugged and some of our

South Africa – The Quinn Tapes

blokes developed an inferiority complex, which you can't have playing international rugby. It was my job to sort that out.

I'd had experience with the Afrikaaners. They're bully boys at heart. If you stand up to them, you don't have a problem and that's what I instilled into our guys. I said we didn't have to beat these guys, but we needed to stand up to them and not just take it.

I think I threw two punches in the third test, that's all. One was at Chris Koch and one at Jaap Bekker. After that I told the referee to tidy it up. All sorts of stories have been told about that day, most of them untrue. Winston McCarthy once told me a story about me taking off my wedding ring and giving it to Bekker and telling him to get a gold tooth made out of it. Well, I'm still wearing that ring today and it hasn't been to South Africa in the meantime!

Another writer, Esmonde Doherty, put in the *Auckland Star* that I'd told Ian Clarke to let me go over to his side [of the front row] so I could fix Bekker. That wasn't quite true. At halftime I asked Ian how he was going and he said he wouldn't mind a spell, so I took over the tighthead, and Ian switched to mark Chris Koch. I swapped sides of the scrum, but not so I could go over and sort out Bekker. That sort of thing is exaggerated so often it almost becomes the truth in some people's minds.

KQ: Jaap Bekker has told us you threw so many punches you demoralised the Springbok team.

Well, he's wrong. I warned Chris Koch for coming through and he did it again, so I whacked him. He was a good mate of mine and gave my family tickets to the Dunedin test and sent flowers to my mother, but I let him have one. Then old Jaapie kept trying it on, so I gave him a wee nudge, too. That was the end of it. After that I asked the ref to sort it out. I might have threatened a few – Salty du Rand and so on – but that's as far as it went.

KQ: Jaap Bekker has told us about a plot before the fourth test to get you during the game. What is your reaction to that?

Well, I didn't go into the series looking for trouble, but I wanted to make sure everyone was given a bite of the cherry and I wasn't going to put up with the antics that Frank McAtamney and Mark Irwin were put through.

On the Tuesday before the final test, I was in a combined team that played the Boks at Rotorua and Jan Pickard was itching to get me on the ground, but couldn't. In the fourth test, I saw the boot put into Tiny White's back, but I didn't realise until now that it was meant for me. I'm surprised to hear Jaap say that. I don't think I've ever played for any side that's gone onto the paddock to do that to anyone. It's sad, but good on him for at least admitting it was him who put the boot in. It was a big kick, not just a nudge, and it was with the toe of the boot.

That last test was do or die as far as South Africa were concerned. Peter Jones scored the classic try, brilliantly started off by Ron Hemi. Ron Jarden got hurt near the end and came back on as a floating fullback. That nearly upset the applecart. But we got through and I was thrilled to go out on that note, to know it hadn't been in vain. I wouldn't have liked to go through another tour like that, where there's so much feeling and where you're so wound up all the time. Really when it gets to that stage, sport has to take another look at itself.

It was intense stuff in 1956, following on from 1949 when we matched them pretty well but lost the four tests. They're pretty passionate about their rugby, the South Africans, and they came here with lots of passion in '56, but we matched it that year and came out in front for a change.

Ross Brown
played for the All Blacks from 1955-62.

I'd never want to go through that situation again [the 1956 series]. Everyone put pressure on us, the press, the public. Nowadays you go to a game and half the public are probably for the other side, but in 1956 the whole of New Zealand was right behind us, even Terry McLean.

Legends of the All Blacks

The Boot

Don Clarke
was New Zealand's main points-scorer on the 1960 tour of South Africa.

Don Clarke

I regard the second test in Cape Town in 1960 as my best performance in an All Black jersey. They beat us 13-0 in the first test and we were lucky to get nought, so we had to win the second test. I had one of those days when everything went right. I was kicking into touch and making seventy or eighty yards. I kicked a penalty, a conversion and a drop kick. It was really unbelievable. Just one of those days…

•

The third test in 1960 was really interesting. We were six points down with six minutes to go, so we were in a very difficult position. There was a penalty awarded to us about 75 yards from the posts. Wilson [Whineray] looked back at me and I shook my head. I thought it was too far. So he took a quick tap kick and we claimed the ten yards. Then I put the ball down on the 65-yard mark and let fly and fortunately it went over. Then Frank McMullen scored that wonderful try in the corner. Frank never had great hands, but he took that ball magnificently and was about half a metre inside the touchline. It didn't enter my head that I was going to miss the conversion. I'll never forget my brother Ian on the sideline – in those days the players officiated as touch judges – and the delight he showed when that ball was struck really squarely and was on its way.

Ian Kirkpatrick
Springbok centre from 1960-67.

Don Clarke was a phenomenal kicker. At one stage in the third test he got a penalty under his posts and put it out at halfway. Then he got another penalty at halfway and kicked it over. Then he converted the final try and the game finished 11-11, really because of Clarke. He was a magnificent player who could come in under any conditions and keep his cool.

South Africa – The Quinn Tapes

Wilson Whineray

captained the All Blacks in two series against South Africa – in 1960, and in 1965. He retired from test rugby in 1965.

I've never quite understood how we let the third test against South Africa slip in 1965. We won the first two tests and were up 16-5 at halftime in the third, at Lancaster Park, which was an unbelievable situation to be in against a Springbok team. They just sort of chewed at us in the second half. We missed some tackles and suddenly there we are looking down the barrel of this great big middle row forward, Tiny Naude, standing there with a kick to win the game. I thought to myself, "I'd really rather you didn't kick this goal, old boy." But he did. He banged it over and they won 19-16.

So we went to Eden Park with the series still alive and on a good firm ground, we scored five tries and beat them 20-3, which was a good win to end the series. And that was the finish for me, my last test.

Colin Meads

toured South Africa twice as a player, in 1960 and 1970.

I learnt in South Africa in 1960 that you don't show your cards too early. We played great rugby at the start of that tour, but the test wasn't till the thirteenth game. We'd won some warm-up games by huge margins, but they just picked us off, picked players to match the All Blacks. They got to know our moves down to a "T". Old Danie Craven and the selectors had camps and they called in anyone who could help. So by the time of the tests, they were waiting for us. It was a hell of a shock. I suppose it's probably what New Zealand did to them in 1956.

Wilson Whineray and Brian Lochore against South Africa, 1965.

Legends of the All Blacks

1970: Shattered Dreams

Earle Kirton
finished his All Black career in South Africa in 1970.

People said the team to South Africa in 1970 was as good or better-looking than the 1967 side, but I didn't think it was. We were missing the great Ken Gray and the rest of us were quite a bit older. We were still okay, but we'd just lost the gas a wee bit.

Brian Lochore
captained the All Blacks to South Africa in 1970.

We'd been looking forward to the 1970 tour for a long time. It was every New Zealand rugby player's ambition to play in South Africa, against our traditional rivals. The team started very well, although I didn't. I broke my thumb in Perth and spent the first three weeks in plaster. Every time we moved, I'd go to a different doctor to see if the hand had improved sufficiently to take the plaster off, but each one would tell me to wait a few more days. In my first game back, at Springs, Colin had his arm broken.

It was a tough tour, but we played well early, and our lead-up to the first test was excellent. We thought we had the Springboks sussed, but we forgot what players they are when they pull on that green jersey.

Colin Meads

I was getting a bit long in the tooth by 1970 and a lot of people were saying I was over the hill. But in the early games on that tour of South Africa I played some of the best rugby of my career. I was captaining the team because Brian Lochore had broken a bone in his hand and I found it very challenging. I was loving my rugby. Then, in Brian's first game back, I broke my arm.

I was a bit superstitious and if I wasn't captaining a team I'd always run out last. There were about four times I didn't, and something bad happened every game. At Twickenham once when I was playing for a

Colin Meads and the most famous broken arm in rugby.

world team, I went out early to introduce Prince Charles to the team and then I hurt my back. Well, in South Africa, Lochore insisted I went out second behind him, because I was the vice-captain, and I broke my arm.

I had all my weight on the arm and then got a kick right in the back of it. The normal reaction is to grab hold of the boot and hang on to it to see who it was, but I knew something was terribly wrong this time. There were pins and needles right up my arm. I went to see a doctor, who said it wasn't broken, so I stayed on. But I couldn't grip. I played out the game and then we found out the consequences afterwards.

One thing I learned was that when you're injured on tour, it affects your rugby. You become part of the

South Africa – The Quinn Tapes

social team on tour. Here's me, Colin Meads at the end of my career, and I'm off invited everywhere – schools, clubs, functions at night. I didn't mind. I felt it was my duty, but it doesn't help your fitness or well-being. You put on weight and your training doesn't have much meaning any more.

I thought I might as well play just in the Wednesday games, to help out. So I found a friendly doctor in Cape Town who said I could play as long as the South African board passed the cast I'd had made for it. They duly did that. The cast was a perfect fit. The only thing it stopped me doing was catching the ball from the kick-offs. I couldn't bend my wrist and used to spill those. It didn't hurt too much, just an instant jab of pain, but not constant pain. I never expected to get back in the test team, that wasn't my desire at all.

Neil Thimbleby
was an All Black prop on the 1970 tour of South Africa.

It's easy to be wise in retrospect, but I feel we didn't change tactics from the midweek games to the tests in 1970. We had nothing left up our sleeves. Perhaps it was because we didn't have a back on the selection panel. The Africans analysed us thoroughly and then picked players to counter our style.

Ian MacRae
played four tests for the All Blacks in South Africa in 1970.

If we'd toured South Africa in 1967 with Fred Allen as our coach, as were supposed to do, I think we would have won. The other big difference was that in 1970 Ken Gray had decided he wasn't pro-South Africa. In 1967 he might have been with us. I regard the fact that Ken wasn't there and Fred wasn't the coach as the main reasons we didn't win the series.

Colin Meads

We found in South Africa that in the provincial games, the referees would be nice and kind to us. You could talk to them, talk them into things. Then they'd get picked for a test and do a complete U-turn. So the referees got to us in the tests in South Africa. We swear to this day that Frank McMullen scored a try in the fourth test in 1960.

But there were still things we could have done. In 1970 we had a good enough team to win, but with their home crowd, their referees and their conditions, it's a tough, tough challenge. In 1970 their fullback, Ian McCallum, kicked the crucial penalties. I remember saying to Lochore when he lined up one near the end from about 50 yards, "The little prick won't kick this." But he did and that was that.

Sid Going
was an All Black halfback in South Africa in 1970.

We had some important injuries on that tour, and there were some selection issues, but you'll have injuries and selection problems on most tours. It was said we had the forward power at the time, but I was playing at halfback and I know I was pushed out of the road by some of our forwards. Some of the forwards wanted all the glory – we had No 8s picking up the ball and running, centre kicking and things like that, instead of letting the backs do that sort of thing. We went from a team to a group of individuals and started to play as individuals. To me, that was our downfall.

Fergie McCormick
toured South Africa with the All Blacks in 1970.

We did lose our compass a bit on that tour. We had some dissension, a split in the side. Bruce McLeod challenged Ivan [Vodanovich, the coach] over me not being picked at fullback for the fourth test. There were some incidents with Billy Davis and Alister Hopkinson having words with Ivan. I think the 3-1 series loss came down to selection at vital times, and Ivan Vodanovich was the kingpin there.

Legends of the All Blacks

1976: Whistling an Unhappy Tune

Andy Leslie
captained the All Blacks to South Africa in 1976.

I'll never forget that moment in the first test in South Africa in 1976 when I could have scored but for the ball rolling around the goal post. I got a telegram from one of the more colourful characters in Petone who said: "The trouble with you, Leslie, was that your head was too bloody big to get between the posts!"

But more seriously, we had moments in most of the tests that year where we could have scored and things didn't go our way. In the last minute of that first test I was penalised for being offside in the ruck and we were just about to roll over and would, I think, have scored. Or in the last test when the ball blew over when Sid [Going] was lining up to take a penalty and the referee wouldn't let him place it again. He awarded the penalty against us instead.

In another test there was a drop kick of theirs that went outside the upright and all the Coloureds down the end of the ground were cheering because the ball had missed. They always pulled strongly for us. But the referee interpreted their cheering as the ball going over and awarded the kick. In the fourth test we had a couple of incidents where penalty tries that could have been awarded to Bruce Robertson. But they weren't. You know… if the dog hadn't stopped, he would have caught the rabbit. You could go on forever wondering about it.

Kit Fawcett
was one of the less conventional All Blacks. He toured South Africa in Andy Leslie's 1976 team.

KQ: Kit, tell us about that story at the start of the 1976 tour, when you were quoted as saying you would score more off the field than on.

We arrived at Johannesburg after a long flight that involved us going from New Zealand to Europe and then down to South Africa. We were dealing with autograph hunters and the media. Then I met a woman reporter named Viv Prince from the Johannesburg *Women's Weekly*. She asked me if I had a minute to answer a few questions. I said, "Fine." Then she asked me about my attitude towards socialising on the tour. She said when the 1974 Lions were in South Africa they had a trophy for the most scoring off the field. I said, "Well, I'm only 21. I haven't really got a preference in terms of different types of women. It's a bit like a cheeseboard at the end of the meal. It's optional if you order it, though you know it's available." I was trying to be diplomatic. Then she asked me who were the romantics in the team. I had a little bit of a think and said all the guys would be romantic if they met the right woman at the right place and time, meaning that it was a very personal thing. Then she asked me how I was going to go. I said, "Well, I'm a fullback and I hope to score more on the field than off."

I was rooming with Laurie Mains when the paper came out the next day. It was all over the front page – "All Blacks hope to score more off the field than on, says 21-year-old fullback Kit Fawcett, who likes blondes, brunettes and redheads and wants them all to come to the hotel." Laurie told me I was in the shit. I hoped it wouldn't get back to New Zealand, but the same day about 250,000 *New Zealand Heralds* went out with the same story in it. I went down to breakfast and couldn't figure out why nobody was sitting with me. But what had happened was that all the wives had rung up overnight and asked what was going on over there.

The quote was turned around, but she was obviously looking for a story. And it was a bloody good story because it went around the world and probably ruined my career. But what can you do? Do you hold up the white flag and say, "This ain't fair."? You have to take it on the chin and get on with life.

To give credit to Andy Leslie, he did come and sit with me and say, "Bad luck, Kit." He explained about the wives being upset and so forth. I had only been trying to do a little PR, but I had no idea of the consequences. She wanted a story and marketed it all around the world.

South Africa – The Quinn Tapes

Kit Fawcett in South Africa, 1976.

Viv Prince turned up on the last week of the tour and wanted to do another interview about how I'd got on, which I thought was quite cheeky of her. She knocked on the hotel door and said, "Hi, Kit. I'm back. I want to do an article about how your tour's been." I said to her very politely that she'd probably caused enough problems and could we just leave this one. She agreed, but some of the other press saw her at my door and wrote a little story about her returning. You couldn't get away from the press.

Ian Kirkpatrick
toured South Africa with the All Blacks in 1970 and 1976.

It was more disappointing to lose the series in 1976 than 1970. We certainly had the team to win, but we didn't have a goal-kicker [in 1976]. That was a huge minus. If you don't have a kicker, you go down. We had some refereeing decisions, but with a good kicker, we'd have overcome the refereeing.

JJ Stewart
coached the 1976 All Blacks to South Africa.

The nationalism was intense in 1976. The Olympic boycott happened while we were there. Here's South Africa, being told they're the rubbish of the world, no-one had any time for them, no-one was interested in their economy. So they think, "We'll show you on the rugby field. We'll prove we're tops." But I don't want to be too picky, because it was really the same situation when they came to New Zealand in 1956.

Quite frankly, in retrospect, that tour [1976] shouldn't have gone on. It didn't do our game any good. It set us back. There's such an anti-rugby lobby in New Zealand, always ready to express itself, and teachers, for instance, were then able to say rugby had supported this terrible apartheid in South Africa, so they didn't want anything to do with the sport.

Bruce Robertson
played at centre in all four of the All Blacks' tests in South Africa in 1976.

I thought there were two reasons why we didn't win in South Africa in 1976. First, we were playing away and secondly we were playing the opposition referees. You've got to play well enough to beat the opposition above what they are going to dish out to you. In 1976 we came away disappointed with the referees and their attitudes to the games they refereed. The Lions had been there in 1974 and won an historic series there, so obviously two series losses at home wouldn't have done the South African ego any good. We went over there with high expectations, but it didn't turn out that way for us and I don't think the refs helped us in any way.

The fourth test is the one that's often spoken about. ▶

Legends of the All Blacks

1976: Whistling an Unhappy Tune

There were a couple of times when I'd kicked the ball through. The first one was from a loose ball and one of their players just came across in my line and took me right out of the play when I thought I had more than a reasonable chance of scoring a try before the opposition got there. In the second half I got the ball – we had quite a good breakout with the whole team contributing. We ran to within the opposition 22. I put a chip kick over and somebody just took me out completely and the ref ruled penalty, but not a penalty try. It comes down to the referee's judgment, but in my opinion, we'd have scored a try. It would probably have given us the game and meant a drawn series. That would have been a lot better than losing the test series.

The Robertsons. Ian of South Africa and Bruce of New Zealand, 1976.

KQ: You went to South Africa, and then you decided that you didn't want to play the South Africans any more. Why was that?

When I was in South Africa I was fortunate enough to be able to visit a lot of places where there were only Coloureds and black people. I looked at the facilities they had and the opportunities they had to promote and play rugby, and they were zilch basically. I thought they weren't getting a fair kick at life. So after that I made my stand: until they sorted out that side of things and all people had the equal opportunity to play, I wouldn't play against them. That's why I made myself unavailable to play against the Springboks in 1981. It's hard to say if it was the right decision. That tour, with all the protesters, turned into a mess for rugby in New Zealand. It put the sport at an all-time low here. In the long run, I hope that my decision, and those others made along similar lines, made a difference and helped lead to South Africa changing its internal practices. Maybe that's wishful thinking, maybe it's true. I don't know. But I'm very glad they have made the transition and that South Africa is back in the rugby fold. They are our traditional rivals, our main opposition. When we meet, it's like a clash of world champions.

South Africa – The Quinn Tapes

1981: Behind Barbed Wire

Graham Mourie
was the All Black captain, but would not play against the 1981 Springboks.

The South African issue had always been a major one for New Zealand rugby, but had become much more important by 1981. I'd looked at what happened when the Springboks toured Britain in 1969-1970 and Australia a year later.

It seemed to me a tour of New Zealand by the Springboks would not be good for rugby, or for New Zealand society. And I had a basic belief that sport shouldn't be subject to legislation in terms of whether people would be allowed to play for their countries. Those three issues made it very difficult for me to play against them happily. Had we been going to South Africa, I may have been available, because there would have been just one issue. Having the South Africans tour New Zealand created problems within New Zealand. Had I been selected in 1976, I would probably have toured South Africa.

Another factor was that as captain of the All Blacks, I felt there was a leadership issue and that leaders should make judgments on right and wrong, rather than leading where they thought the team wanted to go without considering the issues.

Andy Dalton
captained the All Blacks in the tempestuous home series against the Springboks.

Peter Burke asked me if I would captain the side when Graham Mourie stated he wouldn't be available, and I was quite relaxed about it. I do recall two of the senior All Blacks coming to me on the eve of the first test to tell me the team talk I was about to give would be the most important of my life, which I didn't particularly appreciate at the time, given that I knew damn well myself. During the series the senior guys, particularly Mark Shaw, were very helpful. Mark Shaw was a real asset to the team. It's black and white with Mark. He has a very simple philosophy: you just do it. There are always backs who have plenty to say, but Mark cuts them dead in the water. I've always had a lot of respect for the guy.

•

There weren't any of us in the squad who didn't have family members or close friends who were against the tour. It certainly alienated the country. I believed it was important it went ahead, on the basis of the freedom in your own country. They were invited here legally and I felt we had every right to play against them. If people didn't want to watch, they didn't have to.

There were a lot of pressures on us socially. A number of us were under police protection. It was said they [the anti-tour protesters] intended to kidnap one player, and clearly the only player they could carry off would be Allan Hewson, given his weight. So he was under armed guard. It was a tough time.

Then to run onto the paddock at Christchurch for the first test and see barbed wire and cops all around the park – it was just so foreign to New Zealand, and I struggled with that. It was sad it had got to the stage where some people would try to ruin a legal pastime for others.

Wynand Claassen
captained the 1981 Springboks to New Zealand.

We knew there were going to be a lot of political undertones, but we didn't expect it would be that bad. The Springboks went through the 1969-70 tour in Britain, the so-called "demonstrators' tour" and there was trouble in Australia in 1971. But in South African people's minds, New Zealand was a rugby nation and they were our friends. I don't think anybody expected it was going to be as bad as it turned out to be. It came as a shock.

Television started later in South Africa and the tours to Britain and Australia weren't televised. All ▶

Legends of the All Blacks

1981: Behind Barbed Wire

you knew was what was in the papers and on radio. In 1981, television brought home the situation a lot more clearly. South African people got up at 4am and sat for three hours waiting for the Waikato game to start. Then the game was abandoned. That was a shock. I'd say that was part of the big change in South Africa. It opened a lot of eyes when people saw a country like New Zealand, that we regarded as a friend, could be so anti the South African system.

Sport has always been so important in South Africa. That 1981 tour opened the eyes of the public and they realised change had to come.

Andy Haden
played for the All Blacks from 1972-85.

The 1981 season was really a dockyard brawl throughout, from one bad memory to another. But there were huge principles involved on both sides. I think rugby grew up a lot in that period.

The protesters felt they had a legitimate reason for protesting and we felt we had a legitimate reason for playing. We knew some of the protesters were being hired and that if you got in a cab and said you were going to a protest, some of the cab fares would be paid. It was quite handy at times. You could get a free cab drive to the protest, which was often outside our hotel! But the protests got completely over the top and as they got more extreme, our attitude to the protesters became a bit bitter.

Wynand Claassen

The day of the Waikato game was dramatic for the whole team. Very early in the morning we went to Rugby Park. We wanted to evade the demonstrators and to get a feel for the field. We were there about seven in the morning. We went into the grandstand and sat in the function hall on the first floor. There were some mattresses lying around for us. I looked at the Springbok head from the '56 tour, when South Africa lost to Waikato, and I thought that we mustn't lose the Springbok head again to Waikato. Little did I realise it would be far worse – there was to be no game at all.

It was a frightening experience, even more so when we went into the changing room. Our manager, Johan Claassen, came in and told us there were quite a few people on the field and that they were being removed and that the game would start a little late. It just dragged on and on. We'd warm up, then sit down, warm up again, then sit down. Finally I went out into the tunnel and saw what was happening. It was frightening. I realised there was no way they would get those people off the field.

At one stage when we were all curious to know what was happening, we pushed the medicine table against the back wall, where there were some small windows. We stood on the table and could see several big trucks parked there, trucks that farmers had put there to keep out the demonstrators. A lot of demonstrators came around the back and started to push one of the big trucks over. That was really frightening. Thankfully it didn't go any further than that.

•

In a strange way, the unusual conditions we encountered before the second test at Athletic Park actually helped us. I mean the conditions were awful – Athletic Park is very old with corrugated sheeting and all that. But we stayed in the function room, and we had nice heaters. It was carpeted. The beds were about a metre apart. There were television sets and we watched videos. We had two pool tables and played some games. So for team spirit, it was actually good. We stayed close and we had a woman cooking for us. The management stayed with us and we just made the best of the conditions. In the end I think it favoured the Boks.

South Africa – The Quinn Tapes

Andy Dalton

I felt most comfortable going into the third test [of the 1981 series]. Our selections were sorted out and our build-up was better. It turned out to be the most incredible game I've been involved in. There were dramas getting to the ground, then the game itself was incredibly exciting and there was the plane flying overhead dropping flour bombs and Gary Knight being knocked over by one bag. Clive Norling called over Wynand Claassen and I at one stage and asked us if we wanted to stop the game because of the flour bomb interruptions. As we were leading, I thought it was a sound suggestion, but Wynand wasn't having a bar of it, so we carried on.

Then the clock went past full-time with the scores level. I asked Clive Norling how long there was to go – this was after about four minutes of extra time – and he said, "I don't really care, I'm having so much fun." Then we got a penalty close to the posts, although Hewie would probably say it was out on the side of the track 50 yards out. Hewie was so very confident and kicked it sweetly through. Then we had another two minutes of the hardest football of my career before we won. After all the dramas and traumas, I don't know how I could have handled a team that had lost that series.

Wynand Claassen

The third test was one of rugby history's most epic and dramatic matches. You had a series even between the two greatest rugby nations in the world, and there were the demonstrations and that plane buzzing around over the park.

And the match itself was very good – it was so close and should really have ended in a draw. It says a lot for the two teams and their spirit, for the way they played that match.

We were trailing 6-3 at halftime and reasoned it out like this: in the first half we played against the flight of the aeroplane. It was alright for the forwards who were busy with the game, but the players in the backline would often be standing there watching the plane. We came back strongly with the plane behind us. Maybe by then the All Black backs were busy watching the plane!

In the last minute Naas Botha had the chance to kick the goal that would win us the match and the series. It wasn't an easy kick, but not too difficult for him. But ▶

Claassen and Dalton prepare to play out the final scene of the '81 tour.

Legends of the All Blacks

1981: Behind Barbed Wire

after Ray Mordt scored that last try there was quite a long break when Dave Loveridge got injured after Mordt fell on top of him. It took time to get Loveridge off the field and to get the replacement on. The plane was still circling and I think Naas probably lost concentration a little. The kick could have won it for us, but it would have been unfair if we had won the series. I was very happy for a drawn match and series. The All Blacks dominated the first test and we did the same in the second. In the third test the first half belonged to the All Blacks and the second half to us, so a draw was a fair result.

That's how it should have been. We were very unhappy with that last penalty awarded by Clive Norling. We still question it. Allan Hewson stepped up and kicked it and that was that. In the books it says the All Blacks won, even if we didn't feel it was right. We were very unhappy with the way Norling handled that test, especially the last bit. Here we were – the two greatest rugby teams in the world, playing a fantastic test under unbelievable circumstances. Why, in that sort of situation, does a referee feel he has to make a final decision that will decide the outcome of the series? I'd rather have played all three tests with a good New Zealand referee like Paddy O'Brien in recent years, a referee I could trust. O'Brien is a fantastic ref, happy to stay in the background. He's not a show pony. He lets the game flow.

Clive Norling

refereed the decisive third test in 1981.

It was the most remarkable game of rugby I have ever refereed, with the barbed wire and the plane buzzing and the flour bombs. I had to act as not only referee, but aircraft spotter as well. After the game Andy Haden told me I'd caused him great problems at one lineout. He said Andy Dalton had signalled for him to jump for the ball just as I'd said, "Oh, God, boys, here he comes again! Duck, duck, whatever you do, duck!"

With eight minutes to go I asked Wynand Claassen and Andy Dalton if they wanted to call off the game. Andy was rather silent. Wynand was adamant he wanted to play till full-time, which was the eight minutes remaining, plus eight minutes of injury time. If Wynand Claassen had asked that we call it off at the end of normal time, it would have been a draw.

KQ: What about that injury time penalty?

It was ironic. The Springboks had done the same thing in the second test and been penalised and Hewson had kicked the goal. I had talked to them about it after the second test. There was dummying by the scrumhalf, Serfontein, and foot up by the hooker – two offences. When this happened in the third test, I gave a free kick. Donaldson took a very quick tap penalty, sprinted into midfield and passed to Rollerson. I kept my arm out for advantage because the Springbok three-quarters had not retired ten yards. Rollerson then got tackled and I penalised the Springboks for not retreating ten yards. In those days that was an automatic penalty. Hewson kicked the goal and the rest is folklore.

Clive Norling

South Africa – The Quinn Tapes

I suppose the controversial end added to the drama of the whole series and the tour. If you look at that season and what New Zealand and its people went through, maybe it was fair enough that they won the series.

John Reason
English journalist.

The result of that third and final test in 1981 was the biggest travesty of justice I have ever seen. Five minutes into injury time, it should have been the end of the game. But [referee Clive] Norling

Demonstrators outside Eden Park.

restarts it, not ten yards, then the fullback kicks the goal. Poor old Clive Norling had the misfortune to be sitting next to me on the plane on the way home, and all the way from Auckland to Singapore I flattened his ear. "Well, you know, John," he said, "it was my watch that was at fault." I said, "Clive, that's rubbish. You were rowing the boat for the opposition, the way Welsh referees always do. The Springboks deserved a draw out of that. They were the better side, they had better players behind the scrum. Naas Botha and Danie Gerber were in a class by themselves." I told Clive what he'd done would remain forever unforgivable.

Gary Whetton
played for the All Blacks from 1981-91.

I got called in to partner Andy Haden after the All Blacks were beaten in the second test at Athletic Park in 1981. It was very unexpected. I went into camp and met all these great All Blacks, really for the first time – Dave Loveridge, Andy Dalton, a real leader, Stu Wilson, Murray Mexted. Andy Haden, I knew of course, from Auckland. I was lucky enough to be rooming with Murray Mexted. In those days you had a great big bed for the six foot six guy like me and a little, wee bed for the smaller guy. Murray, being the gentleman he was, said, "That's your bed – the little, wee bed there."

It was a different atmosphere to anything I'd known before because there were police everywhere. Our hotel was surrounded twenty-four hours a day for the next five days. When we went to training, we had van loads of police behind and in front of us. We'd go to the field, we'd train intensively with Peter Burke and the Red Squad would be there, often training on the ground beside us. We had ready-made opposition.

For twenty-four hours a day there'd be chanting outside the hotel, people not wanting to let us sleep. My mother was getting abusive and threatening calls because her little boy was going out to play South Africa. My father's best friend, like a second dad to us, was against the tour and it split up everything. It was a very emotional time. All I wanted to do was wear the black jersey with pride. ▶

Legends of the All Blacks

1981: Behind Barbed Wire

The normal time to go to the test match was about twelve or one o'clock. We were up at six-thirty in the morning, in our tracksuits, told to have all our gear ready. We left at seven in a huge convoy. There was a police car in front of our bus and a mini-van full of police behind us with another mini-van. A huge bus full of another sixty-odd police was behind further, and another big truck, an army truck with a helicopter, lifting gear and so on. We had to go to the stadium early because they were afraid the protesters might block the harbour bridge. And here I was, trying to prepare for my first test. To be honest, I wasn't thinking about rugby. We were in a war zone. We got to Eden Park and there was barbed wire and containers everywhere. We went to one of the big reception rooms, which had mattresses on the floor. We tried to relax, but it was a long day.

Just before we went out, Mr Norling, the referee came in wearing his tight shorts and said, "Good afternoon, guys, the name's Norling, Clive Norling. To you, Mr Norling. Let's have a good game."

As we started going into the tunnel, he held us because there was a problem with the plane. All of a sudden, the Springboks came out of their changing room beside us. I was between Andy Haden and Murray Mexted. Out came Hennie Becker and the guy just about had to get onto his knees to get through the doorway. He was about six foot eight. I thought, "Oh, my God." and Mexted said, "Don't worry, you're not marking him. It's Haden's." All of a sudden, out comes Louis Moolman, the big Afrikaaner from Transvaal, a miner and a farmer and he had a big flaming orange beard and yellowy eyes like a big lion. Mexted said, "That's yours, buddy."

It was a hell of a game. We started brilliantly as a pack and before you knew it, it was half-time. I was everything – tired, emotional, pumped up. I think Moolman must have smacked me three or four times, but, hey, I was playing in my first test.

Then it got very close in the second half when the Springboks started to run it at us. Ray Mordt scored three tries. Finally it came down to Botha's conversion. As he was lining it up, I stood under the posts thinking, "This could be the beginning and the end of my All Black career. If he gets this kick over, I could be a one-test wonder."

Then Mr Norling, in his wisdom, kept the game going and we got three points. Then it was over. Relief, excitement and a belief that I'd arrived.

Andy Haden

In the Auckland test, I thought the plane passed overhead only three or five times, but it was apparently five times that many. We were very focused on trying to win the game and were very caught up in the drama within the confines of the rugby field, oblivious to what was going on around us. In normal circumstances that would have been one of the epic tests of all time, but the things that went on outside the test far overshadowed the publicity of the actual contest. Yet it was probably as good a test as I've played.

Naas Botha
champion Springbok flyhalf and goal-kicker.

There was brilliant play by both New Zealand and South Africa in the last test, but no-one's going to talk about the rugby. It will go down as the flour bomb test and for the Clive Norling penalty. That's sad because we had a long, hard tour and it all came down to flour bombs and a referee. Both teams deserved better.

Andy Dalton

I'd do the same thing now as I did in 1981, but I'm much happier with the current situation where South Africa have been accepted back politically. I've got strong beliefs in terms of sport for sport's sake. I believe it's possible to keep politics out of sport, though it's not easy sometimes. I've never questioned the politics or religion of people I've played against. You get into all sorts of bother if you do that.

South Africa – The Quinn Tapes

Allan Hewson lands the greatest kick of his career.

Peter Bush
New Zealand's best-known rugby photographer.

The 1981 tour should never have happened. It was the closest this country ever came to civil war. I received some of the vilest comments I've had thrown my way. At the Waikato ground, I was whacked in the middle of my back by a drunken oaf who leaned over and tore a paling off the fence. A couple of cops moved in and stopped me climbing over the fence to give it back to him. That Waikato game – or non-game – really proved to me that it was hopeless cause – drama, after drama, after drama.

Francois Pienaar
captained the Springboks from 1993-96.

It was a difficult series to follow and difficult for the Boks to play in, but it made us proud of the guys who went to New Zealand and played in those conditions. It was only later that I realised it was necessary for that to happen. It was necessary for the world to see there was something wrong that needed to be changed.

Legends of the All Blacks

Rugby of a Cavalier Fashion

Andy Dalton
captained the Cavaliers on their unauthorised 1986 tour of South Africa.

My first ambition in rugby was to get in the All Blacks, and my second was to be in a team that won a series in South Africa. My father having been in the team that lost 4-0 over there in 1949 was probably a large factor in that. I saw 1985 as my last opportunity. With Brian Lochore as the coach, it was all falling into place. The team had been named, our businesses had been organised and then we got the news that the injunction had been granted. It was devastating. There was confusion the next few days and then when it was finally stated that the tour was cancelled, it was absolute disappointment and anger – a dream that wasn't going to happen. I felt robbed and I'm still sceptical about the process by which that injunction was granted.

Then there was all this talk of rebel tours and we received quite a deal of encouragement from various sectors, including political and even the Rugby Union, to proceed with an unofficial tour. Finally I made a decision with another player that it [later in 1985] wasn't the right time to go. The opportunity arose again the following year, and that became the Cavaliers tour.

Andy Haden and I had kept in close contact and there was a lot of interest for the tour to go ahead in 1986 on the basis that it was the same team. Andy and I were quite adamant about that. The biggest disappointment was Brian Lochore not being able to accept an invitation to go as coach because he was an official of the New Zealand union and would be in breach.

Gary Whetton

It was a major decision to tour [with the Cavaliers]. I was hugely worried. I spoke a lot with my parents and friends, my employers. You didn't know what would happen to your rugby career afterwards. Did I want to end my All Black career? It was a possibility. It was an easier decision for the older guys, but us younger guys had more to weigh up. And a lot of it had to be done behind the scenes. We were unable to approach certain players who were friends. You didn't want any leaks. It was a very stressful time.

We went down to play Canterbury in a Super 6 game, and were leaving straight after the game. Our team didn't know, though in the end we let a few of the players know. Unfortunately, our coach, John Hart, had been kept in the dark a lot of the time.

We were in a hotel room and Tane Norton knocked on my door on the morning of the game and said, "Hi, guys, got any luggage for me?" We gave him a big bag of luggage and he said, "Right, this is going on the plane." Then we went out and played the game. It was a hard game, as Auckland-Canterbury games are, and Albert Anderson and I ended up in a bit of a tussle. We were on the ground and I looked at Bert and said, "We've got to get on a plane in an hour and a half." He said, "I know." I said, "Well, don't harm me." And he replied, "Don't worry, I don't want to hurt you."

As soon as the game was over, we rushed into the showers, got changed, said our good-byes to the team and were gone. I felt really bad about it. We had taxis waiting. We rushed to the airport and ran the gauntlet at the airport. One old man jabbed me with his brolly and said, "Shame on you for going."

It wasn't the best way of doing it, but we were determined to go. I have no regrets about going. I had a fantastic time, played good rugby, got to see the country, as it was then. I went there to play rugby. I'm not a politician.

•

I must have told my employers two or three times that I might not be there the following Monday, and that I'd be back in a couple of months. Their attitude was, "We're a large company. We'll just put you on unpaid leave." My bags were continually packed for two weeks. It was hard trying to do everything else at the same time – play rugby, do your job, lead your life.

South Africa – The Quinn Tapes

Grant Fox in action for the Cavaliers in 1986. Other Cavaliers pictured are (from left) Andy Haden, Murray Pierce, Mark Shaw and Gary Knight.

Robbie Deans
All Black fullback from 1983-85.

The first time we decided to make a tour of South Africa was a comedy in its own right. It was a time of great stress and obviously we players were betwixt and between. There was a great desire to go to Africa and play against an historically great rugby nation. But also we were aware that we were doing something that didn't have the full support of the New Zealand union. We did have one aborted attempt. All the Canterbury contingent met up at our place and we left from the farm at about 2am to drive to Picton where we would catch the ferry. We had been travelling a couple of hours, with not a soul on the road, when these headlights came up behind the van. It was Jock, [Hobbs] who was reasonably stressed at the time. He had other issues as well – Nicki [Hobbs' wife, Deans' sister] was pregnant – so he was highly strained and he said, "Christ, they're on to us." But we got up to the Picton terminal. We were in disguise, wearing hats and shades and thought we were very well camouflaged. But Wayne Smith, one of the last players to get on, passed his ticket over to the ticketing man who said, "Hell, we've got half the Canterbury team here tonight." So our disguises failed miserably.

We got to Wellington and got off the boat and were hiding all around the dock. Finally a Honda Civic came to pick up eight players, plus all their luggage, so that was a disaster. They took the gear and we players were still there. We finally got up to a house where all the curtains were drawn. There was a lot of conjecture: it was off, it was on, it was off. Ultimately it was off for good at about 4pm. We threw open the curtains, which was a source of much relief, because the whole thing was very poorly planned. It seemed like a good idea because of the opportunity it presented, but the reality was it was just a disaster. So that trip was aborted and we went up to Masterton to play Wairarapa on the Wednesday. Only half of us ended up playing the ▶

Legends of the All Blacks

Rugby of a Cavalier Fashion

game. The other half were deemed to be in no mental state to do so.

I can recall vividly the second effort to get away. Jock came up to our cricket ground in north Canterbury. I thought it was a bit unusual for Jock to get so far out of town in February and knew something was up. I approached the vehicle in the lunch break and he said, "It's on again." I thought that crikey, we'd been through two attempts, the official one and the first aborted attempt, so the rebel tour didn't inspire me a great deal at that point. I was sceptical it would happen at all, even when we got to Hong Kong en route. There were various players coming in from all parts. Kieran Crowley was coming from Italy… it still didn't feel like we were going to get there. Until we got there, a lot of us didn't think it would be a reality.

Andy Haden

We were primed for a tour [in 1985] and it was a huge disappointment when the tour was called off. I remember sitting aside from the rest of the players in Wellington after we got the news and saying, "I don't think we can sit here and take this. We have to make our own way in the world, stand up for ourselves."

•

The South Africans were the people who had the plan [for the rebel tour]. I was their main contact in New Zealand and flew to Hong Kong for a meeting with Louis Luyt, Andy Dalton and Colin Meads…

We put together an agreement, advising all the players who had been selected for the tour [in 1985]. There was no pressure on the players to go. Grant Fox was unsure whether he would go. He used to ring in the morning and say he wasn't going. I'd say, "That's fine, I'll ring Frano Botica." Then he'd say, "I'll ring tonight to confirm." If he was out in the morning, he was back in at night. If he was out at night, he was back in the next morning. I never did ring Frano and Foxy came. David Kirk and John Kirwan elected not to go. There was no pressure put on them.

KQ: How did the name Cavaliers come about?

I felt we couldn't call ourselves the All Blacks, but we had to have some name. I spoke to Ian Kirkpatrick [team manager] and Colin Meads [team coach] and suggested the Cavaliers. I even wrote them a page to deliver at our first press conference explaining why we were there and mentioning the name Cavaliers. It was just a name which popped into my head and I liked it.

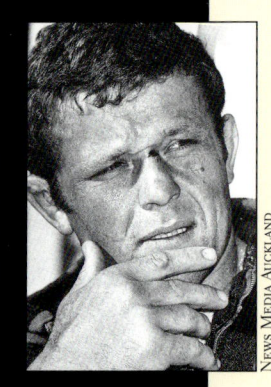

Andy Dalton

I would much prefer to have gone as the official All Blacks. It's not in my nature to go against the establishment, so I struggled with that issue. We were not the New Zealand team; we emphasised that and I was upset when it was publicly stated over there that it was the All Blacks. We made it clear we weren't. Having said that, we played it as close to internationals as we could, with the build-up, the disciplines, the determination, the commitment and dedication.

Jock Hobbs
All Black loose forward from 1983-86.

When I first heard about it, my inclination was not to go and I now regret having gone. I respect the decision of my fellow players who went on the tour. We believed at the time it was the right thing to do. On an academic intellectual level, you could debate either side convincingly, but I regret not having followed my first inclination. I have learnt from that and it has had an impact, certainly some influence with respect to the

South Africa – The Quinn Tapes

crisis in 1995 [when Hobbs negotiated with the All Blacks over professional contracts], even though they were very different events and circumstances.

These are not regrets that I had ten or thirteen years later. I had regrets through the tour and they continued immediately afterwards. It comes back to a gut instinct and I feel that rugby came under a great deal of pressure because of it. I suspect that the majority of people in rugby supported the tour, but it did cause distress, which didn't help the game. That's the first issue. Secondly, on a bigger scale, the black majority didn't want us there and I think that should have been respected.

KQ: You could be criticised, like Chris Laidlaw has been, for touring South Africa, enjoying the good life, then coming back and changing your mind.

That's a possibility. Indeed, one could be far more critical of me because I had concerns and my inclination was not to go, yet I did. I deserved more criticism than the player who from the very beginning thought this was right, still feels it was right, and went.

David Kirk
made a late decision to pull out of the Cavaliers team for the rebel tour of South Africa in 1986.

I was selected for the tour of South Africa in 1985 and was happy to go. I had examined my conscience and my approach quite seriously, but in the end decided that it was a New Zealand representative team going to play rugby and made the decision that in the end major political systems and approaches aren't influenced by sport. That was my position in 1985. I was disappointed when the tour was called out.

A number of things caused my change of heart over the next year. In 1986 it wasn't an All Black tour, so there wasn't the same pull there. We weren't going to be going as the New Zealand All Blacks to beat the Springboks. There was talk of money which for me was also a downside as it inevitably gave the tour a different flavour. By then my own sense of the rightness of making symbolic acts regardless of whether they worked or not had emerged. I thought I should not go if I felt it wasn't the right thing to do, regardless of whether it was going to ultimately influence the political system. It is probably easier to talk about after the event than at the time, when it was just some kind of emotional amalgam that made me say that in the end I didn't want to go.

David Kirk

I feel that for most of the players the main reason they wanted to go was to beat South Africa. They were rugby players who were able to totally separate themselves from any wider agenda or wider context. Some of the senior players who had not had the opportunity to go there before and had really been very successful through the early 1980s now wanted to go to South Africa, to climb that final peak and win a series on South African soil. Most of the players went absolutely for those reasons, but there's no doubt the taint of money was an added complication.

KQ: What do you think of players who toured with the Cavaliers and now say they regretted it?

I think that's honest and courageous of them. I mean I, who changed my mind between 1985 and 1986, ought to salute people who in hindsight say they made an error and shouldn't have gone. Good for them.

KQ: Did pulling out of the Cavaliers team affect your future relationship with many of those players?

When the players went they hoped and believed that ▶

Legends of the All Blacks

Rugby of a Cavalier Fashion

the tour would be successful and would be viewed by the New Zealand public as a fair enough thing to do. They'd been denied the chance to tour the previous year by a sort of foul means. They were just a bunch of guys who wanted to go over there and win for New Zealand. It would be televised, people would be interested, the tour would be accepted as an appropriate activity. But my recollection is that most New Zealanders – certainly all the administrators and many supporters – felt this was a wrong tour and the talk of money at the time was a big part of that.

So the players felt set upon and felt a bit defensive about the fact that they were now kind of outsiders. I'd made a separate decision when I had been part of their group and they saw me as someone who had in a way benefited from their pain after the event and that set up a strained relationship with some of the players.

There was a lot of tension during the Bledisloe Cup series in 1986 because of that. I captained the team for the first two tests of the season, one against France and one against Australia, when those players were either unavailable or suspended. Then about twelve of them were selected for the second test against Australia. There was nothing particularly overt, but within a group you either acknowledge that there's a leader and you're part of the team, or you're not. It was fairly obvious, because the team was then dominated by players who had been to South Africa – and they had become a very tight group when they were away – that my capacity to lead them was pretty low. I felt excluded. Some of it was my own sense of defensiveness about it, but I definitely felt excluded, like I was an interloper as their captain. Although I'm sure they tried not to give that view, it was hard not to, particularly among the forwards, who really were predominantly African touring players.

Robbie Deans
was an All Black fullback from 1983-85.

I have no doubt that some members of the New Zealand union were aware we were about to make a rebel tour of South Africa. We had administrators come into the shed after our South Pacific fixture against Auckland at Lancaster Park and wish us well. Those same people were being quoted on Monday as saying, "What's happening? We weren't aware of this."

Danie Craven

Andy Haden

KQ: Did Danie Craven know about the Cavaliers' tour plans?

Absolutely. I spoke to Danie a couple of times. I know he fell out with Ces Blazey over that and said he never knew about the tour. But he talked to me.

Ross Turnbull
a former Wallaby and IRB member.

The announcement came through over breakfast that the All Blacks had arrived in South Africa and there's both these old men [Danie Craven and Ces Blazey] saying they didn't know anything about it, which was ridiculous. Of course they knew everything about it. It was just the way the game was played.

South Africa – The Quinn Tapes

INTO THE NINETIES

Laurie Mains
coached the All Blacks from 1992-95.

KQ: How was the feeling before the test against South Africa in 1992, the first in eleven years between the two countries?

It was just sensational. I remember coming out of the dressing room and going into the stand and the hair on the back of my neck stood up. The atmosphere in the stadium was fantastic, and then when the crowd burst into *Die Stem*, it was something I'd never even close to experienced before.

Sean Fitzpatrick
played for the All Blacks from 1986-97.

KQ: Tell us about the famous ear-biting incident at Athletic Park in 1994.

It was bizarre. It's not the sort of thing you expect to happen on the field and I couldn't believe it had actually happened. We'd got on Johan's [le Roux] case a bit in the previous test at Dunedin and wound him up to breaking point. I'm a huge believer that you give as much as you take and I take a fair bit. My message to him was if you can't take it, don't give it. We went into a ruck, cleaned him out, and held onto him. He didn't like it and retaliated.

After the game, that was the end of it. I had a beer with Johan and nothing was mentioned. But it went on further for him, and he got suspended.

Louis Luyt
was the South African Rugby Football Union president in the mid-1990s.

I remember in Auckland when I handed over the Tri-Nations trophy [in 1996], I was booed. Then Mr Bolger, the Prime Minister got up and he was also booed. I said to him he'd received a bigger boo than me, but he said, "No, yours was bigger!" It's sad for me that New Zealanders, who have been my friends, feel like that about me. I was only joking during the speech I gave after the World Cup. I explained that to Colin Meads and he accepted it, but apparently other New Zealanders haven't.

Sean Fitzpatrick
was a favourite target of South African spectators during the 1990s.

I enjoyed the way the South African fans loved to hate me. We New Zealanders are so similar to them in our passion for sport and getting right behind our national team. It got to the stage in South Africa where I never used to walk onto the ground before a game because it used to almost cause a frenzy within the crowd, with the booing. I can remember a man at King's Park telling me I was the JR Ewing of world rugby, the player that we love to hate, which was fine with me. They were the sorts of things which motivated me. Allan Border once said to me that if he came to Eden Park and they didn't boo him, he'd be worried. That's how I felt about South Africa.

•

KQ: In 1996, Sean Fitzpatrick achieved what every All Black captain had aspired to – victory in a test series in South Africa.

Pretoria in 1996 was very special for me, the greatest moment of my career. We were one up in the series. We'd already beaten them three times so far that year and it was difficult to believe we still had to play another one to win the series. We had to beat them at Pretoria because the last game was going to be at Ellis Park. We had to really struggle to win the series. Every match was a ding-dong affair and you couldn't rest and enjoy the game.

To win at Pretoria was the most amazing feeling. With a minute to go, I had visions of them scoring a try and converting it, which would make the game a draw, and then they'd go to Ellis Park and win the next game to draw the series. They took a quick tap and ▶

Legends of the All Blacks

INTO THE NINETIES

The long wait is over – Pretoria, 1996.

van der Westhuizen, the halfback scored. Thank goodness the ref pulled him back and said he hadn't taken it from the mark.

At the end it was sheer elation, to finally win over there. It'll be part of New Zealand history that will go on forever. I walked back to the dressing room and saw past All Blacks crying, the media coming into the room, everyone so excited. Before I went to the game, I got a call from a chap in Gisborne who said, "Fitzy, we're having a party here. The whole of New Zealand is behind you." Looking around the ground at the end of the game, and the number of New Zealanders there following us, it was just fantastic. What really amazed me was how gracious the South Africans were in defeat, not only their team, but their supporters.

I remember Ian Jones being asked to compare the World Cup and the series win in 1996 and he said, "You are only world champion for four years, but beating the Africans on African soil for the first time – that lasts forever." I'd dearly love to have won the World Cup in 1995, but to be the first All Black team to win a series there, that's etched on my mind as one of the great moments of my career.

John Hart
became the All Black coach at the end of 1995.

Winning a series in South Africa was something we'd never done, and when that's your first task as an All Black coach, that's pretty daunting. The key decision was taking thirty-six players.

I have three memories of the game at Pretoria – Jon Preston coming off the bench and immediately putting a penalty right between the posts from forty-five metres; Zinzan Brooke's brilliance in dropping a goal that put us seven points ahead; and the last minute when the All Blacks defended with every sinew of their bodies working overtime. The South Africans threw every bit of their history at us to try to keep the series alive. When it was over, some of the All Blacks were so exhausted they could hardly move. It made me so proud, not just to be the All Black coach, but to be a New Zealander.

Colin Meads

We were sitting at home watching the telly when we finally beat South Africa in 1996. I remember saying we should go and have a drink because there were a lot of people in New Zealand with the same thoughts as me – "At last we've beaten you buggers." I felt so much pride watching Fitzy and Zinny and the rest of them. It was a great feeling.

The Captains

Taking the Lead

By Ron Palenski

A captain, Graham Gooch once wrote, has to combine the qualities of a tactical guru, sergeant-major, thoughtful counsellor, supreme man-manager, excellent player, diplomat, inspirational gambler and consistent motivator and be skilled in media relations and overflowing with luck.

Gooch, as captain of England and Essex, was writing about cricket of course, but he might as well have been writing about the captaincy of the All Blacks – and thrown in a few more desirable qualities, such as having the patience of a saint, the hide of a rhinoceros, the sensitivity of an accomplished artist, the verbal skills of the most practised politician and the negotiating skills of the sharpest lawyers.

They must keep their own counsel yet be gregarious at the same time; self-effacing yet be able to forcefully state their case.

Do such people of contradictions exist, especially in a physical contact sport such as rugby in which, shorn of the politically correct niceties, the ultimate respect is paid to those players who put, to use the time-honoured phrase, their bodies on the line?

Remarkably, they do, and New Zealand, much more than any other rugby country, has been blessed with the quality of its captains.

The only other job in New Zealand that comes under such public scrutiny, when detractors and supporters are all self-proclaimed experts, many of them with justification, is that of prime minister. And there have been occasions in New Zealand's rugby history when the All Black captain has known public debate over his tenure, the like of which many prime ministers never experienced, or would want to.

What New Zealand prime minister, for example, has been vilified on the front and sports pages of the British newspapers for imagined wrongdoings, accusations of sins of omission or commission that cloaked rampant chauvinism and parochialism? The answer is none. Yet several All Black captains, from the mists of time and in recent memory, have known such public enmity.

There have been and are people in New Zealand who have much more diverse, enduring and immediate impact on the way New Zealanders live than All Black captains, yet none has been as microscopically scrutinised, examined, dissected, analysed, criticised or praised as an All Black captain.

When an All Black team is announced and the magic (c) is added to a

Legends of the All Blacks

player's name, that player forever foregoes the status of his peers, he is marked for life. If it's true, and it demonstrably is, that whatever else an All Black may do in his life he is forever known first and foremost for having been an All Black, then it is doubly so for a captain.

One player who captained the All Blacks briefly, Chris Laidlaw, attained high office in a number of spheres, including such weighty responsibilities as advisor to the Commonwealth secretary-general, confidant of a prime minister, diplomat and race relations conciliator. For all those accomplishments, he once lamented, he was more often described in later life as former All Black captain or, more commonly, former All Black.

Wilson Whineray became chairman of one of New Zealand's biggest companies, chaired the Hillary Commission, the quasi-government body charged with encouraging sport for all in New Zealand, and was knighted, yet he has never lost the prefix, "former All Black captain".

Brian Lochore coached the All Blacks to their only World Cup win – the fact it was New Zealand's only win in a sport it historically dominates is a statistical oddity – and served his country in many diverse ways beyond rugby. He too became chairman of the Hillary Commission and was knighted, but he too is known primarily for his long-ago status as the All Black captain.

It is just not the living former All Black captains who, though their playing days are long behind them, carry with them the mantle of respect and the burden of history that the leadership of the country's national rugby team endows.

Two of the earliest, Tom Ellison and Dave Gallaher, are still, close on 100 years later, frequently cited as authorities on the game and thinkers and leaders ahead of their time. And that's not just in New Zealand, where there is a justifiable pride and an all-consuming interest. Ellison, the man who decided the national playing uniform should be a black jersey with the silver fern, argued long before any others that the amateurism imposed on rugby by the upper middle-class of southern England was impractical and never intended for world-wide consumption. It took nearly 100 years for his views to be heeded.

Gallaher, the captain of the 1905 Original All Blacks – so-called Originals because they were the first All Blacks to go to Britain – and his vice-captain, Billy Stead, wrote a book after the tour called *The Complete Rugby Footballer*. They wrote it over a three-week period between the end of the tour and waiting on a ship to North America, yet such a rush job became one of the standard text books of the game.

Ellison and Gallaher both died young, though Gallaher was also an All Black selector for seven years, and their names are writ large in the history of All Black captains.

There can be few, if any, positions in world sport that carry with them such high status, a status that brings with it such intense public scrutiny. How many captains of Manchester United, for example, have become household names

The Captains

Dave Gallaher, who died in the First World War.

because of their captaincy? Or of another perennially successful team in another sport, the New York Yankees? Or the Brazilian soccer team, a national side with which the All Blacks are most often compared for enduring excellence?

When respected New Zealand rugby journalist Lindsay Knight wrote a book about All Black captains, *They Led the All Blacks*, in 1991, he likened the captaincy to that of the Australian cricket team. It was an accurate observation. Only the Australians with their cricket have vested the captaincy with the type of aura that belongs to the All Black captaincy. And it is neither coincidence nor serendipity that Australian cricket, like New Zealand rugby, is at its best when there is stability with the captaincy.

For all the burdens of leadership and for all the weight of history, it may be reasonable to assume that players strive to be the All Black captain. A logical upward progression for club rugby players would be to first play for their province, then captain their province, then to be chosen for the All Blacks, then the ultimate: the All Black captaincy.

But history, both in the past and contemporary history, suggests this is not so. Once having attained the rarefied status of the All Blacks, the ambition of most players is to remain an All Black, knowing that by so doing they will be "good" or better All Blacks. Improvement and success and a deep-seated drive to not let the side down is what drives All Blacks. Few would consciously set out to become the All Black captain. Money is not a motivating factor in itself. The money in the game now allows the players to devote the time to the sport that it requires and it provides a career for them at a time of their lives they would otherwise be career-building in other directions. Earlier generations, of course, built careers in tandem with rugby careers, but the game is at such a level now that that would be impractical, if not impossible. The payments to players too provide an equitable share of the profits that rugby reaps as a major entertainment.

For all that, many of today's players would continue to play for the All Blacks even if there wasn't money.

The additional money it is assumed an All Black captain earns would not in itself be sufficient motivation for a player to aspire to the captaincy. If the amateur past is repeated in the professional present and future, there would

Legends of the All Blacks

be All Blacks who would not want to be captain. History suggests this would be a valid assumption.

A day after the Original All Blacks left Wellington by ship in 1905 for Britain, Dave Gallaher resigned from the captaincy. He told the manager, George Dixon, that his appointment had been made by the New Zealand Rugby Football Union without consulting the players. Gallaher did not want to be captain, he said, unless it was the wish of the players. Dixon, as a member of the NZRFU, was a little put out and initially refused to accept the resignation, but he eventually bowed to Gallaher's wish and the captaincy became the subject of a seaboard ballot. Of the 29 eligible voters on the ship, 17 voted for Gallaher – hardly unanimous, but sufficient to confirm him in the position and what Dixon described as "awkwardness" was past.

Such reluctance on the part of appointed captains was not purely a foible of the past. Sean Fitzpatrick became the captain in 1992 when Mike Brewer, the player who coach Laurie Mains wanted as captain, was injured. When Fitzpatrick saw Brewer lying on the ground injured in a trial match in Napier, he knew he was the next logical person to be captain, but he was reluctant.

"I really didn't want to be the All Black captain," Fitzpatrick wrote in his autobiography, *Fronting Up*. "It wasn't something I'd ever considered. Now that I had it, I didn't feel good about it. I was excited, but nervous too. I didn't want the pressure of public speaking and the pressure of looking after a new team . . . I wanted to sit back, recapture my form and not have any responsibilities."

Not all captains, either of short or long tenures, have recorded their views when first given the job, but there could have been few, if any, who viewed their appointment with anything other than a mixture of pride and trepidation – pride that they were considered worthy for such a high honour, and trepidation that they could do the job and, importantly, do the job without it adversely affecting their primary role in the team.

And what is "the job"? In these days of corporate organisation, it probably comes with a job description written by someone deskbound who has little feeling for the multi-faceted talents that are required and even less feeling for the sensitivities and personality of the person involved. The job has changed over the years and the demands have become much greater as rugby has determined itself to be part of the wider entertainment industry rather than essentially a Saturday or Wednesday afternoon leisure pursuit watched and followed by committed devotees. The essentials have not changed; the practicalities have.

When Dave Gallaher was leading the Originals in Britain, he was under constant criticism for his playing role as wing forward, a position the British held to be a cheat (though they copied it). He recalled that he was approached in a hotel foyer one day by "a gentleman of the press" (his description) who sought his views on the propriety of the position and of the public criticism of it. Gallaher said he replied a little haughtily that he was

The Captains

not at liberty to say and if any public comments were to be made, they were to be made by the manager, George Dixon.

The 1998 All Black captain, Taine Randell, and many of his predecessors, would probably like to be able to respond in the same manner, but know they could not. The captain is the public face of the team and it is a part of his duty to respond to as many interview requests as are reasonable (and a great many that are not). It is a small role in the wider scheme of the good of the team, but it is a large role in terms of consumption of time, and often a frustrating, boring one because so often the questions a captain is confronted with have been put time and again, yet the captain has to contrive to answer as if each time it is fresh and new.

Sean Fitzpatrick

To say that captaincy is leadership is axiomatic. Of course it is, but it's more than that. The All Black captain has to have standing as a player and he must have presence, the X-factor. It's called the X-factor because the qualities such a description requires are difficult to define. New Zealanders are fortunate to have the Maori word, mana, which perhaps covers the requirements best of all.

The captain's qualities are apparent in the big pictures and in the small pictures. An example of the former was on the 1972-73 tour of Britain when prop Keith Murdoch was, belatedly, sent home for confronting a security guard in the team's Cardiff hotel. Ian Kirkpatrick, a player who bore all the hallmarks of the ideal All Black captain, shouldered much of the criticism that followed the Murdoch affair, yet had little if any responsibility for it. He bore the criticisms with stoicism and with more good grace than could reasonably have been expected in the circumstances.

An example of the latter, the small picture, was when the All Blacks were starting out on their Grand Slam tour of Britain in 1978. On the first Saturday in London, a couple of days after arriving, they went along to Twickenham to watch England play Argentina. After the game, the All Blacks were standing around outside the dressing room area and the captain, Graham Mourie, was besieged both by autograph hunters and

Legends of the All Blacks

by English journalists, anxious for his views of the forthcoming tour. Mourie waved them all away with a smile, "This is Argentina's day, not ours," he said.

It was Mourie who once said he thought rugby devoted more time and thoughtful energy to choosing the right captain than it did to many other decisions it made. "More thought is given to the All Black captaincy appointment by the selectors than there is by the union to electing the council and then by the council itself to some of its appointments," Mourie said.

That was when New Zealand rugby was governed by a 19-man council, but the same may hold true now that it is governed by a nine-man board, set up along corporate lines.

The appointment of Taine Randell to the captaincy had long been predicted. He captained Otago when he was 19 and in 1995, when he was chosen for the All Blacks for the first time, even as a junior All Black and a midweek player, he was touted as a future captain. That was under one coach, Laurie Mains. When the next coach, John Hart, took over, nothing changed. It was always implicit that Randell was the heir presumptive to the long-serving Sean Fitzpatrick. When Fitzpatrick was injured and couldn't play on the 1997 tour of Britain and Ireland, Hart made halfback Justin Marshall the captain and that was seen for what it was: a temporary measure to allow Randell to grow into his role of All Black flanker before becoming the captain. When Randell early in 1998 was named the captain, no-one could have been surprised.

Captain Taine Randell (left) and coach John Hart.

While rugby in New Zealand has more often than not chosen its captains wisely, its methods have not always been characterised by wisdom. A classic example of considering an appointment ahead of the feelings of a man occurred before the All Blacks' tour of Britain in 1924, the team known as the Invincibles. Before the All Blacks left for Britain, they made a short tour of Australia on which they were captained by an Auckland five-eighth, Ces Badeley. It was assumed that he would remain captain for the British tour, but because the All Blacks had been beaten in Australia, the New Zealand union decided otherwise. Its method of advising Badeley of the transfer of the captaincy from him to the Wellington wing forward, Cliff Porter, was brutal. It happened at a parliamentary farewell dinner to the team. Printed on the dinner menu was the name of the captain, Ces Badeley, who was

The Captains

down to reply to the toast to the team. But when the time for the speeches came, the master of ceremonies summoned not Badeley, but the tour captain, Porter, to make the speech. It was the first indication Badeley had that he was not the captain.

Whether the choice was the correct one or not was irrelevant; the method of advising of the change was reprehensible. And for all the success of that team, it remains debatable whether the choice was the correct one. Porter played in only one of the tests on tour, against France, which was then a relatively minor rugby power, the captaincy in the others going to a Southland forward, Jock Richardson. Porter had been injured before the first test, against Ireland, but doubts lingered whether the injury was sufficiently serious to keep him out of the following tests against Wales and England. Perhaps a clue to Porter's omission came a few years later when he told rugby writer Terry McLean that as long as the Invincibles' manager, Stan Dean, held any position of authority in New Zealand rugby, he would have nothing to do with the game.

Porter was not true to his word because Dean was a dictatorial chairman of the New Zealand union from 1922 until 1947, yet Porter again captained the All Blacks in 1929 and 1930. Porter's comments, though, hinted at a personality clash between himself and Dean, a not unlikely conclusion to draw given that both were strong personalities. A factor in tours then too was that there was no coach involved and the manager was in unquestioned charge of all aspects of the tour, including selection.

Cliff Porter

Porter was not chosen even as a player for the 1928 All Black tour of South Africa. The captain then was the great All Black forward from Hawke's Bay, Maurice Brownlie, and his vice-captain one of the most mercurial backs to play for New Zealand, Mark Nicholls. There were, evidently, politics on that tour too and Nicholls, for all his undoubted genius, played only in the final test, which was won. Brownlie was a man of few words, preferring his deeds to do his talking. Nicholls had a sharp tongue and therein perhaps lay the answer to the mystery of why Nicholls played in just the one test.

If the circumstances of the replacement of Badeley with Porter in 1924 were unkind, the lessons were hardly learned by rugby authorities. They may have taken great care in the appointment of their captains, but they seemed to care less when it came to discarding them.

Legends of the All Blacks

After Ian Kirkpatrick had borne the brunt of the criticisms of the 1972-73 team, criticisms which obscured how good the team was and how close it went to becoming the first to achieving the Grand Slam, he was replaced as captain in 1974 by Andy Leslie. He learned of the change in the same way everyone else learned of it – in the crowded function room, usually referred to as the dungeon, at Athletic Park after a trial match. The chairman of the union, Jack Sullivan, announced the team chosen by the new coach, JJ Stewart, to the assembled trialists and live on radio. At the end of the team being named in position order, he said it would be captained by Andy Leslie of Wellington. Leslie and the man he had supplanted, Kirkpatrick, happened to be standing next to each other at the time. Kirkpatrick, showing again the type of man he is, shook Leslie's hand and promised him full support – which, on the following tour of Australia, he gave. And some say that Kirkpatrick played some of his finest rugby on that tour, particularly in the Sydney test, perhaps expressing a relief that he had shed the burden of captaincy.

The union, though, didn't learn even from that lesson. Three years later, when the All Black team was named to tour France, Mourie was named as the new captain and Kirkpatrick, despite still being a dominant figure in New Zealand rugby and having played in each of the four tests against the Lions, was not included. He learned of his omission while sitting in the Poverty Bay team's bus. A deep suspicion lingered that the selectors wanted to ease Mourie into the captaincy without the "pressure" of having a former captain, Kirkpatrick, among the players. But Kirkpatrick had shown amply in 1974 that such petty considerations were not part of his make-up and such a contention would have reflected poorly on Mourie's leadership also.

The past serves the present to plan for the future but, amazingly, New Zealand rugby again got it wrong when in 1990 the All Black selectors decided to drop their hitherto highly successful captain, Wayne Shelford, and replace him with Gary Whetton. Shelford learned of his demotion at the same time as the public did, apparently because of a misunderstanding among selectors about which of them had been deputed to tell him. In the event, none did.

The dropping of Shelford also led to the unprecedented public outcry to "bring back Buck", a clamour that seemed based more on sentiment than on rationality. But it was an indication of Shelford's standing as an exemplar of the type of captain who leads by example, the leader who leads and by his sheer presence, compels the others to follow.

His replacement, Whetton, was in an entirely different category. A fine lock for many years and a great athlete, Whetton did not seem to be a natural leader and his selection as captain owed more to his seniority and longevity than any other factor. History does not judge Whetton's tenure kindly, mainly because it ended at the World Cup in 1991 when the All Blacks were beaten in a semi-final by Australia and, as bad as that loss was seen to be, were regarded as an unhappy, dysfunctional team. Senior players

The Captains

Mike Brewer

such as Fitzpatrick and Grant Fox made no secret of the fact that they considered retiring after the cup because they had had enough.

With the undoubted wisdom of hindsight, the selectors of 1990 – Alex Wyllie, John Hart and Lane Penn – when they chose to rid themselves of Shelford, should have then opted for the perennial captain-in-waiting, Mike Brewer, instead of Whetton. No one can know how the All Blacks would have fared under Brewer, but they could not have fared much worse than they did.

The selection of a player such as Whetton as captain broke the mould for the All Black captaincy. Hitherto, long-term captains (as opposed to those for just odd games or tours) such as Whineray, Lochore and Mourie had been chosen because of their potential as captains. They'd either been earmarked early in their careers as having the difficult-to-define captaincy material, or in the case of Lochore they'd shown on their early tours that they had the presence to command a disparate group of men bound by the single factor of wanting to play winning rugby.

In military terms, Whetton was the type of player who would be an admirable lieutenant, but not one who would aspire to field rank.

This is not to suggest that Whetton could not or did not do the job on the field. He did and it could be argued, especially considering his long tenure as captain of the successful Auckland team, that he was a tactically astute captain, especially adept at exhorting his team to apply pressure when he felt his opponents were teetering on the brink of acceptance of defeat.

Where Whetton had trouble was in the off-field demands of the job, especially in dealing with the media and the other many extracurricular demands that captaincy brings.

New Zealand normally shows great care in the selection of its captains. Sometimes it's just plain lucky. Such a time was the 1987 World Cup when the appointed captain, Andy Dalton, was injured shortly before the first match and the halfback, David Kirk, took over the on-field role. The captaincy then had to be seen in the context of what preceded the cup. New Zealand rugby was a sport divided. Two years before the cup, court action prevented the All Blacks under Dalton from touring South Africa and in the year before, the All Blacks who would have gone organised themselves into a private group they

Legends of the All Blacks

called the Cavaliers and went anyway. Dalton led them but Kirk, who had been chosen for the All Blacks in 1985, opted out of the rebel tour.

New Zealand, and New Zealand rugby, was reunited by the success of the team in the cup, and the stand-in captain Kirk was seen as its public face. Kirk, in the memorable words of the Rugby Union chairman at the time, Russ Thomas, was someone who all young women loved and who all older women wanted to mother. It is unlikely the All Blacks would have been greeted so ecstatically throughout the country if Dalton, the face of the divisive Cavaliers, had played. But Dalton remained the cup squad captain and played a vital role in the team's success. He had recovered from his injury and could have played in the last few games but coach Brian Lochore decided against changing a winning team. It was probably the only time in history that the All Blacks had a dual captaincy – Kirk the smiling public face, Dalton the leader behind the scenes.

It would not have been coincidental that when the New Zealand union wanted a former All Black captain as union president for the World Cup year of 1999 it chose Dalton. It also showed that if it can't always remember, the union can at least forgive.

The Cavaliers episode also focused an unusual attention on one of the great men of New Zealand rugby, Colin Meads. He had through the 1960s been the indestructible face of the game, the atypical epitome of the strong All Black forward, the type who would seemingly grow whenever he pulled on the All Black jersey and intimidate opponents by his mere presence. He too was a lieutenant but he was promoted after Brian Lochore's retirement at the end of 1970 and made captain for the 1971 tour by the British Isles. Meads was the type of captain who led not by the right words in the right ears at the right times or by dint of inherent leadership qualities, but by force of personality and presence. Every New Zealand rugby player knew that Meads would die for his country – he had played a test with a broken arm, after all – and All Blacks in his teams felt they could do no less. They drew strength from his. It was Meads' misfortune that the 1971 Lions were the best organised team to tour New Zealand and had the talent in key positions to complement the organisation. It was also Meads' misfortune, and the All Blacks', that he was injured in a car accident over the following summer and could not tour with the All Blacks in Britain in 1972-73. Had he

David Kirk leads the All Blacks into the 1987 World Cup.

done so, it was widely believed his commanding presence and experience might have helped avoid the pits into which that team fell.

It was Meads' love of rugby and his devotion to the cause that led to his being coach of the Cavaliers in 1986, an action that cost him his job as a national selector, but he too was later forgiven. He was the All Black manager in 1995 at the World Cup. Then later that year, in France, after the All Blacks lost the first test in Toulouse, he delivered one of the sternest reminders to All Blacks that must ever have been delivered. He reminded them of their obligations as All Blacks, the legacy of their jersey, their responsibility to all those All Blacks who had gone before and to all the people back home. The All Blacks won the next test.

New Zealand rugby has been well served by its captains. There have been some who were not successful, but by and large New Zealand avoided, usually by design, sometimes by accident, the former British habit of choosing leaders based on their breeding rather than their ability. There was no greater example of that than the captain of the 1966 Lions, Mike Campbell-Lamerton, an army officer who had all the attributes except the ones necessary to lead a successful rugby team.

Jack Manchester

New Zealand has had captains chosen as a compromise – Jack Manchester in 1935 was one example – or because other candidates fell by the wayside, such as Bob Stuart in 1953. Each of them fitted into their roles well, even though they were both leaders on what were considered losing tours (always given that "losing tours" by All Blacks are those on which not all games are won). There have been what might best be termed part-time captains such as Dave Loveridge in 1980 and Stu Wilson in 1983, but their tours failed for reasons other than their captaincy. There have also been captains who didn't want to continue in the role, such as Kevin Skinner after the 1952 season and Frank Oliver after he led the All Blacks against Australia in 1978 when Mourie was injured. There was a move to retain Oliver for the following British tour, but he demurred, Mourie was brought back and the team became the first to win the Grand Slam in Britain. It's never possible to determine how much of the success of a team is due to its captain, but in 1978 a large measure went Mourie's way.

The captain's role has changed markedly as the years have progressed, but in some aspects it has remained the same as when William Millton led the first New Zealand team to New South Wales in 1884. There have been managers and there have been coaches, but the noble line in the history of All Black rugby is that of the captains.

Legends of the All Blacks

Joseph Romanos
New Zealand journalist.

The question of the captaincy of the 1924-25 Invincibles is interesting. Cliff Porter was the captain, and a very respected leader he was. However, he got injured early on the tour and missed the first test. Jim Parker took his position as wing forward and evidently played outstandingly. When Porter then became available again, this led to an awkward selection meeting. I spoke to Jock Richardson, the team's vice-captain about it, shortly before he died. This is what he said: "There were three of us at the selection meetings, Cliff, Stan Dean, the manager, and myself. We would all agree on every position until it came to the question of wing forward. Stan Dean would vote for Jim Parker. Cliff thought he should be playing. This meant I had the casting vote and I would go for Parker, who was a brilliant player. He was fast enough to play on the wing and was in magnificent form. Naturally Cliff was not happy with this state of affairs and sometimes he would say in frustration, 'What's the use of being captain of the team if I can't play in the tests?' Eventually Cliff was chosen for the test in France just before we came home."

What was interesting was that none of this discord surfaced. I suppose the media of the time was less intrusive and questioning. You could imagine the situation today if the captain was being excluded from the test side and was unhappy about it.

Eric Tindill
was a member of the 1935-36 All Black team to the British Isles.

I wouldn't describe Jack Manchester as a successful captain. He never really exercised any leadership. He hadn't captained Canterbury. He was a side row man, so that wasn't a bad position to captain a team from. But we never heard from him while we were on the paddock. He played some of the other games at lock and we couldn't expect to hear from him there. And he played part of one game at No 8, so he could have led us properly from there. But he wasn't dominating, wasn't really telling us if we were doing anything wrong. And there was certainly no change of plan during the game, as there is today. He was a splendid player himself, absolutely outstanding. He might have said a few words in the dressing room before a game, but it was very low-key. If anything, it was Charlie Oliver, the vice-captain, who issued instructions now and then. He was playing at centre and used to tell us to let it out now and then.

Kevin Skinner
one of New Zealand's greatest props, captained the All Blacks against Australia in 1952.

I'd captained Otago in 1950 and had captained a couple of other rep selections. Next thing you know, the All Black selectors appointed me captain in 1952. Quite honestly, I wasn't very happy about it. I could see what they were planning – that I would lead the team to Britain in 1953-54. I preferred to be away from that job. I felt I could be more use to the team as a player. I didn't enjoy getting up at after-match functions making speeches and that sort of thing. So I asked the selectors to find someone else.

Cliff Porter (left) and Jock Richardson farewell Captain Cameron of the 'Remuera' after landing at Plymouth in 1924.

The Captains – The Quinn Tapes

Wilson Whineray

was just 23 when he was appointed All Black captain in 1958. He led New Zealand until 1965.

The first time I captained the All Blacks [in 1958, against Australia at home], we won quite well and I had a marvellous game, scoring two tries. I thought, "This captaining, it's easy peasy, really. You run onto the field, and you get a couple of tries." Well, I played another umpteen tests and never scored another one. Even so, it was a great start for me. Having said that, we immediately set about losing the next test, which brought me back down to earth with a bump.

New Zealand Rugby Museum

The on-field bit was the easy bit, the part I enjoyed and could relate to and didn't get nervous about. On bigger tours, especially in Britain, there's a fair number of dinners and social off-the-field functions and that can be a burden. It was that side that I found the least exciting. I was able to cope with the social aspects of being captain and got better the more I did it. You get into a routine.

•

The prime responsibility of a captain is to be a leader. People get all tied up with how you do things, but there are times when you've just got to take control of the show. I'm not sure I was a good captain to start with, but I think I became quite a good one because after a number of years there wasn't anything that could happen on the field that I hadn't been involved with before. One of my simple rules of thumb was: if you're losing and time's running out, do something different. It doesn't really matter what, but you're going to end up losing if you keep the same pattern until the final whistle. I said to the players I was with, "Don't question what I do on the field. I don't want to hear from you. Just do it, because I'll take the rap if it's wrong. The coach or selectors will deal with me, but if you don't do what I ask you to do, then you'll take the rap."

Legends of the All Blacks

The Lochore Years

Fred Allen
appointed Brian Lochore as All Black captain in 1966.

A captain has to be a good speaker, and good leader – he has to lead by example. I felt Brian Lochore had something special about him. So I decided Brian was the man. He's got tremendous mana about him. When he talks, it's in a nice manner. He doesn't get too loud-mouthed and you never hear him swear. He just controls the players under him and leads by example. He's still showing the same qualities in the things he's associated with these days.

Gareth Edwards
Wales and British Isles halfback from 1967-78.

The best New Zealand captain I played against was without question Brian Lochore. He was not only an outstanding player, but a great captain. He never panicked and the match was never lost, which I found to my dismay on a couple of occasions when the All Blacks won in injury time.

Brian Lochore
All Black captain from 1966-70.

I was very surprised when Fred Allen asked me to be the New Zealand captain. At the time, if you had a ranking list of how New Zealanders saw the next All Black captain, I would've been fifth highest behind Colin Meads, Kelvin Tremain, Ken Gray and probably Chris Laidlaw. Out of the blue, Fred told me I would be the captain, which shattered me really. I was a very nervous individual and wasn't ready for it mentally, captaining these guys for whom I had absolute respect. But the captaincy was made incredibly easy by the way they accepted me into the family, I suppose, and individually came and offered their support. They gave their support at team meetings and in discussions and it made my life a lot easier.

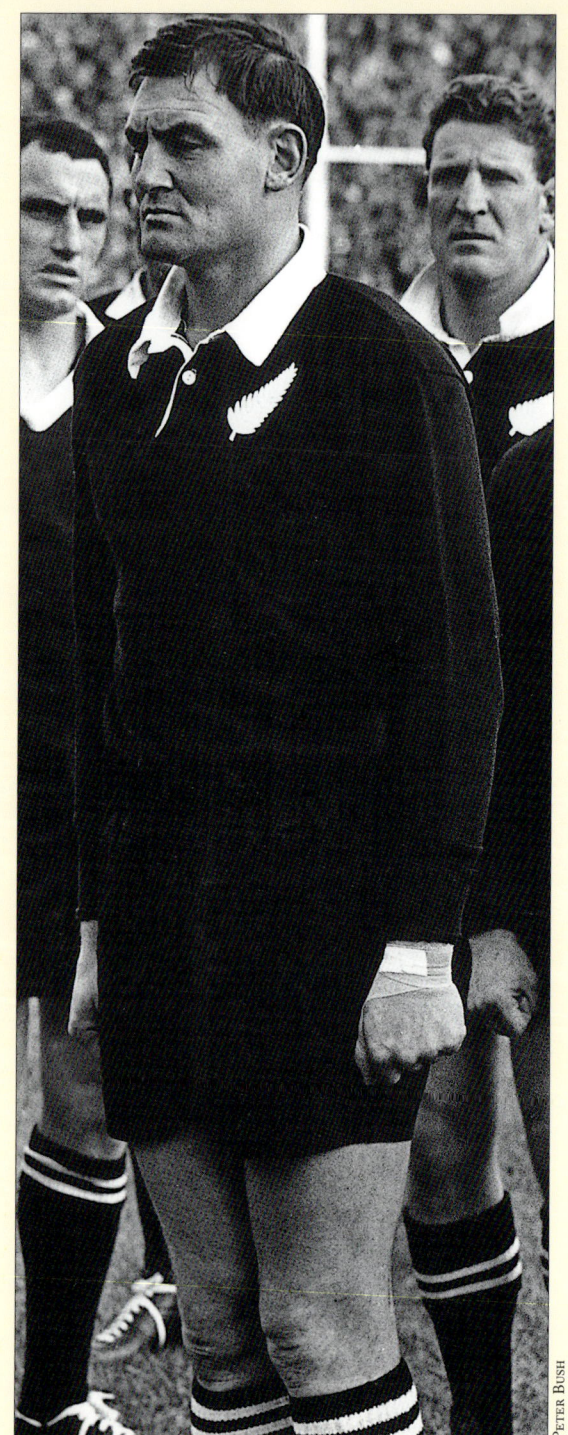

Brian Lochore with Ken Gray (left) and Alister Hopkinson before kick-off in the second test against France, 1968.

The Captains – The Quinn Tapes

Shaky Seventies – Searching for Stability

Colin Meads
captained New Zealand against the British Isles in 1971.

I never aspired to be All Black captain. I loved captaining King Country because that was my style, but to captain New Zealand, I always thought you wanted a guy like Whineray, a great mentor who taught me so much in life. He had a good education, had been to university and knew how to handle himself. I felt I was one of the troops. After I'd played for a few years, I'd be called on to sort things out with the troops. That's how I saw my role. I felt a bit inhibited when I was the All Black captain.

Ian Kirkpatrick
captained New Zealand in 1972-73.

I never sought the All Black captaincy. My big ambition wasn't to captain the All Blacks, it was to get in the test team. Having been given the captaincy, it was a huge honour and I was more than happy to take it on. I wasn't a big ranter or a raver. I probably expected a bit much of the players – to be responsible for themselves. My philosophy was to go out there and give one hundred and one percent without relying on anyone to motivate you or yell at you. You programme yourself so that the eighty minutes on the paddock is for your team and your country. So maybe I was a little too hands-off as a captain.

Bruce Robertson
played under Ian Kirkpatrick's captaincy in 1972-73.

Kirky was a great player and a good leader. He probably didn't get the support of us as players as much as he could have when he was leading the 1972-73 team through Britain. The tour didn't go as well as it should have and looking back, perhaps it was because the players didn't support Kirky as we could have.

JJ Stewart
in a surprise move, appointed Andy Leslie All Black captain in 1974.

We picked the 1974 All Black team to Australia in the broom cupboard under Athletic Park, facing asphyxiation from floor polish, detergent, and dirty buckets. Jack Gleeson, Eric Watson and I had a little table in there to help us select the team. Eric tells the story that when we got there I said, "You haven't got a bad first-five down there in your club in Otago. We'll put the bugger in now and get a cup of tea. That player was Duncan Robertson. We'd had such a disastrous season the year before, being beaten by England, who'd lost to all three provincial teams they met, that everyone's head was on the chopping block. We chose 15 new players out of 25. Jack Sullivan [NZRFU chairman] kept popping open the broom cupboard door and asking where our team was. I finally said, "Well, Jack do you want the team or do you want us to hurry up and just give you some names to announce?" So he'd go away and then return a few minutes later.

When we gave him the team, he said that we needed a captain. He assumed that because Ian Kirkpatrick was the current captain it would be him. But I didn't think Ian really enjoyed the captaincy. He was a great player and a great personality, but I didn't think being the captain was him. So Jack asked who it would be if not Kirkpatrick. We looked down the list and ended up with Andy Leslie. Some people have said Andy was selected to be captain, but that's quite wrong. It was the other way around. I didn't know Andy at all. I'd met him at after-match functions, but kept mixing him up with Dennis Waller, the big Wellington lock. I knew he'd captained Petone on a tour somewhere, and he had played one hundred and ten first class games for Wellington. In 1973 he'd been one of the reserves for the All Black trials. He must have thought the parade had passed him by, but there he was not only an All Black, but the captain. ▶

Legends of the All Blacks

Shaky Seventies – Searching for Stability

Andy Leslie
All Black captain from 1974-76.

Even though I was tremendously delighted to be named All Black captain, and felt there was no greater honour in New Zealand sport, it was one of the hardest moments I have faced. I replaced Ian Kirkpatrick, who was one of the greatest men I have been involved with. He was the first guy up to congratulate me. After the team was announced, some of the established players in the team tended to stick with Ian a wee bit and I had to earn their respect. But Ian never held back. The first letter I received on becoming All Black captain was from Ian's mother and the second one was from Ian. That was absolutely marvellous.

Ian Kirkpatrick

KQ: What were the circumstances when you lost the captaincy in 1974?

There was a story in *The Dominion* prior to the trial in 1974, so I had an inkling it could happen. I certainly wasn't told by anyone in the right places, but I put two and two together. I was probably happier playing without the captaincy, though no-one ever asked me that.

Andy Leslie (right) at a reception for the All Blacks, South Africa, 1976.

The Captains – The Quinn Tapes

Enter Graham Mourie

Bruce Robertson
played under six All Black test captains from 1972-81.

Graham Mourie was the best captain I played with in the All Blacks. He was mentally challenging. He looked at the intellectual side of captaincy. He looked at each game and tried to motivate his players in a different way. On the field he led by example and he was able to make changes when necessary. We won the Grand Slam in 1978 and that was a reflection of his captaincy because he helped lead the team on and off the field, setting standards for the players.

Graham Mourie
captained All Black teams from 1976 to 1982.

I was relatively young when I became captain, but so were people like Wilson Whineray and Taine Randell. That can create problems captaining people you've previously looked up to. I was fortunate to have senior players like Bryan Williams, Bruce Robertson, Andy Haden and Frank Oliver, who quickly became part of that group that leads All Black sides. To be a successful captain you have to have that support.

The leadership issue has become more important these days because there are more decisions to be made on the field. The game is quicker and a little more complicated. There is more public pressure on All Blacks. But some characteristics are still required. A captain must understand the game, understand people and understand issues that are involved in playing rugby and touring.

Clive Norling
Welsh test referee.

Graham Mourie was a super captain. Before the test match, he was a great guy to talk to, at the toss-up, he knew exactly what I wanted and on the field he was a very passionate New Zealand player, but a gentleman.

A bloodied Graham Mourie rallies his troops.

When Graham brought the 1978 All Black team to Britain, they were regarded by the press and rugby supporters as very ordinary, and I think it was down to his captaincy and motivational ability that the side is now remembered as a great New Zealand team.

Andy Dalton
played under Graham Mourie's All Black captaincy from 1977.

Graham Mourie was an aloof character and a highly intelligent person. He used to tell us he was and read some books that I'd never imagine reading, so I'm presuming he was! He was quite unusual in the rugby ▶

Legends of the All Blacks

Enter Graham Mourie

sphere, more of an intellectual-type person. He had very few close friends within the team, but was highly respected. He had an uncanny ability to drop a couple of words in your ear and by the time you'd read in the dictionary what they meant, he made you think. That sounds a bit glib, but I respected the guy greatly. He was always testing people mentally. That was one of his skills as a captain.

Will Carling
is the most successful England test captain.

To be a successful captain, you have to be honest with yourself. You have to have focus and intensity to be successful. I read Graham Mourie's book and thought the guy had standards and principles that he would never compromise and really, that's what it's all about. A guy like that will set out: "This is who I am; this is what I am; this is what I believe in." Players know where they stand. Mourie was an incredible captain. Fitzpatrick was different, probably not as cerebral as Mourie, but by the example he set and the way he pushed himself, he pushed others. People weren't allowed to live in a comfort zone in that New Zealand side. Zinzan Brooke had a lot to do with that as well.

Mark Ella
Wallaby captain 1982-83.

I watched Graham Mourie lead the All Blacks and took note of a lot of things he did. He was an unbelievable captain, inspirational. In the two years I captained Australia, I tried to apply the same techniques.

Andy Dalton
captained the All Blacks in 17 tests from 1981-85.

To be All Black captain, you must have a high standard of playing ability, because you must be able to justify your selection. With that comes respect from the other players. I was a hands-on, follow-me type of leader. Graham Mourie had more of a philosophical approach, testing people's mental status regularly. Cowboy [Mark Shaw] would be the extreme opposite of that. So there's a balance there, but it comes down to respect and values. Nowadays a captain needs the ability to talk to the media and to represent the team. That was just starting in 1985. Once that year, we counted forty-three radio stations that rang our home for comment, and it must be double or three times that now. Public speaking is another important part of the job now, and generally having a lifestyle that's agreeable to the public.

Peter Bush
New Zealand's best-known rugby photographer.

Graham Mourie's tactical appreciation was superb and he had the X-factor that great leaders and military men have. In the last ten or fifteen minutes he could walk down the lineout and ask his men – far lesser players – to lift their game, and they'd go the extra mile for him.

Wynand Claassen
captained the 1981 Springboks to New Zealand.

Andy Dalton's contribution as All Black captain was a good one. We were in the same boat. The All Blacks at the time were an established side under Graham Mourie, a great captain who decided not to play against South Africa. The Springboks were also well-established, under a great captain in Morne du Plessis, who decided suddenly to retire before the tour of New Zealand. So Andy and I became captains under similar circumstances. He made one bad decision, to give us the wind first in the Wellington test. Otherwise he did very well.

•

We admired Graham Mourie for not playing against us in the sense that he stood on his principles. How many players would be prepared not to play for their country because of their beliefs?

The Captains – The Quinn Tapes

Kirk beams in... and out

David Kirk (left) and Dave Loveridge at the 1985 All Black trial.

David Kirk
was appointed All Black captain in remarkable circumstances in 1986 and dropped four tests later.

The major circumstance that put me in the frame to be All Black captain was that so many players went off to South Africa in 1986 [in the Cavaliers team]. There were at least three previous All Black captains on that tour – Dave Loveridge, Andy Dalton and Jock Hobbs. Certainly Dalton and Hobbs would have been considered ahead of me in the queue. It became clear they were not going to be available for the first test against France. I had captained Auckland in Andy Haden's absence and various trial teams, the New Zealand Universities, the North Island. I suppose I was one of the few people qualified to captain the All Blacks in that test. The other two in the team who had played test rugby were John Kirwan, who was out on the wing, and Brian McGrattan, who was in the front row.

•

People say that in major events you remember exactly where you were. I can certainly remember the day I learned I'd been dropped from the All Black captaincy. I was in a flat in Auckland and heard it on the radio. I wasn't listening for it – the radio was on in the background and they announced the team to tour France [in 1986] and said the big item was that David Kirk had been replaced as captain. I was pretty annoyed and disappointed. I got over it pretty quickly. You have to shrug and go on. But I felt let down as I'd done my best through the home series, and now when there was a chance to make a break, go away and meld a new team, they weren't going to give me that chance.

Legends of the All Blacks

The Shelford Affair

Wayne Shelford... immense mana.

Wayne Shelford
captained the All Blacks from 1987-90.

I was twenty-nine and had been there for a couple of years, so I was a little bit wiser than some of the younger guys. I just took it on board like I would a job when I was in the military… just take it on the broad shoulders and go for it.

Gary Whetton
replaced Wayne Shelford as All Black captain in 1990.

Buck was a fantastic captain. He captained in a great era of All Black rugby, so the accolades must go to Buck for keeping that era going. He is a very charismatic person and on the field, that was his strength. It was, "Here we go, guys. Follow me, once more into the breach." He had some great players around him, but he led us and did it very well.

Alex Wyllie
the All Black coach who dropped Wayne Shelford in 1990.

I thought Wayne Shelford was a very good player, very determined. He was a true driving No 8. You couldn't ask for much more from a captain as far as leadership on the field was concerned. He did it himself. He was all guts. Perhaps he didn't talk as much as some people like a captain to, but he did it the other way. He was out the front leading the team and he wanted them behind him.

I know there are always questions asked about whether he should have been dropped or given another chance. But like a lot of players at that time, he'd gone to Italy and when he came back, it looked as if he was carrying an injury, though he denies he had an injury. He just wasn't playing to his best, he wasn't the Buck Shelford we knew.

I can tell you it was a hell of a decision to arrive at, or even think about [dropping Shelford], because if you look back even to 1987, he was one of the players right at the very top, firing away all the time. I've seen him a few times since and I'm sure he understands. He's doing a similar job now where he has to pick and leave out players. It's not easy. I'd certainly rather not have had to drop him. The same thing happened for me at provincial level with Don Hayes. You don't do it to create a sensation. You try to be honest and make sure you are doing it for the best. With Buck, a lot of people felt we were talking rubbish and that it wasn't for the best, but we weren't getting to breakdowns and there was a bit of a gap. There weren't the people there that we wanted. Zinny [Zinzan Brooke] had been pushing for some time. He had come on the year before in the Barbarians game and played well.

I don't like leaving anyone out, especially at home. If you're on tour, you can sit down and talk it through.

They can play mid-week and you have the opportunity to see how their form is. But we didn't play that well against Scotland in the first test [in 1990] and we certainly didn't play that well in the second test, either. There was something missing. It was one of those decisions you would not wish on anyone. I wasn't surprised by the public reaction. Buck Shelford had a huge public following and he deserved that because of the way he had performed.

Wayne Shelford

I believe there was a very big power play in the All Blacks to get rid of me as the All Black captain, and that was the Aucklanders. I was told that for a fact by Mike Brewer when we were having dinner with him in Dunedin one time. He told me that in 1989 they were having meetings behind closed doors to get rid of me. I know the meetings took place; that's on their conscience, not mine. I know for a fact that Foxy and Alan and Gary Whetton were there. They'd asked Mike Brewer, Joe Stanley, guys like that to go to the meetings. It was all Aucklanders. No-one else was invited.

KQ: Mike Brewer was from Otago.

Yes, but he didn't go. He stepped aside and said, "I'm not going to be involved in anything like that. As long as Buck Shelford is performing, I'll back him all the way."

There had to be a reason, there had to be someone else involved. Zinzan Brooke – I love the guy and he's a great competitor and we are still very close – even he didn't know what was going on. But Zinny came to me before the team left for the 1989 tour [to Britain] and said that John Hart had told him he was going to get the test matches on tour. And John was only a selector, not the coach.

Over the next four or five years I pieced things together. The players in these meetings were Aucklanders, no outsiders. They wanted to get rid of me. Maybe I wouldn't bow to their suggestions. Auckland had gone through this big thing with Jim Blair and expected to be able to train in the gym for forty-five minutes to an hour and do everything needed. I turned round and said, "Cut the bullshit and get on with it. Do what the coach tells you to do. Let's get down and do the hard work." There were never complaints from the ▶

Wayne Shelford and Alex Wyllie – captain and coach.

Legends of the All Blacks

The Shelford Affair

players from North Harbour, Canterbury, Waikato, Wellington – only the Aucklanders. Alex Wyllie was the coach, but he was in the dark about what was going on. There was more going on behind the scenes with John Hart. The excuse Alex gave me [for dropping Shelford] when he rang was pretty weak and it had to have come from somewhere else. Grizz made the call, but his hand was forced by other people. I don't think he really wanted to do it at that stage.

When I look back now, I was better off out of it because the bullshit that was going down in the team carried on for another year and a half. That was the downfall at the 1991 World Cup.

Gary Whetton

I was never privy to any goings-on, or meetings or whatever. The selectors were looking at making changes, but what happened was out of my hands. You hear all sorts of conspiracy theories, but I'll tell you: it was nothing like that as far as I was concerned. The first I knew was a phone call, telling me I was the new All Black captain. My first reaction was, "Shelford's been dropped." I tried to get hold of him and couldn't. I rang Peter Thorburn, who told me which hotel he was at, but I couldn't get him. When Buck was dropped, I think most of us All Blacks were thinking mainly of self-preservation. We were relieved it wasn't us, as simple as that. The unthinkable had happened, so how close had we been to it, too?

To lead your national team is one of the biggest honours you can have, but unfortunately for me there was a lot of unfair pressure, a lot of controversy, so it wasn't the happiest time. It was very, very, difficult. I was on my own a lot of the time. The selectors had ducked for cover. They never fronted it. It shouldn't have been my job to answer for them – I didn't even have the answers. So there was more controversy and more rumours. It was unfortunate, the way it happened. I never felt I had the support from my country that an All Black captain can expect to have.

John Hart
was an All Black selector when Shelford was dropped.

Earlier in the season the panel had become concerned about Buck's form. Lane [Penn, the other selector] and I went to Whangarei to watch North Harbour play, then we met Alex, who'd been watching Waikato, at the Koru Lounge in Auckland after the game. We were primarily watching Walter Little, but Alex asked how Walter and Wayne had gone. Lane said, "Very, very average." Then Alex shocked us by saying, "Well, we'll drop him." We certainly hadn't gone to Whangarei with the belief that we were looking at Wayne Shelford to drop him.

It subsequently came out that Alex had spoken to North Harbour coach Peter Thorburn to say that if Shelford didn't front up, he'd be dropped. So obviously without the other two selectors knowing at the time, Alex had it in his mind to drop him.

I was part of the decision-making process, but wasn't happy with the way it was handled. There wasn't much dialogue with Wayne, and there should have been.

KQ: Wayne Shelford has told us there was an Auckland-inspired plot to get rid of him. Is that true?

That's absolute nonsense. The players weren't even talked to about it. It wasn't an issue with them. Gary Whetton got as much of a shock as anyone when notified by Alex that he'd be taking over the captaincy. Buck is way off the mark there. The issue was one involving only selectors, and the final decision was the convener's. I think the decision was the right one in the sense of his form, but people get emotional about it because of the dropping of a great captain and a great player. He was slowing up at the time.

It's ironic that I seem to be blamed for Shelford's demise. I was the one, later, moving for him to be picked to go to Argentina [in 1991] because I thought he could still contribute. I had a lot to do with Shelford's career. I coached him in Auckland, when he first played. On the tour of Japan in 1987 we were pretty close. I'm

The Captains – The Quinn Tapes

Gary Whetton, who replaced Wayne Shelford as All Black captain, with coach Alex Wyllie.

disappointed Wayne still feels that way. There was no plot and I was not solely responsible for his sacking.

Bob Dwyer
Wallaby coach at different times between 1982-95.

We were surprised to hear the talk that Shelford might get dropped. We thought he was pretty important to the All Black mentality. He was a great presence on the field. It was the restricted nature of the way Shelford played which made him so great. His ability to take the ball forward off the back of the scrum was legendary. His ability to command men was phenomenal. We thought New Zealand were the lesser for Buck Shelford's absence.

Gary Whetton

KQ: How did you feel about all the "Bring Back Buck" signs on the terraces and among the crowds?

I noticed them, and it wasn't a good thing when you're trying to play a test match. I thought the whole episode personified an erroneous situation. The public looked at me, the next captain, as having had a role in Buck's downfall, but that was completely untrue. I suppose me being an Aucklander didn't help. People love underdogs and Auckland had been so successful. It didn't help, but it hardened my resolve.

Wayne Shelford

Those "Bring Back Buck" signs – it's quite funny, actually. It started off in Manawatu, some of the university boys did it for a laugh. But it has carried on for ten years. It's wearing a bit thin now, but probably the people might have been right. There was a dirty thing done, and to the wrong person. I've seen the signs in Jamaica, Japan, England, South Africa, Australia, Hong Kong, even at soccer matches in England. People probably look at the signs and say, "Who is this Buck?" But it's a good laugh.

Legends of the All Blacks

Fitzpatrick – the Long Reign

Earle Kirton
was on the All Black selection panel that appointed Sean Fitzpatrick captain in 1992.

The final trial [in 1992] was in Napier, and obviously we were lining up Mike Brewer to be captain. Then he got badly hurt, so we were suddenly bereft of a captain. I said to Laurie that the only man we could really go for was Fitzpatrick. Laurie said, "Well, I don't really know him. When did you have him?" I told Laurie he had been one of my captains in a trial team in Rotorua and that he was excellent. He was good for the young kids and didn't go and mix with just the Aucklanders. Laurie listened, but he wouldn't just take my word for it, not totally. So he went up into the stands to talk to BJ [Brian Lochore], who'd had him as a captain as well. BJ gave him the thumbs up. He was quite categorical, not even a waver. So Fitzy got the job.

Fitzy had tremendous depth and self-discipline. It's a lonely job, being All Black captain, but he grew into it. The All Black captain has to be fair and he was. He left the back seat; he sat up the front of the bus, on his own, not really getting too close to us either, because he didn't want to quite get into our camp. He always maintained that distance because he never wanted to be seen as a selector as well as a captain. He wanted to be able to carry on with the lads. From time to time he'd join them down the back. It's a delicate balancing act. He maintained his discipline and stature the whole way through, and I take my hat off to him. He got better and better and better. He became a great captain as well as being a great player. He never got down to the rubbish as regards discipline in the team. He'd get the oldies to sort it out – Zinny and the rest of them.

•

Fitzy never joined the Auckland clique. He stayed away. He'd love to have spent time with Zinny and Foxy and Kirwan because they'd been mates for years and years, right back to the school days. But he kept to himself to maintain this absolute impartiality and to be fair to the team as a whole. I couldn't speak more highly of the man. He had the self-discipline and was hard-nosed enough to make it work, and he was pleasant with the media, which was a help, too.

Fitzy would never stay for selection meetings. He'd come in, give his opinion and then tell Laurie he really didn't want to hear the discussion. He didn't want it to be said he'd punted for one guy or the other. We appreciated that was the way he wanted to do things as New Zealand captain.

He was an outstanding player and ended up being one of the great players of all time, up there with Ken Gray and Colin Meads. He created a tremendous record. Fitzy looked after himself. He never went out and indulged hugely and he was morally squeaky clean. He was very much in love with his lady, so that made it easier, but it never crossed his mind because he never wanted anyone to have anything on him that might have undermined his standing. He had the discipline to hang off any situation that looked as if it could be contentious.

Sean Fitzpatrick
became All Black captain in surprising circumstances in 1992.

I'd never really seen myself as a captain. I'd always been a follower, never a leader. Laurie came to me in Napier in 1992 and said that Mike [Brewer] would be captaining the team on the tour of Australia and asked if I would captain it midweek occasionally. I was fairly happy about that. Then when Mike got so badly injured in the trial match, the first thing that flashed through my mind was that I could be the captain of the All Blacks. I think Laurie's arm was twisted a bit and I was named captain that night, within a couple of hours of Mike being injured. Laurie didn't look too happy about it, that's for sure. That decision changed my approach to the game and my whole outlook on life.

•

My first match as All Black captain was a bit of a nightmare. It was our centenary year and we had three

The Captains – The Quinn Tapes

A word of congratulations from captain Fitzpatrick for Andrew Mehrtens.

games against a World XV. We lost the first game in Christchurch, my first game as captain. That night we had to go to a function where there were a thousand people, including a lot of ex-All Blacks, and it was a very difficult time. I had my hand badly trodden on and went to get it x-rayed at Christchurch Hospital. I remember sitting there thinking, "I hope it's broken so I can get myself out of this predicament." It's funny to look back on that now, but that was the way I felt, the pressure I was under. It was a difficult time in New Zealand rugby. There'd been a lot of players who had either retired or been dropped and there were a lot of new faces within the team including some players I didn't think were worthy of being All Blacks.

Legends of the All Blacks

FITZPATRICK – THE LONG REIGN

Ian McIntosh
Springbok coach in 1994.

Sean Fitzpatrick epitomises the All Blacks to me. A lot of people said he talked too much on the field, but he gave as good as he got, and when he got it he never squealed. He was the first to play damn hard for a win, and the first to have a beer with you afterwards and the first to want to have a chat about the game.

Sean Fitzpatrick

I don't think people realise the pressure the All Black captain's under. As the prime minister said, "I'd love to be the All Black captain when they win, but when they lose, I'd much rather be the prime minister." You're very much in the public eye. There's a lot of expectation on the captain – maybe the image of the team is seen through the captain.

When I became captain, I felt I had to change. The style I played and the way I related to referees had to be toned down a bit. I had to get to know the rest of the team better and my people skills had to change. One of the hardest things for me was putting some distance between me and the rest of the team. I'd always enjoyed being one of the boys and having a bit of fun, and rooming with the other guys. When you become captain you had to have a room to yourself and stand back a bit. I was fortunate I had McDowell, Kirwan, Fox and Zinzan around and they were a great help in those early days in terms of using them as a springboard and somebody to listen to.

KQ: In 1996, Sean Fitzpatrick led New Zealand to its first test series win in South Africa.

Before we went to South Africa in 1996 somebody said to me that I could become the most successful captain ever if we won the series there. At Cape Town we were down 17-3 and I remember running back to halfway looking at the scoreboard. About 20 minutes had gone and I thought to myself, "Five weeks to go. I could be the most unsuccessful captain ever to visit South Africa."

The captain needs to be a player who dominates his position and has the respect of the team. If he's not the best player in his position, that can leave doubts in people's minds as to his right to be there.

Taine Randell
captained the All Blacks in 1998-99.

The captaincy is nice and it's a huge honour. But to be captain, first of all you've got to be in the All Blacks.

Taine Randell and Sean Fitzpatrick.

British Isles

Battling the Brits

By Ron Palenski

One of the recurring "them and us" debates in rugby, found in few other sports, is the battle for supremacy between the hemispheres, northern and southern. In New Zealand terms, it's us against Britain (and for the purposes of the debate, "Britain" almost always includes Ireland, which in rugby terms means the republic and Northern Ireland).

In recent years, the debate has centred on playing strength as New Zealand, Australia and South Africa have widened the playing and performance gap on Britain, but less noticeably on France.

Historically, the gap has more often been philosophical, especially when it relates to just New Zealand and Britain. There has always been, there still is, and there may always be, a philosophical difference between the rugby cultures of Britain and New Zealand. It has been a source of anger, of wonderment, of frustration. The range of emotions prevalent at the time has been made manifest whenever British and New Zealand teams have met on the field, either there or here.

The differences in the last couple of years as New Zealand and Britain, and especially England, have gone their separate ways in embracing professionalism have just accentuated the philosophical gap.

The reasons for the differences go back to rugby's very roots. They are as easy to pinpoint as they are difficult to resolve.

To understand the differences, the first thing that has to be set aside is the enduring myth that rugby began by the wilful act of one man, William Webb Ellis, when he supposedly picked up the ball and ran with it at Rugby School in Warwickshire in 1823. Ellis, who was more noted as a cricketer at school than a footballer, may well have run with the ball, though no-one has been able to produce any evidence that he did or didn't. What the recalcitrant Ellis did is irrelevant because there is ample evidence, acknowledged by objective historians (into which category England's Rugby Football Union does not fall) that rugby evolved at various public (that is, private) schools in England and Scotland, including Rugby itself, from various forms of folk football that had been played for centuries.

Ellis entered the picture 70 years after his supposed act on the word of one man, Matthew Bloxam, who was keen to prove that rugby was developed by the higher minds of public schoolboys rather than being part of a natural evolution from folk football that was played by the masses. The Old Rugbeian

Legends of the All Blacks

Society seized upon Bloxam's contention because it suited its purposes by defining rugby as an elitist's game, as did the Rugby Football Union which at the time was locked in bitter debate with Yorkshire and Lancashire over players wanting compensation for lost wages while they were playing. The argument became a broader one, the middle class of southern England versus the working class of the North, sport for a well-heeled few versus sport for all. The debate led inevitably to what is known as rugby's Great Schism, with the clubs of Yorkshire and Lancashire pulling out of the Rugby Football Union and forming their own body, which was initially known as Northern Union and then, in 1922, finally became rugby league.

The RFU got its way by enshrining Ellis as the "inventor" of rugby and imposed its imprimatur by erecting a plaque at Rugby School which ensured the myth was perpetuated. And it still is as players from around the world meet at the World Cup every four years to play for the Webb Ellis Trophy.

It was against this background that rugby spread to what was then Britain's colonies, with people in authority such as civil servants and soldiers, many of them old boys of Rugby or other rugby schools, introducing the new sport with its strong ethic of elitism and amateurism. One such introduced the sport to New Zealand. Charles John Monro was the son of the Speaker of the House of Representatives, Sir David Monro, and he was dispatched to a public school, Christ College in north London, to complete his education. Christ's had adopted the rugby rules in preference to the other developing ball sport of the time, association rules (later known as soccer), and Monro became a convert. When he returned to New Zealand in 1870, he persuaded pupils at Nelson College to adopt the new rules rather than to continue to play a variant of football that would be known today as "scrag". Nelson College played the Town in May, 1870 in the first recorded rugby match in New Zealand and a few months later, Monro led his band of pioneers across Cook Strait (after persuading his father to make a government steamer available to them) and introduced the game to Wellington. It spread to Wanganui and Christchurch and, ultimately and remarkably rapidly, throughout New Zealand.

Charles Monro

New Zealanders, then as now, were a pragmatic people and in the course of developing a young country, had not brought with them the class baggage of England. Rugby became the game for all of the people, not a game for those people who could afford it. Though such terms were seldom used in New Zealand, there was no distinction between working and middle class. Landowner packed down with labourer, doctor with sawmiller.

And importantly, Maori people also took to rugby, unlike in South Africa or New South Wales, where rugby also took root. More to the point, Maoris were encouraged to play rugby, unlike in South Africa and New South Wales, where the indigenous populations were seen but not wanted to be heard.

As rugby in New Zealand developed, there was a natural desire to test the development and skill against other countries and matches were arranged with New South Wales in 1884. But the ultimate test became a tour by a British team in 1888, which was closely followed by a tour of Britain by a New Zealand Native team in the northern winter of 1888-89.

The New Zealanders were pleasantly surprised by what they learned from this initial contact. One of the deep thinkers of the game in New Zealand in the 19th century, Tom Ellison, wrote that before the 1888 tour, passing in New Zealand backs had not developed because forwards did not heel the ball back in the mistaken belief that if they did, the forwards would be in front of the ball and therefore offside.

"Beyond learning the minor though pretty and effective trick of feign passing from Mr [Tommy] Haslam and learning to disregard the strict law on offside play as regards forwards in the scrum, I challenge anyone to tell me what else they taught us," Ellison wrote in his revelatory *The Art of Rugby Football*.

The Natives' tour of Britain that followed (so-called because it was to have been a Maori tour, but four Pakehas were included) adduced no further evidence that the British had developed in rugby any better than had New Zealand.

One of the instigators of the tour, Joe Warbrick, who had been on the pioneering New Zealand tour of New South Wales in 1884, found little difference in the standard of play in Britain as the Natives went through an astonishing 108 matches for 80 wins. "I do not think there was much difference and any difference would be in our favour," he wrote. "I feel positive that if we always could have met our opponents fit and well, there would have been even less than 20 losses."

Ellison, who was also on the Native tour, had a lasting influence on the relations and history between New Zealand and British rugby. He successfully moved at the first annual meeting of the New Zealand Rugby Football Union in 1893 that the national team's playing uniform be a black jersey with a silver fern, thus creating the most symbolic jersey in world rugby, and he was active in developing playing strategies as well.

It was Ellison, while playing for Poneke in Wellington, who devised the position of the wing forward in an attempt to stop marauding halfbacks from getting round at scrums and disrupting possession. The wing forward, allied with the old New Zealand 2-3-2 scrum, led to a distinctive New Zealand playing style that created an equal measure of admiration and anger when it was first exhibited in Britain on the Originals' tour of 1905-06.

Ellison also had a hand in the development of the New Zealand five-eighths system which, allied with the wing forward and set forward positions, gave New Zealand an organised playing dominance that the

Legends of the All Blacks

Tom Ellison

British seldom matched and even less often could beat. The British eventually legislated the wing forward out of existence by ruling in 1931 that front rows must comprise three players, giving rise to the oft-stated belief that whenever New Zealand developed a playing dominance, the lawmakers in Britain would legislate it away.

Ellison adroitly fingered another difference between the rugby of New Zealand and of Britain and this struck at the very heart of the game in Britain: the question of amateurism.

Just as the rules and methods of the game were exported, initially to the colonies, either by the British or by "natives" such as Monro, who had been educated at rugby-playing public schools, so too was the underpinning attitude of amateurism, even though the social conditions that applied in Britain did not also apply in New Zealand. Rules and laws of the game were for the most part until relatively recently framed in Britain by Britons who must have had only the most rudimentary knowledge of social conditions and mores in the countries for which they were legislating. For a long time, national unions such as the NZRFU owed immediate allegiance to the English union, not to the International Rugby Board, which had been formed in 1886 as a British appeal body, there to rule on disputes over playing laws or interpretations.

The view that the British legislated for everyone from their own limited knowledge and from their own narrow base is not a new one. Ellison put his finger on it when a tour of Britain was first mooted. "The idea is excellent," he said. "I see one difficulty only and that is getting the best men away without giving them some allowance over and above their actual hotel and travelling expenses – a difficulty due to the stringency of the laws as to professionalism. Personally, I think that these laws were never intended to apply to extended tours abroad…"

And, of course, they were not. The laws were framed to keep rugby elite, to keep artisans and workers out of the game. It was philosophical amateurism. Hypocritically, the RFU had no objection to paying generous expenses or guarantees to "amateur gentlemen" on tours, in much the same way the "amateur" WG Grace could command huge fees for playing cricket.

Ellison argued that to adhere to the English-framed laws on long tours that were not contemplated by the laws' framers would have the effect of

British Isles

players losing their jobs and, in some cases, their homes. By the English ideal, rugby players would not have jobs to lose. Ellison's views on the English idea of amateurism were echoed by a great many other New Zealanders, both then and for years afterward.

They were the root of the philosophical difference between New Zealand and English rugby and were the source of friction until 1995, when the International Rugby Board bowed to the inevitable and allowed players to be paid for playing.

New Zealand's attitude to amateurism, pragmatic rather than philosophical, and the competitiveness it brought to the game, provided the edge in competition between the two countries. A tenet of the English amateurism was that the game was there to be enjoyed for its own sake and by the players alone; it was not for competition and not to be a public spectacle. It was for this reason that the British unions held out for so long against the idea of a World Cup. This was living in a fool's Corinthian paradise, as New Zealanders knew only too well. What earthly point, they contended, was there in playing a game if not to win? The game is there to be enjoyed certainly, but the greater enjoyment comes from winning.

The development of New Zealand rugby, the way it had devised and embraced new strategies and had studied assiduously what could or could not be done within the laws, was there for all of Britain to see on the Originals' tour of 1905-06, a tour that laid the framework for all tours since and that developed a New Zealand ascendancy that has never been permanently diluted. The tour became, by design and by accident, the tour that set the benchmark in world rugby and confirmed in New Zealand that rugby was the national game and was, moreover, a game that New Zealanders could play better than anyone else in the world.

Its importance to New Zealand was underlined by the fact that for the first and only time, the tour was subsidised by the Government. Premier Richard Seddon, an ardent rugby supporter, was convinced that it was through rugby that the world would notice New Zealand. He agreed to a state subsidy of £1963. Seddon's most fervent hopes were realised after the first match, against Devon, which was won 55-4 by New Zealand. The score was greeted with such scepticism in one London newspaper office evidently, that a sub-editor thought it had been wrongly transmitted and turned it around to have Devon, one of the leading English counties, winning 55-4. But it was no mistake, as soon became clear when the following five matches were won 41, 41, 32, 28, 34 without another score against New Zealand, a total of 231 points in six matches against a solitary dropped goal. It was this scoring spree that led to another of rugby's myths, that New Zealand became known as the All Blacks because a typographer of independent spirit on the *Daily Mail* didn't like the phrase used by its correspondent, J A Buttery, in describing the team as "all backs". He figured Buttery must have had in mind the colour of their jerseys so changed it to All Blacks.

Legends of the All Blacks

Buttery, the only journalist to cover the whole tour, was mightily impressed with them and even defended the captain, Dave Gallaher, against the cheating charges that accompanied him wherever he went. Gallaher bore the brunt of the English antipathy to the wing forward position, even when he wasn't playing. In one match, against Surrey, Gallaher was in the stand and George Gillett was the wing forward. The spectator in front of Gallaher spent the match crying out such epithets as "You cheat, Gallaher!" and "Offside Gallaher!". Gallaher remarked that he didn't realise he was so popular.

The All Blacks' stately procession through British rugby was slowed only in Wales where the scores were much closer and where they lost, famously, their only match. The 3-0 scoreline in the Welsh international entered rugby folklore not so much because Wales won 3-0, but because New Zealand didn't score. Whether Bob Deans did score, but was dragged back across the line before the referee could get up to see, became one of the great talking points of rugby history and fostered the keen sense of rivalry that existed between New Zealand and Wales until relatively recent years. Even 70 and 80 years later, New Zealanders visiting the Arms Park in Cardiff would ask to have the spot where Deans "scored" pointed out to them and smiling Welshmen would oblige, even though ground changes had long since caused the spot to reside under the West Stand.

It wasn't just the manner of the All Blacks' play that upset the British. The All Blacks were derisively known as "three bob a day men" because they were paid three shillings expenses a day, a fact that horrified those custodians of British rugby, who were steeped in the excesses of amateurism. The tour made a profit of £9962 and as pleased as the players were with their progress, there was also dissatisfaction. One of the Originals, writing in 1908, highlighted this: "That they, the All Blacks, could scarcely raise £10 in the whole team on their return passage home to New Zealand is well-known, and the fact made a great impression in colonial circles. This brought the question before the colonial public and it was generally admitted that the team were not well treated. Several were men of means, and could well afford the loss of time, but the majority were working men."

Money was also a source of friction when the team was in Scotland. A system of guarantees had been worked out for each tour match with the host team having to pay the All Blacks a set amount to cover team costs. The guarantee for the Scottish international was £200, but for some reason the Scottish Rugby Union refused to agree. The Scots were happy for the game to go ahead, but New Zealand would have to carry the risk. The Scots also decided that they would not award caps for the match, meaning they did not regard it as a full international. Yet another problem was that the ground at Inverleith in Edinburgh was frozen the morning of the match and there was talk of calling it off.

British Isles

The 1905 Originals.

In the event, it went ahead, New Zealand won a memorable game 12-7 and All Black manager George Dixon pocketed all the profit for the New Zealand Rugby Football Union. The Scots, it could be said, were less than happy with this state of affairs and when the All Blacks next visited Britain, in 1924-25, they refused to countenance a match. Those All Blacks beat everyone else and came to be known as the Invincibles and ironically, the Scots then were probably at the strongest in their history and were reckoned to have been the only one of the "home" nations capable of beating the All Blacks. But the Scots, because of their resentment from 1905, denied themselves the chance and they are still waiting for their first victory over New Zealand.

The Originals' tour had far-reaching consequences in other directions. During the tour, the All Blacks watched a game of what was then known as Northern Union and when they were home, they learned that a postal clerk, Bert Baskerville, was forming his own team to go to Britain to play the other form of rugby – the paid form. Baskerville teamed up with one of the most remarkable of All Blacks, George Smith, who had been a champion sprinter and hurdler and who had also ridden the winner of a New Zealand Cup. Smith told Baskerville of what the players had seen and the pair of them began talking to rugby players about a Northern Union tour. "This set me thinking," Baskerville wrote. "Why shouldn't a New Zealand team play the northern unionists? Strict amateurs will answer, 'Because some of their players are professional'. This argument seems weak if we keep in view the fact that in the sister association [soccer], amateurs and professionals often play in the same side and frequently against each other."

It was a simple if naive argument. Had Baskerville properly appreciated the politics of rugby, he would have known that the northern game was always much further beyond rugby's pale than any of the other professional or semi-professional sports.

By the time Baskerville had his team formed, Smith was vice-captain and three of the Originals had been signed up. Several other former All Blacks were also included. They stopped in Sydney on their way to Britain and a series of meetings there led to their borrowing the outstanding Australian rugby player of the day, Dally Messenger, for the tour, and to the formation of league in Australia.

All of this so alarmed the custodians of amateur rugby in Britain that they hurriedly assembled a team in 1908 to tour New Zealand to preserve the true faith and to "save" New Zealand rugby for amateurism. The emergence of a New Zealand league team compounded the worries the British were having about New Zealand rugby, following complaints of violent play by the Natives and in domestic rugby, and by what the Scots saw as the veiled professionalism of the Originals. The team for 1908 was originally to be British, but neither the Scots nor the Irish would have anything to do with it so it became an Anglo-Welsh team instead, hand-picked to ensure they were pristine amateurs and therefore bound to bring the naughty New Zealanders into line. The patronising plans all fell apart, though, and the tour was more of a culture clash than the missionary cleansing of the soul that it was intended to be. The Anglo-Welsh were unfit and happy to be so, declaring the matches would gain them the necessary standard of fitness. The New Zealand union was so appalled by the physical condition of the tourists that it appointed a prominent athletics coach, Tom Leslie, to be their trainer at £3 a week. But because the Anglo-Welsh would have nothing to do with anyone in rugby being paid, they didn't use his services.

They criticised the New Zealanders for the roughness of their play, they were unrelenting in their criticism of the wing forward position and they accused New Zealand referees of favouring the home sides, arguing they were interpreting laws by colonial standards instead of by the (presumably higher) standards of "home".

The Anglo-Welsh team's greatest humiliation came when during the tour the English union banned one of the pristine amateurs, Frederick Jackson, for having played as a professional in the North seven years previously. Jackson was summarily dismissed from the tour and put on the first ship home. Jackson, who had played for Leicester against the Originals, later returned to New Zealand, played league for his adopted country and had a son, Everard, who became an All Black.

British Isles

Britain's clumsy attempt to stop league in New Zealand and to bring New Zealand rugby back into the bosom of home was a failure. No further attempts were made and it was the intervention of the First World War that slowed the development of league and re-established rugby as the pre-eminent winter sport in New Zealand.

Confirmation of rugby's status came in the 1920s and especially with the success of the Invincibles in Britain, the standoffish Scots notwithstanding. The All Blacks lost to New South Wales before they went to Britain and lost also to Auckland, prompting critics to call for team changes and to contend that the team was over-rated. There was not much expectation they would do as well as the Originals but early in the tour, one of the Welsh team who had beaten the All Blacks, Teddy Morgan, wrote: "Already they have demonstrated, to those who know football when they see it, that as a side they compare favourably with their predecessors of 1905… weather conditions have been against big scores, and one must not forget that English football today is about 30 per cent better than it was in 1905. They have youth, brawn and wonderful playing capabilities. No club side will beat them and it will be a very fine international side that will hold them. Their match at Twickenham versus England will be worth seeing."

Morgan was proved correct, more than he may have wished. The All Blacks were beaten by no one and players such as George Nepia at fullback, Bert Cooke in the centres and Maurice Brownlie in the forwards remain exemplars of the best in rugby, their fame not dimmed by the succeeding generations.

There were echoes of the past, too. Captain Cliff Porter was as reviled at wing forward as his predecessor, Dave Gallaher, had been, and it was from that tour that the days of the controversial position were numbered. Porter after putting the ball into the scrum would stay in position, hampering opponents from getting around, but when Jim Parker supplanted Porter in the internationals, he took up a position in the backline after putting the ball into scrums.

The Invincibles entered the record books in an unenviable way too when one of their forwards, Cyril Brownlie, became the first player to be ordered off in an international. Referee Albert Freethy of Wales issued a general warning after some heated play early in the England test and then when he again stopped play, he uttered the line, "You, go off!"

"Our horror can be imagined," wrote lock Read Masters, "when we realised that the remark was directed at Cyril Brownlie. Jock Richardson, our captain, appealed to the referee, but Mr Freethy, who seemed to have completely lost his head for a minute, remained firm and so one of the most good-natured men in our team had to retire." Masters wrote that with Brownlie in the Twickenham dressing room, a new spirit seized the team – "We were determined to avenge the unjust charge."

Freethy later said that Brownlie happened to be the unfortunate player in his line of sight when he blew up a general melee of players. "Cyril Brownlie

Legends of the All Blacks

Cyril Brownlie takes the long walk... the first player to be sent off in test rugby.

was no better and no worse than any of the others," he said. "He was unfortunate that he was the player in my line of vision when I made my decision." It was unfortunate for England too because as Masters acknowledged, the All Blacks played with a renewed resolve against an England team that may otherwise have won. One of the scorers was Brownlie's brother, Maurice.

The last rites for the wing forward, a festering running sore between British and New Zealand rugby for more than 30 years, were played out during the British Isles' tour in 1930. The battle lines were drawn after the opening game in Wanganui when the British manager, Bim Baxter, called the man in the position a cheat. "I won't say he is on the borderline," Baxter said, "he is over it and must be discouraged. He causes irritation to both sets of forwards. I am not speaking of the man playing in the position today, but of a man playing in that position. It is contrary to the spirit of rugby football."

The All Blacks won the series three tests to one, but they were troubling times for New Zealand rugby. The Depression was to force several rugby players to take up league contracts, including the incomparable Cooke and Nepia, and the abolition of the wing forward meant that New Zealand had to totally rethink its forward strategy, including playing for the first time with a 3-4-1 scrum. The forced reversion to England's rules irked New Zealanders, including former All Black Geoff Alley, who wrote: "The lack of desire to change anything in the game is a most galling thing to New Zealanders, who are freed from the bonds of tradition in a way the English mind is not, and we should be false to the idea of progress if we abandoned our attitude."

Shorn of the quick-heeling 2-3-2 scrum and the freedom of movement it

British Isles

had given the backs, New Zealand was in a period of readjustment, almost relearning, through the 1930s and '40s, a period that included the All Blacks' first loss to England.

Captained by Canterbury flanker Jack Manchester, the 1935-36 All Blacks in Britain lost by a point to Wales, beat Ireland and Scotland, and were held scoreless at Twickenham as England scored 13 points in what became known as Obolensky's match.

Alex Obolensky was an aristocratic Russian émigré whose family had escaped to London during the 1917 Bolshevik revolution. Obolensky began playing rugby at Trent College in Derbyshire, then went to Oxford where an uncle, Vadim Obolensky, lectured in French. A track sprinter with a best 100 yards time on grass of 10.2 seconds, Obolensky was immediately put on the wing for the university team and almost as immediately, was selected for an England trial, then named in the team to play the All Blacks. Vivian Jenkins, the 1935 Welsh fullback who followed his playing days with a long career in rugby journalism, recalled Obolensky as "a carefree White Russian Parisian type, full of gaiety, who'd train on champagne and a dozen oysters". He appeared to take this attitude onto the rugby field.

His two try-scoring efforts against the All Blacks have been celebrated in England ever since, in itself perhaps a reflection of the lack of England success against New Zealand and a reflection, too, of the paucity of sparkling English back play.

Obolensky scored his first try by running round, with a nonchalance befitting his aristocratic background, the New Zealand fullback, Mike Gilbert. But it was his second try that was the most celebrated and called the try of the century. Of all the tries of the century scored before and since, this at least deserved the rating. The England first five-eighth, Peter Candler, began the move and passed to centre Peter Cranmer, who gained 30 yards. When he was blocked just inside the All Blacks' half, he slung the ball back to Obolensky, who had come off the right wing at pace. Obolensky continued his diagonal run, sped round the All Black left wing, Brushy Mitchell, and scored in the corner.

Prince Alex Obolensky.

It was not coincidental, contended New Zealand rugby writer Spiro Zavos in 1998 that England's most convincing defeat of the All Blacks was sparked by a man who had never embraced the English way of playing rugby. "Only someone not steeped in the England game could have conceived the eccentric line of running against the flow of the cover defence to defeat the All Black chasers," he wrote.

It was to be nearly another 20 years before the All Blacks were in Britain again, the intervening years including the Second World War, two series defeats by South Africa and a

Legends of the All Blacks

series win against the British Isles in New Zealand in 1950.

The Lions as a fully representative British (and Irish) team had toured New Zealand first in 1930, but it was the 1950 tour that developed their reputation for innovative, sparkling back play that was not, unfortunately for them, complemented by sufficient ball-winning from the forwards. The Lions of 1950, 1959 and, especially, 1971, the only British team to win a series in New Zealand, won respect from New Zealanders for the quality of their back play, but only the 1971 team had the forward power and know-how to enable them to win.

The 1950 Lions had the Irish first five-eighth, Jackie Kyle, and the teenage Welsh fullback, Lewis Jones, the 1959 team had outstanding wings Tony O'Reilly and Peter Jackson, and the 1971 team had the prince of first-fives, Barry John, complemented by perhaps the best Welsh halfback to have played the game, Gareth Edwards, one of the best centres to have played, Mike Gibson, and the best fullback of his time, JPR Williams.

It was because of such players, and others, that singly and collectively, the British countries gained a reputation for producing exciting backs but lacked, until 1971, the forward power to provide them with the stage on which they could properly perform. From the success of the 1971 team, coached by Carwyn James, one of the most gifted coaches the rugby world has seen, there grew a British and especially an English obsession for forward power. The pendulum swung so far the other way, toward the need for possession, that backs in later years were almost unnecessary appendages with the exception of a halfback to get the ball to the first five-eighth, who would then kick.

Captain Graham Mourie and coach Eric Watson in 1979.

The obsession had developed alarmingly by 1979 when coach Eric Watson and captain Graham Mourie led the All Blacks to Scotland and England. By the end of the tour, All Black manager Russ Thomas felt compelled to stand up at the farewell dinner and, in a classically literal case of biting the hand that feeds you, told the assembled authorities of British rugby that until they moved away from big lumbering forward packs and returned to playing rugby, their game would never be any good.

Thomas had also been manager the year before when the All Blacks achieved the Grand Slam of victories over each of the "home" nations for the first and only time. That All Black team is remembered in Britain with a reluctant respect, a notch or two down from the fondness with which the 1967 team is remembered. The 1967 All Blacks had been due to go to South Africa, but that tour was cancelled when the South African Government wouldn't relent on New Zealand

British Isles

wanting to include Maoris for the first time. They went through Britain without a loss, but it was the manner of their play that endured more in the memories than the balance sheet of wins and losses. They surely would have been the first to achieve the Grand Slam but for an outbreak of foot and mouth disease that prevented them from going to Ireland. The 1967 All Blacks played the way the Lions used to play, but they had the forwards who could consistently deliver quality ball. It was not coincidental that the All Blacks were coached by Fred Allen and managed by Charlie Saxton, who had both been in the 2NZEF Army team that revitalised rugby in Britain after the war, playing the same style of rugby.

The old bogey of rugby contact between New Zealand and Britain, amateurism, had never gone away. There seemed always to be a deep British mistrust of New Zealand, even though the phenomenon of "boot money", the stuffing of notes into a player's boots, was uniquely British. At the time of the first World Cup in New Zealand and Australia in 1987, British journalists and administrators were incensed when they saw that some of the All Blacks were appearing in television commercials and there was a serious attempt to have one commercial, which featured All Black captain Andy Dalton, withdrawn.

Two years later, when the All Blacks toured Wales and Ireland, captain Wayne Shelford was vilified in the British press for agreeing to open a supermarket in Wales. This was plain evidence, the criticism went, that New Zealand openly flouted the regulations against players earning money from rugby. Yet the same critics were silent about several British clubs, and most notably Harlequins, paying players.

By then, the amateur days were clearly drawing to a close and it was only a matter of more time and more pragmatism, and the drifting away of a few die-hards, before rugby entered the real world. When it did, England showed it could no more handle the administration of professional rugby than it could amateur rugby. Its allowing players to be contracted to clubs rather than the national union led directly to the farcical tour of Australia and New Zealand in 1998 by a plainly sub-standard team.

A constant companion of New Zealand-British rugby relations has been what could best be described as a robust press, more on the British side than the New Zealand. It has always been so, from the outset when the Original All Blacks were castigated for the wing forward and for their casual approach to amateurism. When New Zealand teams go to Britain, they know that at some stage of a tour there will be an issue that will be inflamed by the competitive British press. Keith Murdoch was painted as an ogre and a wild man in 1972 when he remonstrated with an aggressive security guard in the Angel Hotel in Cardiff; the All Blacks were thugs in 1978 when the Bridgend and Welsh fullback, JPR Williams, was raked by All Black prop John Ashworth; they were thugs again in 1993 when Philip de Glanville, an England centre playing for the South-West, suffered an eye injury in a ruck.

Legends of the All Blacks

Keith Murdoch walks out of All Black rugby and into history.

There's been a similar story just about every time New Zealand and British rugby has made contact. The All Black coach in 1998, John Hart, was even accused by a British journalist of manipulating the judicial system to prevent lock Ian Jones from being punished for an imagined transgression.

For what seemed a generation or two, the leading British critic against New Zealand was a Welshman, Bryn Thomas, who wrote for the Cardiff *Western Mail*. Black was not his favourite colour. His mantle has now been assumed by another Welshman, Stephen Jones, who writes for the *Sunday Times*. Black is not his favourite either, as evidenced by his accusations at various times of All Blacks' systematic cheating (one story even accompanied by a graphic showing precisely how the All Blacks cheated in lineouts) and of how rugby's laws have changed to suit the nefarious needs of New Zealand and turned rugby into balletic basketball. After covering the Lions' tour of New Zealand in 1983 and bemoaning all the while about New Zealand in general and its rugby specifically, he wrote a book called *Endless Winter* which one New Zealand journalist said should have been renamed Endless Whinger. Jones, arriving at Anfield in Liverpool for the All Blacks' match against the North of England in 1993, complained of feeling unwell. "Why?" a New Zealand journalist asked. "Have you been reading your own stories again?"

The philosophical differences over rugby that developed in the early years of contact between New Zealand and Britain, differences over amateurism and exploiting and adapting laws to suit purposes, are as pronounced at the end of the 20th century as they were at the end of the 19th.

British Isles – The Quinn Tapes

Dennis Young (left), Ralph Caulton, and Brian Lochore of the 1963-4 All Blacks inspect the famous plaque at Rugby School.

JJ Stewart
All Black coach from 1974-76.

The William Webb Ellis theory for the origins of rugby is a myth. There's evidence that rugby is a very old game indeed, with elements of it being played in Rome and even ancient Greece. It developed in different parts of Europe, including England, and not just the south of England. Then, in the 1890s, there was a breakaway from rugby union in the north of England, into what we now call rugby league. Elements in the south then moved to emphasise that they had really started the game, not the northerners, so they built up this William Webb Ellis story – picking up the ball and running with it – but it was 70 years after Ellis had been to Rugby school and hadn't been mentioned in the meantime. It's an interesting story and there's a plaque on the wall at Rugby to recognise a feat that didn't take place. Purists like Terry McLean reckon people like me are a pain in the neck for saying it and that it's far more interesting that someone picked up a ball and ran with it.

Spiro Zavos
New Zealand journalist.

The 1905-06 Originals actually invented rugby in my view. Before 1905, rugby was very much like Australian rules and like rugby is now, unfortunately, with turnovers all the time. But the 1905 All Blacks applied a system to rugby. They had position in the forwards and played a particular position in the backs. The backs had moves – cut-out passes, loops, the fullback coming into the line. They invented a system of rugby that was logical and had a pattern.

Legends of the All Blacks

The Originals

Tony Lee
English rugby historian.

Exeter were offered the first game against the 1905 team, but didn't have a lot of money. They were asked for a guarantee of fifty pounds and declined the fixture so Devon took their place. When the All Blacks turned up, they caused an immediate impression because they looked very different to conventional English teams. They wore the traditional strip, but had canvas yokes across their shoulders, wide canvas belts, shin guards outside their socks and a couple wore Panama hats. They got a condescending reaction from the crowd, but they ran riot, winning 55-4, a big margin in those days against a team that had been England champions.

At that early stage of the tour, they weren't known as the All Blacks. Local correspondents called them the "Zeals". Other people referred to them as the Colonials or the New Zealand XV.

Robbie Deans
All Black fullback in the mid-1980s.

Bob Deans was my grand uncle. Max, my grandfather, was Bob's brother. Bob died at 24. It's often reported that he died of pneumonia after playing in the snow at Invercargill, but I understand he got peritonitis, a burst appendix, and died from that. Our family talks about him as being a very respected person, quite religious and carrying a lot of mana within the team. He went to church every week and by the end of the 1905 Originals tour, I understand he had quite a few of his team-mates – even the harder core – attending with him.

Obviously there has been a lot of talk down the years about the try he claimed to have scored against Wales in 1905. The feeling within the family is he would never contemplate lying. If he said he scored, he did.

In 1983, when I was in Britain with the All Blacks, I

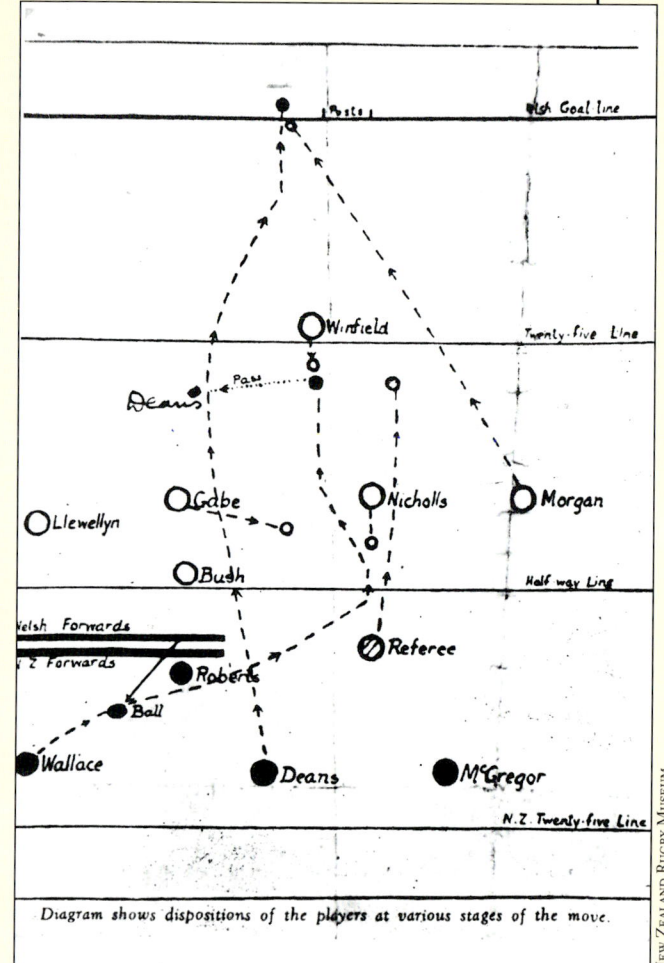

Billy Wallace's diagram of the disputed Deans try.

re-enacted his 1905 try. Wayne Smith, Gary Braid and some others went with me from Bristol, where we were staying, to Cardiff. We were in civilian clothes and no-one would have known we were All Blacks. We got inside the ground and re-enacted the try, just in our long trousers. I placed the ball down over the line, Gary Braid was holding onto my feet and Wayne took the photo. The amazing thing was that a construction worker up on the top storey of the stand yelled, "You're on the wrong side of the line." I suppose that shows how much that incident is part of the Welsh psyche.

British Isles – The Quinn Tapes

Ross Brown
All Black five-eighth from 1955-62.

My father [Handley] was in the 1924 Invincibles team and he told me quite a bit about that tour. He said Bert Cooke was absolutely brilliant and Maurice Brownlie was outstanding. He talked about the winger, Jack Steel, a strong runner, bumping blokes off. He thought Mark Nichols was very sluggish and said they didn't like the manager, Stan Dean.

Fred Allen
future All Black captain and coach.

I was just a youngster when I watched the British Lions play the All Blacks at Christchurch in 1930, but I do remember one incident very clearly. They had two wonderful backs, Aarvold and Morley, and they were running towards George Nepia, the New Zealand fullback. Somehow George just herded them together. It was a certain try because both were speedsters and he herded them together, grabbed them and stopped a certain try.

Eric Tindill
All Black first five-eighth on the 1935-36 tour of Great Britain.

The war dance – the haka – was absolutely out on that tour [1935-36 All Black tour to Britain] because the English Rugby Union said they didn't want us doing it. They thought it was a publicity gimmick and were very critical of it. However, at dinners and dances we were invited to, we did it on request and had a large number of requests for it once word got around that we had a haka.

•

England beat us in what has become known as Prince Obolensky's match. He scored two tries. The first one was just a basic try by a wing three-quarter with speed and he was too fast for the rest. He had space and scored. But the next one was a masterpiece. The ball was going towards his wing and a bit of a scrum was taking place for possession about five metres from their line. He thought to himself there was no point in him staying on his wing, so he went into the normal first-five position, grabbed the ball from the halfback when it was passed, and there was just enough gap for him to get through. Once he got through all he had to do was beat one or two players coming across the backs. He would go infield about ten metres, then another would come across and he'd go another ten. He eventually finished up on his own on the far wing. He scored the try on the opposite wing to his own. It was a magnificent try brought about by his speed and his brains.

•

Inevitably when you lose two internationals out of four and you lose another game to Swansea, plus the draw with Ulster… well, our record didn't compare very well with those of the Originals and the Invincibles. It was fairly common among press comments that they thought the standard of play in the British Isles had improved since 1924, and we were playing against combined counties, not single counties as previous teams had. Also we had to struggle with the three-man front row. So overall I thought we did fairly well. We scored 431 points and had only 180 against us. Over the whole tour – 28 games – we kicked only 16 penalties, not through bad kicking, but because so few penalties were awarded to us. I think history has been a bit hard on us. There were 29 of us in the team and 14 of us were brand new All Blacks like myself, just learning. The injury to Brigadier Page, as he became, hurt us because he was the main runner ▶

Eric Tindill

NEW ZEALAND RUGBY MUSEUM

Legends of the All Blacks

at first five-eighth. He got injured right at the start of the tour and after that was really a passenger. So they brought in the second five-eighth, Jack Griffiths, to help out and he played ten games. I played 13 and Dave Solomon played two. So internally we were struggling. We weren't the greatest team in the world. However, we lost only three of our 28 tour games and two of those were internationals.

KQ: Were their class distinctions in Britain then?

To a minor degree. For example, our baggage man, who was very popular with us, was not initially allowed to travel in the bus with us, and he certainly wasn't allowed to eat with us. Eventually he was allowed to travel in the bus with us when we made representations to the authorities there.

Kevin Skinner
All Black prop from 1949-56.

The 1950 series against the Lions was excellent. They were good rugby players. They had a good forward pack and we were lucky to come out of the first test with even a draw. In the second test, in Christchurch, we played better and won well. But the most remarkable test, probably the most remarkable I ever played, was the third, in Wellington. Johnny Simpson came off the paddock with a broken leg. Later on, Ron Elvidge came off and we played a lot of the game with thirteen men. The pitch was a quagmire. Then Elvidge came back on as a sort of floating fullback and scored that famous try that helped us win 12-6. It was a dramatic day's rugby.

John Reason
English rugby journalist on the controversial first test against the British Isles in 1959.

Tony O'Reilly says of that match, "New Zealand kicked six penalties and if it had been necessary for them to kick seven, they'd have had every opportunity."

Wilson Whineray
captained the All Blacks against the Lions in 1959.

That 1959 Lions team was a super team, maybe the best collectively that I played against. But they had no coaching at all. They had a manager and a secretary, who paid the bills and looked after administrative matters. The captain selected the side and disciplined the side. It was a huge burden to put on Ronnie Dawson. Their backline all had the ability to beat their opposite number and they were quick. David Hewitt, the centre, ran in the Irish track team and Tony O'Reilly and Peter Jackson were quick wingers.

Don Clarke
All Black fullback against the British Lions in 1959.

People often ask me about that test against the British Lions in Dunedin in 1959. They scored four tries and I kicked six penalties and we won 18-17. That Lions team was one of the best sides I'd seen. We struggled in the first test. We lost Jones and Finlay, two of our loose forwards, through injury. There were no replacements then and they played very little part in the game, so we were basically playing with thirteen men. The penalties came along and I was able to bang over six of them. It was difficult for the Lions to swallow, that they had scored four tries and still lost. I felt sorry for the referee, because they criticised the ref for giving penalties. Just because I had an on day and kicked the goals, the referee copped some very severe and unjustified criticism.

British Isles – The Quinn Tapes

WHINERAY'S MEN

Earle Kirton (seated top right) in pensive mood during an All Black 'court' session on the 1963-64 tour.

Earle Kirton
played his first game for the All Blacks against Newport in 1963.

It was the third match of the tour, and my first game. As usual I had no sleep before the game. We didn't play particularly well that day as a team, and I was absolutely terrible. I didn't see the ball leave Monkey Briscoe's hands at times with almost sheer hysteria, or physical trauma. I must have dropped the ball fifteen or twenty times. There was no show of us winning because I didn't give them a chance. So I became pretty much responsible for the loss. I accepted that and never tried to pass the buck. I couldn't believe we got as close as we did [3-0].

I was also unnerved because I was playing against a chap for Newport who was a bit small and looked frail. I thought I'd be able to handle him on defence. But I found I had no show. The guy was almost skipping across water, he was so fast, and I couldn't get near him. He did this to me several times. Turned out his name was Dai Watkins and I'd played him into the Welsh and Lions sides. When I inquired about him they said, "Sure he can run. He's the fastest man in the valleys!" ▶

Legends of the All Blacks

Whineray's Men

The hardest and saddest thing was that the oldies didn't speak to me. Whineray did speak to me, but the others just sort of grunted. I was persona non grata for a couple of days. They'd grunt "Gidday" in the morning and that was about it. I was rooming with Bill Davis, which wasn't very pleasant that night, either. He'd played on the wing – it was just his second game and he couldn't believe the All Blacks had been beaten, because he'd been brought up to believe they never lost. Here he was half-pie crying into his pillow. So I said, "For goodness sake, stop that. How on earth could you have any influence on the game? I couldn't even catch the bloody thing to give it to you. Forget it. You'll have me crying in a moment."

Wilson Whineray
captained the 1963-64 All Blacks to Great Britain. The team lost only one match on the tour, to Newport.

Earle Kirton didn't have a very good game against Newport, but then a number of us didn't. Earle has felt that somehow he was victimised for that game, which is not true. One of the problems on that tour was that we took three first five-eighths because the selectors decided to play Don Clarke as often as possible at fullback. The big guy needed the work. His back-up was Mac Herewini, and there was also Bruce Watt and Earle as first-fives. So by sheer numbers, the best player is going to get the tests and maybe some of the top club sides. Then you divide the rest by three and if it had worked out like that Earle would have got perhaps eight or nine games. In fact, he got thirteen.

Colin Meads
made his first tour of Great Britain in 1963-64.

Earle didn't have too bad a game [against Newport in 1963]. It was just because he was a new All Black. and it was his first game. But it wasn't only him who was affected. Brian Lochore played that day – I think it was the third game of the tour. He played only one of the next eight. I recall him coming to me and asking what he had to do to get a game. I told him the one thing he had to do was train because an opportunity would come and when it did he had to be ready. Sure enough, he was brought in at the last moment for the test against England, so things did change.

Earle Kirton

I was told I'd have to wait for my next game because they realised I could be a ginormous liability. So I waited four more games before I got picked again, against Cambridge University. This was alright. We had a fairly heavy pack, and Don Clarke was at fullback, and it wasn't a bad day, so I thought I'd get a bit of confidence back. For a while it was alright, then early in the second half, I raced after my opposite number and just couldn't get near him. Only a stiff-armed coathanger from Don Clarke stopped him from scoring. So I thought I'd go a bit wider on him and come back at him on the angle, but he did me again, beat me hands down. I got beaten three times by this chap. Later I found out his name was Michael Gibson. So within two games I'd played against the two best first-fives Britain had produced in probably twenty years. Gibson was still playing at forty, but they never knew he was any good until he played against me and I showed them. After I finished with him, he was playing for Ireland and the Lions!

Wilson Whineray
scored a famous try in the Barbarians game.

It was a nice way to end the tour and the edge was taken out by the Barbarians including Ian Clarke, which was super. We scored thirty points against a Lions side in the second half, which takes some doing. I think what I saw from our team was some of the best rugby of the era.

The game was well won by the time I did my thing, otherwise I might have done it differently. The ball fell loose after a big tackle by John Graham following a

British Isles – The Quinn Tapes

lineout. Paul Little picked it up, cut through and I called to him, just to let him know I was there. He flicked me the ball and then I heard a call from Colin. I was going to pass it, I really was. Then as I looked back just to check where the defender was, I saw he'd gone past me and had almost committed to Colin, so I managed just to hold the ball. It was right on my fingertips and it just stuck. I've often thought I must have been within an inch of fumbling it, which would have been stupid. The defender was gone and I could just walk over and score. It was just lovely really – the crowd and the team reaction.

Wilson Whineray is chaired off the field after the Barbarians game.

Colin Meads'
memories of the Whineray try.

By the end of the Barbarians game, we'd loosened up a bit and were all out there looking for plums. I remember Whineray's try because it was me that he sold the dummy to – I was outside him. A few weeks earlier against France, I got tuned up for not passing at one stage. So I whispered to Willie [at Cardiff], "And you said I was a greedy bugger!"

Don Clarke
fullback for the 1963-64 All Blacks to Great Britain.

The Barbarians game in Cardiff in 1964 was a wonderful afternoon, full of emotion. Ian, my brother, was asked to play for the Barbarians. I think Nick Shehadie of Australia had been asked to previously, and there might have been two or three since, but it was a special honour. The Barbarians game is the windup for the tour. They select what they think are high-class, talented players to play the touring side. Ian provided one of the highlights of that game because he drop kicked a goal. I knew he could drop kick, place kick and so forth, but it surprised a lot of people. I dropped out and kicked a little bit far for our forwards to get under it. Ian caught it. In those days you could mark anywhere on the field, and he marked a drop out. We knew it was coming and he let fly and the damn thing cleared the bar by about 20 feet! That was the only points they got. New Zealand went mad then and we scored six tries and converted all of them. Our last try went to Wilson Whineray, our captain. By then we were really stretching the Barbarians' defence and the ball was being moved a lot because we had players like Nathan and Tremain who were wonderful movers and runners of the ball. The ball went to Whineray, who was running up to Stuart Wilson, the Scottish fullback and he feinted the dummy. Wilson took the dummy, so Whineray kept on running for another thirty or so metres and scored the try. It capped off the entire tour. The crowd sang, as only Welshmen can, *For He's A Jolly Good Fellow*. It was a very moving moment as Wilson was chaired from the field.

Legends of the All Blacks

Joseph Romanos
New Zealand journalist.

One amazing incident that occurred in 1967 was when the All Black selectors picked 31 players for the team to go to Britain and France. They gave their team to the Rugby Union chairman, Tom Morrison, to read out under the grandstand at Athletic Park, in the time-honoured way teams were named after All Black trials. But fortunately before Morrison read out the names, he counted them and found there was one too many. So he went back to Fred Allen, the All Black coach, and explained the problem. Fred and the other two selectors then had a hastily reconvened meeting along the corridor and eventually took Wellington fullback Mick Williment's name off the list.

When the team was named, therefore, it contained only one real fullback in Fergie McCormick. Williment was the incumbent, so his omission was a surprise. It would have created an even bigger stir if people had known at the time the full circumstances of his non-selection.

Mick Williment

Gareth Edwards
was a Welsh and Lions halfback from 1967-78.

One of my earliest games for Wales was against the All Blacks in 1967. It was the first time I played with Barry John and it was a baptism of fire. But one incident gave me hope for the future. I chased an up-and-under and collided with Ian MacRae, who was a big man. Our heads clashed and the front of my head hit him in the eye. I remember blood pouring down the side of his face and thinking, "God, they actually do bleed." It's a funny thing to say when you are 19, but we'd been brought up on huge helpings of trying to understand these giants from the other side of the world who were as tough as teak, big as mountains.

This man actually bled and it gave us hope.

That day in Cardiff it was all blood and thunder, both sides going for victory. I was under yet one more ruck. I had foolishly dived on the ball and the whole pack landed on top of me. Fortunately the Wellington flanker, Graham Williams, dived on top of me and pulled me in as both sets of forwards stormed in and said, "Get in there, young man. You'll be safer under me." And he actually put his body over the top of mine. That's something I have never forgotten.

Graham Williams
All Black flanker from 1967-68.

In those days we used to do a lot of genuine rucking and if you were in the wrong place, you actually got rucked out. On that particular occasion I was in a position where I could offer Gareth some protection, but I wasn't going to let him out, either!

British Isles – The Quinn Tapes

PINETREE FELLED

Colin Meads
became the second player in test rugby to be sent from the field when referee Kevin Kelleher gave him his marching orders against Scotland at Murrayfield in 1967.

I was on a formal caution – like a yellow card now – after a lineout scuffle earlier. Then a ruck formed. We rucked harder then than they do now, but not as hard as we had done ten years previously. Anyway, I ploughed in there, over the ruck, rucked a couple back out of it and kicked at the ball. Then the ref had no hesitation in saying, "You're off." I was stunned. "Who, me?" My reaction was one of shame and shock. They always have a big pipe band at games in Scotland and I got in under the tunnel but couldn't get into the dressing room because it was locked. The baggage man couldn't get down in time to unlock the door, so I was standing in the corridor under the stand waiting. Then one of the band members came in. He hadn't been watching the game and had obviously drunk a fair bit of Scotch. He looked at the bandage on my head and he said, "Have you been hurt, my boy?" I tried to tell him to bugger off politely, but I was very angry and in the end I had to tell him where to go.

I felt as if I'd let down the family, but the New Zealand team were tremendous. I didn't know what to do, what to say, where to go. Charlie Saxton was marvellous. He was probably the greatest manager I toured with. When we got on the bus to leave, the Scottish officials were scared. They kept the referee away from me. I don't know what they thought I was going to do to him, but when I hopped on the bus, there's Alister Hopkinson halfway down the aisle saying, "Of all the dumb, useless, stupid idiots I've met…" It took me a while to realise he was talking to me. So that broke the ice. He said, "All you had to do was limp off, you bugger, and the crowd would have clapped you." The humour helped me.

There was a hearing in Cardiff and Charlie fought for me. I waited around all day on tenterhooks. I was never called in. Charlie came out, found a few reserves who weren't playing the next game and told them to take me down to a bar and have a few drinks. It was a sad occasion, and something you'd never want to go through. But the whole of New Zealand was great. All telegrams and letters – I got some marvellous letters from past players and past opponents – helped ease the burden. Over there I was branded for kicking a player, but I'll swear to this day I actually kicked the ball. When I got back from Scotland, they held a reception for me at Te Kuiti and I said then I didn't want to be remembered for the Murrayfield incident, I wanted to be remembered as an All Black.

Brian Lochore
captain of the 1967 All Blacks to Great Britain.

Colin Meads' sending off was one of the saddest occasions I've had to endure in rugby. Pinetree did absolutely nothing wrong in that incident. I understand that he had been warned some minutes earlier for over-vigorous rucking, but I think Kelvin Tremain and I might have contributed to that. I was having trouble at the back of the lineout with their captain, who kept pushing me and pulling me every time we threw the ball to the back. So I suggested to my friend Bunny [Tremain] that he might help me a bit – you couldn't have two captains having a swing at one another. So Kelvin did, but he was never a fighter on the field and I don't think I was a very great one either. Eventually we dealt with this guy, after warning him several times – and he sneered at us each time – until Tremain gave him one in the bread basket which knocked the wind out of his sails. I turned around to see Tremain about 25 metres away and had to go back and be sympathetic to their captain. Obviously the referee, Mr Kelleher, hadn't seen what had happened and thought he had lost control a little. A minute or so later, the Scottish ▶

Legends of the All Blacks

PINETREE FELLED

captain got up, no problem at all. He'd just lost his breath. Well, it was only a minute later that the incident with Colin happened. I just wonder whether Mr Kelleher perhaps felt he'd lost control, which wasn't the case at all.

I couldn't believe it. I was at the bottom of the ruck and by the time I'd got up, Colin was walking away, and the guys were saying to me, "BJ, you've got to do something about it. Pinetree's been ordered off." That's when Colin came back and we went to Mr Kelleher to see what the problem was. He was in no doubt and I respect that. He was in control, and what he saw was different to what Colin did.

The really sad part was what happened afterwards, the kangaroo court. We had the halfback, whom Colin was supposed to have kicked, come into our dressing room and apologise, saying Colin had not even kicked him. He knew it wasn't meant to be a kick at him at all, that Colin was merely having a crack at the ball, but his evidence was never called. I don't think Colin even had the opportunity to explain in court.

Fred Allen
coach of the 1967 All Blacks in Great Britain.

Colin Meads' sending-off was one of the worst things that happened in my career. He did not deserve that. He was wearing a skullcap from when Plantefol had kicked him in the head when the ball was miles away from him during the test the previous week in France. They didn't like Meads over there in Britain from the previous tour and were agin him. But Meads no more kicked that fellow, Chisholm, than fly to the moon. If you look at the film, he was leaning back when he was kicking the ball; he wasn't going forward over the top of him. It was a terrible tragedy when Kelleher sent him off in the dying stages of that game. It was a grey sort of day and I couldn't believe it. Nobody could. But the crowd roared and it must have sparked Kelleher.

I remember later at the Edinburgh hotel, John Reason, one of their well-known rugby reporters, was

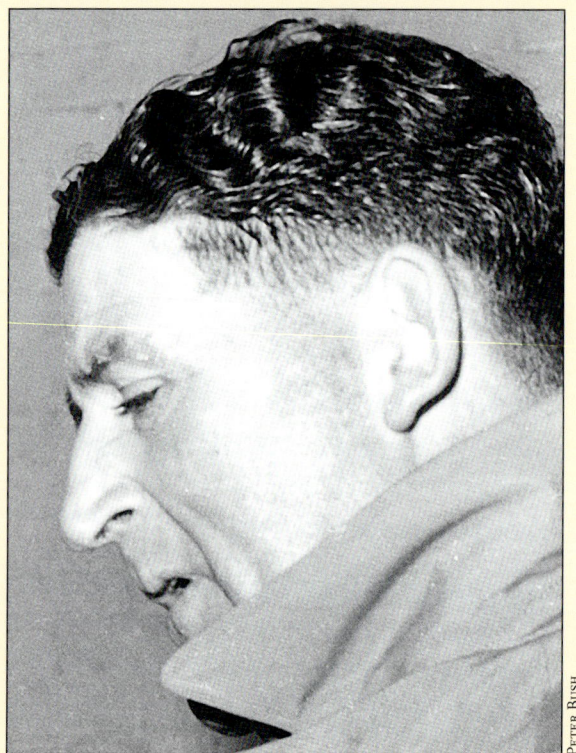

Fred Allen: "I couldn't believe it."

standing in the lounge. I came back in after going to see Pinetree in the bar. Piney was very sad, but Reason, a very sarcastic fellow, said, "Meads should have been ordered off many times." With that I jumped over the settee and the next minute there were two sets of strong arms holding me back, Tremain and Lochore, which was just as well.

John Reason
English rugby journalist.

KQ: What were your views of Meads' sending off in the Scotland test in 1967?

Unfortunate. It was one of those things, a mistake that referees make. They're under a lot of pressure. The more you see the replay, the more it doesn't look so bad, but it looked awful at the time. The referee didn't have five minutes or two years to think and talk about. He

British Isles – The Quinn Tapes

Colin Meads heads for the dressing room.

had to make a decision and he did. I wrote at the time that Meads was indifferent as to whether he kicked the bloke or the ball. And there was no doubt about that.

Bill McLaren
Scottish television commentator.

The Colin Meads ordering off was controversial and threw a pall over the game. The Scottish people knew one of the great New Zealand forwards had suffered an indignity, and they felt for him. I was sorry for the referee. I don't think he wanted to send Meads off, but having cautioned him earlier on, he felt obliged to do it.

Colin Meads

I don't know how it started, but the referee, Mr Kelleher, and I began to correspond. He wrote to me to say he thought he was doing his job. Then it developed into an annual exchange of Christmas cards every year. Then they brought him out for a *This Is Your Life* programme. So I've met him several times. He was a nice man. It's easy to criticise referees and I was probably an expert at it – told them all their pedigrees – they're like us and doing it for enjoyment. I suppose at times we've got to stop and think, "Hey, he could be right."

Legends of the All Blacks

The Danny Hearn Incident

Ian MacRae
was involved in a tragic incident early in the match between the All Blacks and Midlands, London and Home Counties in 1967.

The first time I got the ball in the match, I received a ferocious tackle from Danny Hearn. I was hardly aware of who he was at the time, but as I passed the ball I swung my hip and received a tremendous bang on the hip bone. Both of us went down. I was quickly aware that he was badly hurt, but for a start I was more concerned about myself, because I could feel a fair bit of pain, too. It was lucky that Danny was aware enough to tell people not to shift him, because that saved things from getting any worse. If he'd been moved without due care at that stage he could have been killed.

After the game it was confirmed that he had a serious neck injury. It was shattering and I didn't take it all that well at the time. I wanted to go and see him on the Sunday, but the team management wisely said it wasn't a good idea. So Brian Lochore and the management went along to the hospital to see him. It wasn't until the end of the tour that my friend Bill Davis and I visited Danny at the Stoke Mandeville Hospital. I was a bit apprehensive about the sort of reception we would get, but Danny made it very easy for us. There were no recriminations from his point of view. He explained that it was either him or me. He had intended cutting me in half, hoping to make an impression and be selected to play for England ten days later. Unfortunately he got his head in the wrong place on the tackle.

I felt very sorry for him, as you would for anyone who ends up in that situation. But during our association, I've been so impressed at the way Danny has turned adversity into strength. He takes it so well and has carried on with a very full life.

Danny Hearn
was an England centre. He had his tragic accident while playing for Midlands, London and Home Counties against the All Blacks in 1967.

My head hit Ian MacRae's thigh and that jerked my neck backwards. I was semi-knocked out. I remember one of the All Blacks, Brian Lochore I think, saying, "Stand him up." In self-defence I said, "Don't touch me." Of course, that's the absolutely key thing when anyone has a neck or a spinal injury.

I had one night in the Leicester Infirmary, and then went to Stoke Mandeville, and I was there for nine months. A group of Kiwis who followed the All Black tour sort of made me their project. Every single day, one of them would write to me and that made a huge difference to me. I also got hundreds and hundreds of letters from New Zealand and that was tremendously important to me at the time.

It was an accident and you have to get on and make the best of your life. I've been lucky, I've had a super life since. I mean, I wouldn't wish it on my best friend, but although it's changed my life, other windows have opened. I wouldn't change anything. There's no point

Ian MacRae

Danny Hearn at home in England.

having regrets. What's happened has happened. It's hopeless to lie down and feel sorry for yourself.

I would never want Ian to feel guilty that he caused my accident, because he didn't. And I'm sure he doesn't feel guilty about it. Nevertheless I suppose he will sometimes reflect on how fate has worked. It was my body against his body and I came off worse.

Ian MacRae

It's ironic that of all the players I've played against over the years, the association I've kept up most regularly is with Danny Hearn. We correspond and he's been out to New Zealand and stayed with us a couple of times. It's a close thing. One of the first Christmas cards that gets written in our house is to him, and it's always very nice to hear from him. Even though we're a long way apart, I regard Danny and his wife Jean as very good friends of ours.

Danny and his wife were here in 1981 and were watching a one-day cricket match against Australia with us. This was the infamous underarm incident and we were pretty annoyed. But our reaction didn't match Danny's. He was absolutely outraged, and he thumped the table and used some English expletives such as "You rotten cads" and "You bounders". It was a typical English reaction to bad sportsmanship.

Danny Hearn

I always correspond with Ian and his wife Marilyn at Christmas time and I've stayed with him twice. If there'd been no accident, I'm sure we wouldn't be writing to each other. It was a fairly unique accident and it has inevitably drawn us together to the point where I consider us good friends.

Legends of the All Blacks

Fergie McCormick
All Black fullback from 1965-71.

KQ: Fergie, you were criticised for your play in the first test of the 1971 series. What are your memories of the game?

The Lions were winning up front and got more than their share of the ball. Barry John, their first-five played well, putting kicks just out of my reach. But our wingers that day didn't do their work and some of our loose forwards didn't do their work either. It ended up with me being caught on defence. We lost and the finger got pointed at me. That was the end of my test career, even though I felt I was playing well enough to get another test.

Ian MacRae
All Black to Britain in 1963-64 and 1967.

It was fantastic for the Newport club when we went back there in 1967. They hosted us out at the club and most of the team we had played were there. Four years later they were living legends, sporting cigarette lighters with the score engraved on them. There was a big mural on the club room wall. It shows the magic drop kick going over the bar, but the funny thing is that the mural shows the kick flying over and a green field and a bright, sunny day. The ball actually wobbled over and it was a grey, murky, ugly day.

Fred Allen
coach of the 1967 All Blacks to Great Britain.

I really wanted to go to Africa in 1967. We were going there but with the apartheid, it was cancelled and replaced with a short tour to Canada, UK and France. I was naturally very disappointed. But Charlie and I decided we were going to play 15-man rugby. None of this 10-man stuff where the wing three-quarter throws the ball into the lineout and gets pneumonia the rest of the time standing out on the wing. Charlie and I decided we'd play the same brand of rugby as we had in the Kiwis, where you attack from your own goal-line, use the ball. The papers rubbished us for a start, but in the end they admitted it was a great side. We were also a wonderfully behaved side, which is what you would expect with Charlie and I both strong disciplinarians.

Gareth Edwards
the No 1 halfback for the British Isles on their 1971 tour of New Zealand.

Barry John's contribution to the Lions' tour was immense. He was the linchpin of our victory. His belief in himself, the confidence he gave the rest of the team, his match-winning goal-kicking, his audacity, and the aura he brought to the side really helped us.

British Isles – The Quinn Tapes

WINTER OF THE MAFIA MEN

Ian Kirkpatrick
All Black captain on the 1972-73 of Great Britain.

KQ: How do you recall the Keith Murdoch affair?

It should never have happened. He should never have been sent home. Certain authorities over there wanted to see the back of Keith for whatever reason and when this came up they took their chance. They certainly swayed Ernie Todd [the All Black manager]. They had it in for Keith even before the tour started, and maybe Ernie Todd did too. Yet Keith was a great team man.

On the Sunday morning, Bob Duff [the coach], Sid Going, Ernie Todd and I met. We established that Keith wasn't going home. I think Ernie would like to have sent him home, but we came away knowing he wasn't going to be. Yet whatever went on during that night, that decision changed. It was a shock to us. Looking back, I should have said that if Keith went, we all went. That's one of my big regrets and I've had to live with it and it's been difficult.

Alex Wyllie
All Black loose forward on the 1972-73 tour of Great Britain.

The 1972-73 tour was the first to have live TV coverage, so the rest of the media had to go looking for other stories, because people had already seen what the game was all about and didn't need to read a description of it. I know of a couple of reporters who were told that if they didn't start finding some real news about the All Blacks, they'd be on their way home.

•

Keith [Murdoch] had toured South Africa in 1970, hadn't played much in 1971 because of an ankle injury, then came back in 1972 and made the touring team. He was training hard and playing hard. They couldn't move him in the scrums because he was so strong. I believe the Home Unions saw this. The incident he was sent home for happened in Wales, but it was done by the Rugby Union, as they call themselves. It was disappointing for the players. We'd had a team meeting the night before, and realised that we had to settle down and get things right. Then suddenly it was over – the next morning Keith was going home. That was a hell of a shock.

I haven't seen Keith since, which is a great disappointment. I was rooming with Keith at the time. After the team was named [for the Wales test] we went away and had a couple of beers together and talked about how we were going out there to make it happen on Saturday. Then that happened.

I was sorry he didn't come back to New Zealand because if he had, I think he would have been very well treated. He had the support of all the players. We've all been over it a hundred times. The whole incident arose because of a security guard who had been causing trouble in the hotel. He'd actually attacked some of the Welsh supporters that night. We were in the team room and Keith said, "I'll go down to the kitchen and get some food for us." The guy came in and grabbed hold of him. Well, I mean, that's a stupid thing to do, to grab hold of a player. You can talk reasonably to him and say, "C'mon, I know you've had a good win, but you're not allowed in here." I'm sure had he done that, nothing would have happened. But this guy thought he was going to deal with Keith. It was a silly thing to do.

Sid Going
the No 1 All Black halfback on the 1972-73 tour of Great Britain.

Our 1972-73 All Black team was ear-tagged before we even got to Britain. They were accusing us of this and that and everything else. Poor old Keith [Murdoch] never had a chance on that tour.

The British complained about the amount of strapping we used. We spent 500 pounds on strapping and they really did their nana about it. We didn't have ▶

Legends of the All Blacks

Winter of the Mafia Men

any physios or doctors with us and were trying to strap our ankles and so on. I got injured in the first training session. I was supposed to play in the first game, but had done my ankle. The doctor I went to see wanted to put it in plaster. I told him there was no chance of that as I wanted to be playing within a fortnight and I was. I had to sit and watch the Llanelli game [Llanelli beat New Zealand 9-3] and I can tell you that watching that made my ankle get a lot better very quickly! I managed to play against Cardiff in the third game, but the ankle was never right. I managed to strap it for the whole tour, but the injury kept recurring.

Alan Sutherland, Tane Norton and Alex Wyllie 'keep their heads warm'.

We got a tremendous amount of criticism about everything and really withdrew from the media. I recall an occasion when four of us got a ride from Porthcawl to Cardiff in a taxi. We talked among ourselves, not realising the guy who was driving us was a press man. The next day we read about this so-called interview in the paper. It absolutely stunned us. That sort of thing was happening all the time at bars and wherever we were. People would listen to what the group were talking about and the next thing you know, you'd be reading it in the paper. That's why we withdrew from the media.

But some of the writers really went after us, really eye-balled us. For instance, I'd never been penalised so many times for putting the ball into the scrum incorrectly. But that story about me feeding the scrum incorrectly was all over TV before we even got there. I got penalised thirteen times in one game for that. In the end I gave it to the referee and said, "You put it in because I can't." He penalised me again, though he didn't say what for.

It was a very difficult tour in a lot of ways. We had tremendous team spirit considering the criticism we got. A lot of it was silly. You know, I got razzed for wearing a hat. But I had a bald head and it was cold. Now the All Blacks get hats given to them. It was childish really.

They really went after Keith Murdoch, but he was a good bloke. I'm a non-drinker and at every team function or meeting, he made sure there was orange juice for me. He would make sure everyone in the team had a drink before he put one to his mouth. He was our bar manager if you like, and he was a good guy. It was really sad to see him have to leave like he did, and grossly sad that he felt he couldn't come back to his own country.

Gareth Edwards
Welsh and British Isles halfback from 1967-78.

It left a sour taste and detracted from the tour. The All Blacks went out of their way to make themselves unpopular, whereas they didn't have to be. I knew a lot of them and found them to be decent guys, but it's a fact they were out to prove something they didn't really have to prove.

British Isles – The Quinn Tapes

GREAT GARETH, SUPER SID

Gareth Edwards dive-passes ahead of Sid Going during the second test of the 1971 series at Christchurch. Ian Kirkpatrick follows the action.

Sid Going

Gareth Edwards was a tremendous player, a great player. He was a cocky sort of guy, a bit bigger than me, probably faster. The press always made a huge deal out of our rivalry. I had enormous regard for Gareth. I played against him many times and prided myself on getting the better of him in most of those tests, possibly because our forward pack generally held the upper hand. I've always had a streak of stubbornness and enjoyed playing against Gareth because it brought out the best in me. There were a couple of games where he had it all over me. In the third test of the 1971 series, he had a great game. Another occasion was in the Baabaas game in 1973.

Gareth Edwards

Sid Going was without doubt the best scrumhalf I played against. We had a battle over a long period of time and some he won, some I won. He was a great competitor, so dangerous, a match-winner. You had to keep such a close eye on the man.

John Reason
English rugby journalist.

Sidney Milton Going played thirteen matches against Gareth Edwards and won twelve of them. Gareth is in the International Hall of Fame, but I saw all thirteen of their contests and the only one Gareth won was the Barbarians game at Cardiff when Sid went onto the pitch with an injury so bad that nobody else would have gone on without a crutch. Not only was Sid Going a better player than Gareth Edwards, but I should say that since the war, New Zealand have had four halfbacks better than Gareth. Kenny Catchpole of Australia was better than all of them.

Legends of the All Blacks

Andy Leslie
captain of the '74 All Blacks to Ireland and Great Britain.

In 1974 the All Blacks were over in Britain. We played the Barbarians at the end of the tour and we had the after-match function at the Hilton Hotel. Later Willie John McBride and I were through the streets of London. That night a few bombs had gone off – the IRA were playing up in London at the time. A bobby walked past and saw Willie John and stopped to chat. Willie John said, "You know, if we could all be playing a game like we played today, there would be no problems in this world." I thought that wasn't bad. Here I was, an All Black, walking with Willie John McBride, the captain of the Lions and Ireland. Rugby was the only game that brings Ireland together. It made me think rugby was not a bad game to be playing.

Sid Going
All Black halfback from 1967-77.

Sid Going

I could see the writing on the wall [in 1977]. There was very little communication from the coach [Jack Gleeson] towards us and I was getting that cold-shouldered feeling. There was a huge push from the South Island to put Lyn Davis in ahead of me. Scaley and I had been great mates really since very early on – I was reserve to him in the Colts way back in about 1965 – and we're still good mates. But I could see after the Christchurch test that I was being blamed for the loss. I don't know why… probably I could have scored once, but I passed it and they dropped it. I played for the Maoris against the Lions at Eden Park and scored two tries, but I knew after that after-match function that the game was up. Jack Gleeson was at the match and they announced the third test team from the venue. I knew I wasn't going to be selected because he wouldn't say a thing to me and walked the other way. It's totally different from today's situations, I suppose.

Billy Bush
All Black prop from 1974-79.

The test against Scotland at Eden Park in 1975 was played in huge pools of water. I was marking Ian McLauchlan, Mighty Mouse, and we were in about a foot of water at times. Every time the scrum went down, which was quite often, we would pull up one another's head and make sure the other guy hadn't drowned.

British Isles – The Quinn Tapes

The Mighty Men of Munster

Tom Kiernan
coach of Munster in 1978.

Munster beating the All Blacks in 1978 generated tremendous enthusiasm for rugby in Limerick city for rugby. We compete in Ireland with several sports. There's soccer, Gaelic football, hurling and rugby is fourth. But Limerick is the only city in Ireland where rugby is No 1. We had a number of schools who formerly played hurling and football changing gradually to rugby, with the result that one of the Limerick clubs, Shannon, has won the Irish national league five times on the trot and another Limerick team has won it on three occasions. It was a great shot in the arm for rugby. I just wish it happened more often!

Brendan Foley
who played for Munster on the greatest day in the team's rugby history.

We expected about five thousand because the game was on a Tuesday afternoon and Limerick is not a rugby city. But we couldn't believe it. We got twelve thousand in Thomond Park, which has swelled since to about two and a half million. Everybody you meet was there that day. They were everywhere, on trees around the ground, on walls, on roofs overlooking the ground. And they were still there an hour after the game, unable to believe it. It was a great day.

Moss Keane
long-serving Irish test player and a senior member of the Munster side in 1978.

KQ: Moss, what is your over-riding memory of that great day for Munster rugby?

That was the day our scrumhalf's father died. If the news had come through before the game, we'd have all panicked because Donal Canniffe was a key player – he played like a back row forward as much as a scrumhalf. When the game was over, he was told that his father had died suddenly in Cork. So that incident lives in my mind, from the elation of victory to the deflation when we heard that news. We'd all met the man and felt terribly sad. It was like the harsh reality of life thrusting itself out at us. But it has tended to add mystique to the whole day. There is something slightly unreal about it. If he had died two hours earlier we probably wouldn't have beaten the All Blacks.

Graham Mourie
was the All Black captain from 1976-82.

If we had to lose on that 1978 tour, we'd rather have lost to an Irish side than anyone else. They were such good winners, and their happiness was so evident.

Munster hero Moss Keane (left) is surrounded by jubilant fans.

Legends of the All Blacks

LINEOUT CAPERS

Andy Haden
All Black lock against Wales at Cardiff Arms Park in 1978.

We had talked at training about how to clear up the obstruction that was going on in the lineout. One of the boys mentioned a match between Taranaki and King Country when Ian Eliason dived out of the lineouts three or four times and got a penalty each time against Colin Meads. He mentioned it more in jest, but with a minute to go in the test match the following day, those are the sort of things that come into your mind if you are of fresh mind and thinking quickly.

With a minute to go we were 12-10 down, yet we were a better team. I thought about what Eliason had done. It doesn't actually say in the rules that it's cheating, but it was certainly a variation in tactics. Given the same circumstances, even with the maturity of the last 20 years, I would do it again, unfortunately, because it's the way I think. You do what you can within the rules to win. I didn't want to go back to my dressing shed and sit there and say to myself that there was something else I could have done to win the test.

There was an injury to Doug Bruce and a collection of players gathered. I said to Mourie I was going to dive, and he knew what I meant straight away. Then I went back and told Frank [Oliver]. When the lineout took place, I heard the referee's whistle before the ball had left the hand of the thrower. He can say what he likes, but I'm sure he was attracted by the noise that went on at the same time [as Haden and Oliver dived from the lineout]. Had the lineout proceeded without us diving, I have no doubt there would have been no penalty.

Brian McKechnie's winning kick against Wales, 1978.

Brian McKechnie
who kicked the winning goal for New Zealand in the test against Wales in 1978.

I'd been in the reserves for the Irish test and was dumped from the reserves for the test against Wales. I was fairly dejected and had a few beers with some of the other All Blacks. We went on until the early hours of the morning. I was told during the evening that I might be required in the reserves because Mark Donaldson had an injury, but I didn't think that was very likely. It was quite late the following morning, about 10 o'clock, that I was actually told I was in the reserves. Because of that I never had time to get caught up in the hype of playing a test against Wales, who weren't a bad side. I hadn't followed the traditional night-before routine.

The test turned out to have a fairly heated start. Clive Currie, our fullback, got caught under a high ball and ended up with a broken jaw, which finished his tour. So there's me: 10 o'clock on the morning I'm told I'm in the reserves, then 10 minutes into the test I find myself in the middle of the match. I think at that point it was 6-0 to Wales and things were fairly tense out there. We reserves had already had a few spats with the crowd in the early moments of the game.

It turned into a memorable occasion for me. The first kick that came my way was a high floater that dipped away on me at the last moment. I bent down and caught it on my finger tips and booted it 10-odd metres upfield into touch. That felt good because it was my handling under the high ball that had let me down early in the tour. Then I had a goal kick that struck the posts. Through the rest of the game, things flowed my way.

It came to the last few minutes and we were down 12-10. There was a lineout on their 22. I think they went to throw the ball in first and the ref asked that it be thrown again. I didn't see what actually happened and it wasn't until under the stand later that we saw the incident replayed and saw what had happened. I remember walking up to take the shot. The ball wasn't there. I'd seen Clive take a shot against Cardiff early in the tour and the ball fell over a couple of times. All I could think of was, "Get up there and take this as quickly as you can." I was confident enough and didn't want to muck around. As soon as I kicked it, before I looked up, I could tell I'd hit it well. When I looked up and saw it was going dead centre, I thrust my arm in the air, more in relief, because I knew at that stage we would probably win after having been behind for 79 minutes. That gesture was unusual for me. I'd never really done that. But it was the realisation as I turned to run back that we'd won a test and I'd been part of it.

After the game I was taken into a room for an interview. That's when I saw the lineout incident. I don't think they got a word out of me at the interview because I was so stunned at what had taken place out there.

Because of the drama surrounding that kick at Cardiff Arms Park, and then the cricket underarm incident in Melbourne a couple of years later, I've been associated with a couple of the more controversial incidents in New Zealand sport. I feel I'm the innocent party. I would much prefer at times that the underarm thing faded away, but it crops up more than the Welsh thing. Probably it's because of the Australia-New Zealand relationship. Having said that, I've had some fun with Trevor Chappell over the last few years with various bits and pieces we've been involved in.

Andy Dalton
All Black hooker.

Andy Haden on lineout duty against Wales in 1978.

I couldn't believe what had happened. I threw the ball in and suddenly both Andy and Frank just flew out of the lineout. It all happened so quickly, I didn't see much of it. We got the penalty. Everyone talks about Andy, but Frank's not a very good actor! I suppose Andy has to live with what he did. There is talk that it was discussed before the game, but I wasn't aware of it and was surprised as the Welsh team and the referee to see these guys flying out of the lineout. It set a precedent I wouldn't like to see followed. I'd be a lot happier not having to win games like that.

Graham Mourie

We believed that Andy had an inner ear infection and had lost his balance! On reflection, maybe Andy wouldn't want to do it again, and as a team we wouldn't want him to, but these days the ethics of the game have become a greater consideration.

Legends of the All Blacks

Robbie Deans
was an All Black fullback from 1983-85.

My test debut was at Murrayfield in 1983. We had our team talk and from there it's straight onto the team bus. Through some circumstances I don't want to go into because it'll get me angry, I missed the bus. I arrived at the front door as the bus was pulling out, which was fairly traumatic, though at least it got my mind off first test nerves. I got a taxi and was heading to the ground. Then the guys on the bus realised I wasn't on board and turned the bus around. They passed me going the other way, back to the hotel.

I got stuck in traffic heading towards the ground, whereas they had a police escort. When I finally arrived at Murrayfield, I had to convince the man on the gate that I was playing. Obviously others had tried to have him on because he took some convincing!

Bruce Robertson
New Zealand's great centre of the 1970s.

The Scotland test sealed the Grand Slam for our team in 1978. It got darker and darker during the second half. We charged the ball down on our own 22, kicked it through and eventually I managed to score the try. It was amazing because even the players weren't aware of who'd scored. Graham Mourie went up to BG [Williams] and said, "Great try, Beegee"

Sean Fitzpatrick
All Black captain, 1992-97.

After playing reasonably well to win the first test against the Lions in 1993, we played very poorly in the second test at Wellington. It was a terrible performance. At the end of the game, I said to Gavin Hastings [the Lions captain], "Gavin, you wait for this week. You'll never see a team dealt to by the press in any other country in the world the way they are going to deal to us." It was the worst week of my life. I felt lucky to be selected a week later for the third test.

There was a lot of soul-searching and it was a pretty glum bunch that came together in Auckland on the Tuesday to prepare for the third test. It was a tough week; the media had really got into us. On the Friday, I remember Laurie standing in the front of the bus as we were heading to Eden Park for a look at the ground and saying, "What, are we going to a funeral?" I looked down the bus and the guys looked absolutely shattered and terrible. Laurie said it wasn't that bad and told us to cheer up and enjoy the moment. The team gained a lot of resolve out of that and played really well to win the third test.

Will Carling
toured New Zealand with the British Isles in 1993.

It was amazing to experience rugby life in New Zealand. We went to the Bay of Islands when we arrived in 1993. I went into a chemist on the first morning to buy a tube of toothpaste. There was a lady of about seventy behind the counter who said, "Are you with the Lions?" I said we were and she went through the squad. She thought our loosies were a bit slow, our wingers were quick etc. Unbelievable! She analysed our whole team, and was spot on. It was like that throughout New Zealand. You can't get away from rugby in New Zealand.

The Coaches

Makers of Legends

By Joseph Romanos

The battles over the All Black coaching position over the past few years have been described as a side-effect of the advent of professional rugby, but that's far from the truth. During 1998 there were dozens of newspaper surveys and public polls about whether John Hart should be retained as coach. Talkback callers and newspaper letter writers had a field day. As is often the case with things rugby in New Zealand, everyone seemed to have an opinion. The fate of John Hart was apparently of more pressing concern than that of the demise of the coalition Government, the economic crisis or the future of the health system.

But then the job of New Zealand coach has been causing controversy since 1905. Down the years there have been many public wrangles about the All Black coach:

- Should Jimmy Duncan have been sent as coach of the 1905 Originals?
- Why was Vic Cavanagh ignored for the coach's job after the Second World War?
- Why did Fred Allen, unbeaten in the job, feel pressured to step down with a major tour of South Africa looming in 1970?
- Why was Jack Gleeson shunned from 1972-77?
- Who should be coach in 1988, Alex Wyllie or John Hart?
- Was it a good idea to have co-coaches for the 1991 World Cup?
- In the early 1990s, who would make the better coach, Hart or Laurie Mains?
- Should Hart have been dumped at the end of 1998?

These have been just some of the disputes over the All Black coach that have exercised the public mind this century.

There have been more than 15 official New Zealand coaches, and many others who were co-opted for a specific match or series. Some did the job only moderately, others were very good. But four stand out as being the great All Black coaches of the century – Fred Allen, who towers over everyone, Jack Gleeson, Brian Lochore and John Hart.

Let's examine the history of the position and see what made these four coaches so outstanding.

Legends of the All Blacks

The first New Zealand coach

Before the New Zealand team played its first home test, against Great Britain at Athletic Park in 1904, the players spent nearly a week preparing in camp in Day's Bay under the eye of fitness expert Dorrie Leslie and coach Jimmy Duncan. On the morning of the test, the New Zealanders caught the ferry across the harbour. While they were on the water, Wellington was hit by a big earthquake and when the team berthed they were shocked to find much damage to buildings and people running about in panic.

In the great traditions of New Zealand rugby, the test carried on regardless and New Zealand won 9-3. This decisive victory over the inventors of rugby is often said to be the most crucial result in our rugby history.

An elderly Jimmy Duncan (left) chats with former Otago and All Black representative Laurie Haig.

The idea of having the test players in camp, working on strategy and fitness, was adjudged a success. So in 1905, when the New Zealand team was to tour Australia, then Britain and France, it was decided a coach should accompany the side. For the Australian leg, brilliant Taranaki second five-eighths Jimmy Hunter was appointed captain-coach despite heated objections, especially from Auckland. The number of players taken to Australia was cut from 26 to 25 to accommodate Hunter, who played only three of the seven tour matches. Before the team was confirmed for the big trip to Europe, Hunter was selected as a player, Dave Gallaher was promoted to the captaincy and Duncan was selected specifically as coach.

Duncan, a brilliant tactician and an early advocate of the five-eighths system of rugby, had been one of the dominant figures on the New Zealand rugby scene for a decade. The Otago man had captained the South Island in the first inter-island match, in 1897 and led New Zealand in its first official test, against Australia at Sydney in 1903. He later became an international referee and was one of the ablest and most outspoken administrators of his time. A prematurely balding figure with an impressive moustache, Duncan became the centre of considerable controversy even before Dave Gallaher's 1905 tourists left for Britain. His appointment annoyed some rugby followers – particularly those outside Otago – who would have preferred to have taken an extra player.

The Coaches

There were some strong personalities in that 1905 team and many of them resented Duncan's presence and let him know it. It is difficult to be emphatic nearly a century later, but rugby lore has it that before a training session had taken place, Gallaher told Duncan that he was to play no part in coaching the side. Gallaher intended taking charge of the forwards and vice-captain Billy Stead would work with the backs. Auckland lock Billy Cunningham and Wellington utility back Billy Wallace also helped with the coaching and training, while manager George Dixon did some of the organisation. Duncan must indeed have felt like a spare part.

Instead of being a coach as we now understand it, Duncan became a sort of public relations officer-assistant manager for the team. With his trademark cloth cap (which he even wore when playing, to cover his lack of hair), he delighted the British media with his scathing criticism of the wing forward position. "The innovation should be abolished because it spoils the game and is responsible for continual offside play," he said. This comment can hardly have pleased Gallaher, who was the team's wing forward.

There are conflicting reports on Duncan's feelings about the 1905 tour. Billy Wallace wrote later: "Jimmy put in a lot of hard work behind the scenes. Not only has he been a clever player, but he was able to impart his knowledge to others. He was a keen observer and could quickly pick out the faults of the different players. Jimmy's coaching, especially early in the tour, when we were working out our plan of campaign, was of very great value to us and helped weld us into a very powerful attacking combination. Jimmy put in a lot of time with the injured players and assisted with the baggage."

Duncan, on his return, said publicly he had enjoyed the tour but privately expressed his resentment at his treatment, complaining that he had been made to feel useless. Some players, such as utility back George Gillett, were less complimentary about Duncan than the affable Wallace. While officially things were smoothed over, one fact remains clear: it was to be some decades before another officially-designated coach was sent away with an All Black team.

The 1905 Originals were an innovative side, one of the most important teams in rugby history. They introduced set positions for forwards at a scrum, honed lineout play and came up with a dazzling array of backline moves. Players like Charlie Seeling, George Smith, Wallace, Fred Roberts and Hunter captured the imagination of the British critics and the team lost only one of their 35 matches, a disputed 3-0 defeat by Wales.

Gallaher and Stead, who wrote *The Complete Rugby Footballer* after the tour, were given credit for the fresh, forward-thinking approach of the team and Duncan's role was dramatically down-played. What can't be denied is that Duncan was the first in a line of leading Otago coaches who made a major impact nationally. Others who followed included Vic Cavanagh senior, Vic Cavanagh junior, Charlie Saxton, Eric Watson and Laurie Mains.

Legends of the All Blacks

The Years Without a Coach

The famous 1924 Invincibles coached themselves. Wellington five-eighth Mark Nicholls, acknowledged as one of the best thinkers on rugby that New Zealand has produced, was responsible for much of the tactical planning. It was Nicholls who took 19-year-old George Nepia in hand and showed him the requirements of the fullback position. Nepia, a novice in the position, learned his lessons well – he played every match of the tour and became so good he is now one of the legends of All Black rugby.

The 1924 team was led by another Wellingtonian, Cliff Porter and included the great Hawke's Bay player Maurice Brownlie. These two and vice-captain Jock Richardson took charge of the forwards.

While the no-coach policy worked well with the brilliant 1924 side, the wheels began to fall off after that. Brownlie was left to captain and coach the 1928 All Blacks to South Africa. He had a poor manager and was often at loggerheads with his vice-captain, Nicholls, and in the circumstances did very well to secure a drawn series. It took the All Blacks nearly 70 years to produce a better series result in South Africa.

The 1935 All Blacks to Britain were sadly deficient in leadership. Jack Manchester, a forward from Canterbury, captained a side that had few outstanding players. The manager, Vincent Meredith, was chosen more for his social status than his rugby knowledge. One of the younger members of that team, Eric Tindill, recalls the desperate lack of coaching. "We were an inexperienced team, and desperately needed some good coaching. but we never got any. We'd turn up to training and throw the ball around a bit. But there was no planning or advice. It was the biggest hurdle we had to overcome on that tour."

Usually during home series, a coach was drafted in to help prepare the All Blacks. Alex McDonald of the Originals, assisted in preparing New Zealand for the 1921 series against the Springboks and another of the Originals, Billy Wallace, helped coach the 1937 All Blacks for the home series against South Africa. Canterbury forward Jim Burrows also assisted in the preparation of the All Blacks for this series. But it wasn't until after the Second World War that the coach took on a more formal role.

The great man in New Zealand coaching in the years after the war was Vic Cavanagh of Otago. His father had been a towering figure in Otago coaching in the years between the wars – and a New Zealand selector in 1913 – and young Vic, as he was known, carried on the family tradition, putting together the champion Otago side which kept a firm grip on the Ranfurly Shield from 1947-50.

Cavanagh should have been given the job of coaching the All Blacks to South Africa in 1949, but in one of those strange political decisions which defy logic, the position went to 66-year-old Alex McDonald, who had been

The Coaches

a forward in the 1905 Originals, back in the days of the 2-3-2 scrum, and had been a national selector from 1929-32.

"Alex was a lovely old chap," says Fred Allen, who captained the 1949 team, "but he was far too old and out of touch to coach us. We all wanted Vic Cavanagh. He'd proved his worth with Otago and was the man we needed in South Africa."

Vic Cavanagh (left) with other great Otago and New Zealand rugby identities Arthur Marslin, Bill Duncan and Charlie Saxton.

Cavanagh was a particularly fine coach of forwards and the Otago pack was known for the quality of their play, especially their ferocious rucking. They bound well, drove low, maintained their balance and continually kept the opposition at full stretch until the gaps opened and the Otago backs, Ron Elvidge in particular, were able to take the chances. Instead of winning renown as one of the great All Black coaches, Vic Cavanagh has become known as the best coach who never coached the All Blacks.

In South Africa, Allen himself had to coach the side. It was a tough job and the South Africans shaded his team in each test. Allen gave a glimpse of his ruthless side when he dropped himself for the final two tests. "I'd done all I could. I thought we might do better if someone else had a go," he said. It's doubtful if it was the correct decision, for Allen was a fine player in a team that did not have great five-eighths. But it did give an indication of the uncompromising way Allen approached his rugby.

Through the 1950s an assistant manager was named to travel overseas with All Black teams, his role being mainly to help coach the side. At home, the convener of selectors generally coached the team, though for the really big series of the decade, against South Africa in 1956, Bob Stuart was co-opted as coach by Tom Morrison, Jack Sullivan and Arthur Marslin, the selectors. "They wanted me to work with the forwards," recalls Stuart. "They were concerned they had become too loose. I was very keen to help, but said I couldn't work with forwards in isolation. The whole team has to know what's going on.

"We lost the second test of that series so it was 1-1, and there was a push by the New Zealand union to have me moved aside. But Tom and the other selectors stood firm, saying they had co-opted me so it was their call. I stayed and we won the series 3-1. It was a great series and the All Blacks played very well. I'd spoken to some of the Lions who'd been in 1955 to try to find out where South Africa might be weak, and that knowledge helped.

"They had good backs and were good scrummagers, but we concentrated on driving forward and used the blind a lot. Peter Jones became a key player for us but the unsung hero was Bill Clark, who was so astute tactically and was brilliant at organising the forwards."

Stuart had captained the 1953-54 All Blacks to Britain, where he had coached the side, with assistance from Laurie Haig and Bob Scott in the backs. Jim Fitzgerald, a qualified PE teacher, ran the fitness work. "In those days you used what you had. You looked through the personnel in a team and used the experience that was on offer."

With rugby still amateur, some outstanding potential coaches never took the All Black job. Charlie Saxton, the next in the line of great Otago coaches, Tom Morrison and Stuart himself, all had to decline the opportunity to coach All Black teams because of their work commitments.

Jack Sullivan coached the 1960 team to South Africa and Neil McPhail got the job for the tour of Britain in 1963-64. McPhail became noted for his stirring team talks, often harking back to his own wartime experiences in his efforts to inspire his troops.

Fred Allen – The Needle

Then, in 1966, Fred Allen, who had been a national selector since 1964, stepped into the role of selection panel convener and therefore coach (though on tour the role was still designated as assistant manager).

Through his record and forceful personality, Allen became a dominant figure in New Zealand rugby. He is the greatest coach in New Zealand history, not only because his team never lost, but because he exerted such influence.

Allen had been a hugely successful Auckland coach. After a stuttering start, his Auckland team had gone on to enjoy a record Ranfurly Shield reign of 25 defences from 1960-63. He became known as "The Needle", a tag which suited him as he was prepared to take on any player in a confrontational way. He had some tough decisions to make as Auckland coach, including opting for Bob Graham ahead of All Black skipper Wilson Whineray as his captain.

It is true that Allen, while a good analyst of rugby and a person schooled in the technique of the game, did motivate by fear. There are many famous examples of him stirring up his players. And not just the newcomers, either. He was content, eager even, to take on legends like Kel Tremain and Colin Meads. "Thorney," he would say to ebullient and cocky Grahame Thorne, "we've got other wingers."

"I told some terrible white lies," Allen recalls. "For one Canterbury game I had a real brainstorm. I woke up in the middle of the night with one of my best ideas. We always used to have our Auckland team talks in the Station Hotel and I would bring along the Shield to have it on display there during out talk. But this day I didn't bring the Shield.

"When the players asked me where it was, I told them the Canterbury manager had asked if they could borrow it. I told them he'd said they wanted to get a photo of it, so they could have the picture ready for

The Coaches

Fred Allen makes a point to the All Black front row of Brian Muller, Bruce McLeod and Alister Hopkinson, 1967.

publication when they got back to Christchurch with the Shield. That one really got them steamed up!

"Another time we were to play Wellington. I told my team I'd walked into the Wellington dressing room and been fired out bodily. What they weren't going to do to us, I'd said."

It is hard to describe the tense atmosphere in an All Black dressing room while Allen was speaking. He stared straight at his players, many of whom could not meet his eyes. No-one was spared, not even the captain. "He would have a go at the skipper," says Brian Lochore, "but he'd have let me know beforehand what was going to happen. Everything was done for effect, and Fred was masterful. He didn't go in there and just rant and rage. He knew what he was doing. Some players he inspired by fear. With others, he built up their confidence. He was a tremendous motivator, and his methods would have worked with any generation."

Allen, stern and decisive, coached New Zealand in 37 matches and they never lost one. All 14 tests were won. He was a masterful coach, at pains to be fair and always looking for an opposition weakness to exploit.

He made some significant decisions, including appointing the relatively unknown Lochore as All Black captain ahead of the likes of Meads, Ken Gray and Kel Tremain. In 1967 he dropped Chris Laidlaw and Kel Tremain for Sid Going and Ian Kirkpatrick for the test against France. "Laidlaw and Bunny were going to the physio too much. They didn't have their minds on rugby and needed a shake-up." In 1967 he also opted for Earle Kirton ahead of Mac Herewini as his first five-eighth, a critical decision as it meant he really had to pick Laidlaw ahead of Sid Going, whom he felt was the better player. (Kirton and Laidlaw were provincial team-mates and Kirton much preferred having Laidlaw as his halfback.)

Legends of the All Blacks

Allen had three years of runaway success with the All Blacks, then stood down at the end of 1968. "I'd love to have taken the All Blacks to South Africa in 1970, but I'd heard rumblings I was for the chop, and I always think it's better to get out before they dump you."

New Zealand Rugby Union officials were apparently annoyed with Allen for allowing journalist Alex Veysey into the All Black dressing room before a test in Australia in 1968. Allen says he was never a darling of the Rugby Union – he was too much his own man. So in 1969 he was succeeded by Ivan Vodanovich, a lovely person who had a deep love of rugby and had been an All Black prop in 1955. But few would rate Vodanovich in the same class as Allen as a coach.

Vodanovich had charge of an ageing All Black team that lost major series to South Africa in 1970 and the Lions in 1971. It would have been interesting to see what Allen might have done with those teams.

Allen's methods worked at all levels, not just for Auckland and New Zealand. He assisted Hawke's Bay and Marlborough, would take over lower grade club teams for a month or two and for years took away the *Rugby News* youth team. The one unchanging fact was that whoever he coached did well. His knowledge, personality and motivational skills made him a giant of a coach.

It is doubtful if New Zealand ever sent away a better duo than in 1967 when Charlie Saxton was manager and Allen coach (assistant manager) of the team Brian Lochore captained through Britain and France. Allen and Saxton were very close – both had served in the army, where they'd had instilled in them the qualities of discipline and teamwork. And they'd been members of the famous Kiwis Army side which revolutionised rugby after the war. Saxton captained that team and preached the three Ps credo: Position, Pace and Possession. Allen embraced those principles and based his coaching on it.

The early 1970s were not great years for New Zealand rugby, or its coaches. After Vodanovich's undistinguished reign, Jack Gleeson had a brief stint, Bob Duff took the 1972-73 All Blacks to Britain, then John (JJ) Stewart, a penetrating critic of the game, swept into power.

Stewart, a laconic character who'd coached a New Zealand Colts team to Ceylon as long ago as 1955, cast aside many established players and removed Ian Kirkpatrick from the captaincy. There followed a grand tour of Ireland and Britain in 1974 when New Zealand played Ireland and, effectively Wales and the Lions (in the guise of the Barbarians) within a week, drawing with the Lions and winning the other two.

But the big challenge was South Africa in 1976 and Stewart's team lost that series 3-1. In hindsight the team was not well selected, being deficient in two key areas – fullbacks and loose forwards. While the All Blacks were toiling in South Africa, a second-string New Zealand team was touring Argentina under coach Jack Gleeson and captain Graham Mourie.

The Coaches

The Jack Gleeson era

It was the start of another great era for New Zealand. Jack Gleeson had been a good provincial player, but he was a great coach, even if his methods were vastly different to those of Allen.

Both men understood rugby and were innovative thinkers, but Allen ruled by fear. Gleeson was a more low-key character who used reason and was more obviously democratic. He was a man of his times, for his team included individuals like Andy Haden. By the late 1970s players liked to have more say in what went on in a team, and Gleeson's style suited those requirements. He encouraged players to think for themselves and used to seek the opinions of his players at team sessions and was a good listener. Gleeson was never afraid to delegate, yet there was never any question of his relinquishing power. He had the respect of his All Black team and he was the boss.

It was his second stint with the All Blacks. He led them on a nine-match internal tour in 1972, had never been beaten, then was unaccountably dropped and sent to rugby oblivion for several years.

Yet he was always a discerning rugby watcher who concentrated on quality before quantity. His training sessions, after the players had warmed up, did not last longer than an hour, and he continually stressed the need for zip and zest. With these short, sharp sessions, he ensured his players retained their sting for the matches. In this regard, Gleeson's methods were diametrically opposed to those of Vodanovich.

Gleeson, who lived in Feilding, was a dry-witted man who described himself as a hotelier rather than a publican because, he said, publicans were named as

Coach Jack Gleeson and captain Graham Mourie... a formidable combination.

sinners in the Bible. He took the fledgling New Zealand side through South America undefeated, a good effort, then masterminded a narrow 3-1 win over the Lions in 1977, a split series in France and, his major triumph, the Grand Slam tour of 1978.

For a variety of reasons, the All Blacks had never been able to beat every Home Nation in one season. Wales won a disputed match in 1905, Scotland wouldn't play New Zealand in 1924, Wilson Whineray's 1963 team could only draw with Scotland, an outbreak of foot and mouth disease prevented the 1967 side from travelling to Ireland, the 1972 side drew with Ireland.

But in 1978 Gleeson and Mourie guided a team that did not look especially strong on paper to a succession of cliff-hanging victories. It was remarkable how often the major matches were won in the last minutes, a tribute to Gleeson's planning and Mourie's leadership. Mourie really fitted Gleeson's often-expressed summary of the ideal player: someone who could play the game at pace and be a thinker. The respect was mutual – in his autobiography, Mourie, not a man given to over-the-top statements, said he came to revere Gleeson.

That 1978 team was renowned for its superb tackling, a direct result of the tackle bags Gleeson introduced into every training session on tour.

Gleeson sought to move the All Blacks on from their traditional game of relentless forward power, wanting to use every player on the field and to run the ball whenever possible. To that end, he dropped Sid Going, the great halfback, after the second test of the 1977 series, replacing him with Cantabrian Lyn Davis. While Davis was not nearly the player Going was, he was a better passer and Gleeson was seeking to include his backs wherever possible.

In 1977 the All Blacks were out-muscled in the first test against France at Toulouse. The French side, packed with giant forwards, looked too big and strong for New Zealand. So a plan was devised. Short lineouts, scrums, quick taps… always moving, moving. The big French forwards tired and New Zealand scored a 15-3 series-equalling victory at Paris.

The management of the 1978 team – Gleeson, Mourie and Russ Thomas – ushered in a new era of All Blacks, far removed from the unsmiling giants of previous teams. Bryan Williams described it as the most congenial team he toured with. This tied in with Gleeson's philosophy that the team would be a lot happier if the backs were kept involved on the field.

At the start of the 1978 tour, Gleeson told the cynical British media that the All Blacks would play open running rugby. He remained true to that philosophy, but after a shock defeat by Munster, reassessed slightly. He asked the players if they still wanted to run it, and when they affirmed they did, he adjusted his plans so that the All Blacks would run the ball in the opposition territory, but would be more careful about moving the ball in their own half.

Gleeson took some bold decisions during his coaching stint. Besides Going, he dropped Ian Kirkpatrick before the 1977 tour of France, a decision that must be viewed as a mistake, as his replacement, Dick Myers, was clearly not in the same class. And on the Grand Slam tour, he dropped Bryan Williams for the test against Ireland. Though he was quiet and understated, he was anything but soft.

Tragically, the 1978 tour was Gleeson's swansong. He was already suffering from cancer and died the following year. It wasn't a long era, but his impact was extensive. Not only did he introduce players like Mourie, Stu Wilson, Andy Dalton, Andy Haden and David Loveridge to test football, but he gave the All Black coach a more human face. He was an intelligent, witty man who was always good company. He won 47 of his 51 matches as All Black coach, a formidable record and Terry McLean described him as a "master technician".

The All Blacks paid their own special tribute to Gleeson after he died in November 1979. At the time they were on tour in England and were set to take on Midland Counties. There was a moment's silence before the game in Gleeson's memory, then the All Blacks set out to play rugby as Gleeson had wanted it played. The score – 33-7 with five All Black tries – was their way of acknowledging their old coach.

Brian Lochore and the 1987 World Cup

After Gleeson's departure, Eric Watson, Peter Burke and Bryce Rope had short stints at the helm, but the next significant figure was Brian Lochore.

As with most things he has done in life, Lochore made a success of the job, but it was a close-run thing for a while. As an outstanding All Black captain and a successful coach of Wairarapa-Bush, he had the credentials when he took over as coach in 1985. But his timing was most unfortunate.

New Zealand rugby that year was torn asunder by the debacle of the cancelled All Black tour of South Africa. Lochore was left to coach an understandably lacklustre All Black team to Argentina. The following year things got worse: the rebel Cavaliers toured South Africa and those players were declared ineligible for one test and banned from another. Lochore's fellow selector Colin Meads was severely reprimanded for his part in the tour.

The All Black camp was split into those who toured and those who didn't. Not surprisingly, New Zealand then lost a series to Australia and had the worst of a drawn series in France, being hammered 16-3 in Nantes. At this stage Lochore's reign was not looking too promising, particularly with the World Cup just around the corner.

But it all came together for the All Blacks in 1987 and Lochore, with his chairman of the board approach, must be given much of the credit. He had as his fellow selectors the country's two most successful provincial coaches of the 1980s, Alex Wyllie and John Hart, and they formed a strong panel.

The defeat by France became a strong motivating factor, and the catch-cry "Remember Nantes" was repeated often among the All Blacks in the

Legends of the All Blacks

Brian Lochore... did much to provide a winning atmosphere.

months before the World Cup. "Losing at Nantes was the best thing that could have happened to us in terms of the World Cup," says Lochore.

Exciting young players like Michael Jones, John Gallagher and Sean Fitzpatrick cemented their spots, and Grant Fox became a match-winning kicker. Lochore, faced with the tricky decision of choosing between two world-class first five-eighths, Fox and Frano Botica, opted for the more conservative Fox, reversing the decision he'd made in France. Though he loved the way Botica played, Lochore was pragmatic enough to realise Fox's machine-like place-kicking gave him a match-winning edge. Even the loss of skipper Andy Dalton to injury couldn't halt the All Black juggernaut through the 1987 World Cup.

Perhaps Lochore's greatest success was in keeping such different personalities as Hart and Wyllie working in harmony on the panel. He used

The Coaches

Wyllie while the team was in the South Island and Hart when the team was in the North. But though they helped Lochore, they were not designated assistant coaches: Lochore was very much the main man. Lochore did much to provide a winning atmosphere. He had his players stay a night on farms in the Wairarapa to help them relax during the Cup campaign, and when players were in their home city, they were permitted to live at home. It was all aimed at keeping things as low-key as possible and when the results are reviewed, Lochore's tactics must be judged an outstanding success.

As a man without noticeable ego himself, Lochore sought the same in his players and this helped to overcome some lingering ill-feeling from the Cavaliers tour.

Lochore brought admirable qualities to his coaching. He'd played under Allen, so knew the value of a stern word when required. But he was a more moderate character, so blended his own personality. In addition, he had such stature as a famous All Black captain that players followed him unquestioningly.

1987 World Cup skipper David Kirk breaks against Argentina in Wellington. Other All Blacks pictured are, from left, Zinzan Brooke, Bernie McCahill (12), Terry Wright (on ground), Andy Earl (8) and John Drake.

The selectors in that World Cup year devised the tactics they wanted and then chose the players who would fill that role. "We wanted to play an expansive, fast game that would not only win us matches but be attractive," says Lochore. "Our forwards weren't big enough to foot it with the French and Australians, so we devised other tactics. One of the essentials was that our players were superbly fit so they could play the game at pace. We enlisted the help of fitness expert Jim Blair, who had worked so well with Alex and John in Canterbury and Auckland."

Legends of the All Blacks

The Battles of the Last Decade

Wyllie took over from Lochore and had an increasingly undistinguished reign. The great team of 1987 gradually wore down so that by the next World Cup, in 1991, many of the legendary figures in the team were past their best. The result was a disappointing defeat by Australia in the semi-finals.

Though Wyllie was one of the characters of New Zealand rugby, the stress of being All Black coach for four years took its toll. He appeared to suffer personal problems and gradually became afraid to make bold selectorial decisions.

In a last-hour bid to halt the decline, the New Zealand union appointed Hart his co-coach for the 1991 World Cup, but this was not a successful move. The All Blacks had slipped too far, and Wyllie and Hart made uncomfortable partners.

Hart had several tilts at getting the All Black coaching reins, the first when Lochore resigned. He went very close in 1991, but the New Zealand union's council overruled the recommendation of its own sub-committee and opted for Otago coach and former All Black fullback Laurie Mains. Hart in 1987 had not endeared himself to some by refusing to be a selector if he wasn't coach, citing business commitments. He had another crack at the All Black job at the end of 1994, but again Mains, who was struggling in the position, hung on.

Mains, a rather dour character who exuded suspicion, made an inauspicious beginning to his term when he dropped incumbent captain Gary Whetton without telling him, then lost his first test, to a World XV. Over the following few seasons, world-class players like John Kirwan, Grant Fox, Michael Jones and Graeme Bachop were dropped by Mains as he struggled to find a combination that might take out the 1995 World Cup.

After three troubled and controversial years, it came together fantastically in 1995. At virtually the same time, Jonah Lomu, Andrew Mehrtens, Glen Osborne and Josh Kronfeld arrived to give the side much-needed spark. New Zealand looked the best team at the 1995 World Cup, and pulverised England in the semi-final, with Lomu contributing four tries and turning himself into the most famous rugby player in the world.

In the final, New Zealand lost to a fired up South African side in extra time. Some of the New Zealanders were suffering from a food poisoning bug and the side did not display the fire it had earlier. The Springboks, urged on by a home crowd, scored a nailbiting 15-12 victory in extra time and denied Mains a fairytale climax to what had been a mediocre four years in charge.

The Coaches

The Arrival of John Hart

John Hart, so often rejected, finally got his chance in 1996 (though he had coached an All Black selection to Japan at the end of 1987), as much by a process of elimination as from any great insistence that he be coach. His arrival coincided with the introduction of professional rugby and proved to be a case of "cometh the hour cometh the man".

With his background in commerce and man management, Hart had the organisational and media skills to handle what had become a huge job. He also had the benefit of a salary of about $250,000 a year to help him through those sleepless nights.

There weren't too many of those in Hart's first year as the All Blacks steamrolled their way through Tri-Nations and Bledisloe Cup matches without defeat. When the All Blacks beat South Africa 33-26 in Pretoria to win a series in South Africa for the first time, Hart was fit for canonisation. Television commentator Keith Quinn, recalling the great South Africa-New Zealand battles of the previous 75 years, described this as the greatest day in All Black history.

The All Blacks had just one loss in 1996, the last test in South Africa, when the series was already decided. They went one better in 1997, going through unbeaten, with only a draw in the final test against England to spoil a perfect record.

John Hart in his early coaching days with Auckland.

At this point Hart was acclaimed as a master coach and rugby people wondered why he hadn't been given the job years earlier. He had united a rugby country split through the Mains era and was enjoying tremendous success. His public relations was a dream.

By the end of 1997, Hart had never really known a bad time as a coach. He emerged from his five years as Auckland coach (1982-86) with 78 wins in 90 matches, turning around a team that had been playing without pride or success when he took over. Auckland won three national championship titles and began their record Ranfurly Shield era under Hart. In 1983 the All Blacks that toured Scotland and England included not one player from Auckland. By 1986, there were a dozen Aucklanders in the All Blacks. Hart unearthed talented youngsters like John Kirwan and Michael Jones and made the critical – and far-reaching – decision to play Joe Stanley ahead of the brilliant Steven Pokere.

Legends of the All Blacks

By the end of his time with Auckland, he was an accomplished coach. He'd been a feisty, abrasive player, a halfback who represented Taranaki and Auckland. In his early years of club coaching at Waitemata, he says he was something of a shouter and tried to rule more in the Fred Allen mould. But in time he grew to understand the importance of reason and forcing the players to take responsibility for their own actions and those attributes have marked his time with Auckland and the All Blacks. After completing his time with Auckland, he had notable successes with various sides, particularly New Zealand Colts.

With the All Blacks, Hart ushered in a new professional era in which the All Blacks were notably more amenable to the media and the public, and spent a lot less time on tour drinking and mixing with women. The example came from the top.

Hart displayed a mixture of impatience with the old order and shrewd thinking for what would be required to keep the All Blacks at the top of the tree. He fought and won the battle to be able to take 36 players on tour, enabling him to rest his test squad for midweek matches, and had the number of reserves increased to seven so that he could make better use of the new substitution rules. He showed flair in the way he used his major weapons, too. Jonah Lomu played more as a fourth loose forward in the first test against the 1996 Wallabies, and often the two wings, Lomu and Jeff Wilson would swap sides.

He also introduced a whole new language to rugby, expressions culled from the corporate sector, and suddenly we became used to hearing the All Black coach talk about "accuracy of tackling", "upskilling", "growing" a player's confidence and so on.

Who would have believed at the end of 1997 that within nine months there would be a huge national debate about whether he should be sacked? In 1998 the All Blacks beat England twice, then lost five successive tests – unheard of. Hart, so slick and assured, began to look like a man haunted. His selections were criticised, especially when he doggedly stuck with ageing and injury-prone flanker Michael Jones and ignored new blood; he became testy with the media; criticised some of his players publicly; and, worst of all, could not put onto the park a team that could win a test.

Once again the position of All Black coach – the highest profile sports job in the country – had become the centre of controversy.

In the end, the New Zealand Rugby Union, after appearing likely to sack Hart stuck with him for the 1999 World Cup. The controversy quietened, but the doubts about Hart remained. Was he a super-coach, as some had previously claimed, or was he over-rated? Did he rank alongside Fred Allen, Jack Gleeson and Brian Lochore on the top pedestal of All Black coaches, or would he finish his term largely discredited? For Hart, the 1999 World Cup would be all-important.

The Coaches – The Quinn Tapes

Eric Tindill
was one of the first five-eighths in the 1935-36 All Black team to Great Britain.

All we did at practice was just run the ball from the halfback to the wing three-quarter. There was never any tactics, never any scheduling or scheming or planning. We were poorly handled in that area. We had a new captain, Jack Manchester, who had never captained a side before. He probably didn't have any ideas about how we should approach any particular game. Vincent Meredith was the manager and a selector. We really didn't do anything at practice except get used to handling the ball, which is amazing when you think of what they go through today.

Fred Allen
captained the 1949 All Black team to South Africa. New Zealand lost that series 4-0. He was unbeaten as All Black coach from 1966-68.

Charlie Saxton was a wonderful All Black team manager in 1967. He was a great coach, probably a better coach than me. But we had an understanding when we left that Charlie was the manager, I was the coach, and I could always ask Charlie for help if I needed it. We'd been in the Kiwis together and got on like a house on fire. He was a little man who had a very big heart. One time we were in the Midlands and I asked Charlie to have a yarn to Sid Going, who was showing a lot of potential. Sid was fairly young and I knew we'd be looking at him for the test side, so I asked Charlie to give him some extra passing tuition. Charlie was delighted. He had been itching to help out, but he would never interfere. Anyway, he came down and put Sid right in about twenty minutes. He gave him the correct position to have his feet, all that sort of thing. Charlie also altered our lineout before the test match against the French, one of the greatest test matches I've ever seen. Charlie moved our lineout back a bit and it really did fool the French. He was such a very good thinker, was Charlie Saxton.

•

In my playing days, the management and particularly the coaches were too old. They were fine gentlemen, but didn't know very much about coaching. I'd be busy trying to play for my own position and would have to take over the coaching and make the best fist of it I could. In Australia in 1947 we had Norman McKenzie, who was a very shrewd tactician and a great old man, and Harold Strang. In South Africa in 1949 we had Alex McDonald, who'd been an All Black in 1905 and had coached a 1921 side.

Before the team for South Africa was named, I was called over to the centre of Athletic Park, very muddy it was, and asked who should be coach. Naturally I said Vic Cavanagh, because he's been one of the greatest coaches that never coached an All Black side, no doubt about that. They said they couldn't name Cavanagh because he wouldn't get on with the Auckland players, which was nonsense. At that stage there were going to be eleven or twelve Otago players and about eight or nine Aucklanders. Alex McDonald was going to go as manager, but then Jim Parker decided he wanted to go, so he went as manager and Alex as coach. Vic Cavanagh, a great character who knew rugby like the back of his hand, was left behind.

Alex was 66 years of age on that trip and was sick for a lot of the time. The high altitude and the heat made it difficult for him. Things were different to what he knew. The grounds were rock hard, there were lots of injuries. The travel was enormous – at one stage we spent 10 days out of 13 on a train, playing two games in between. We had the odd hard case who took old Alex on a bit, but generally his health wasn't up to it. He was interested in coming home and in the days of flying, he might have. But he struggled on. You could actually seeing him going downhill. Having said all that, I was very fond of Alex McDonald and Jim Parker. It's just that they weren't the right people for the job in South Africa.

Legends of the All Blacks

The Needle

Brian Lochore
was captain of the New Zealand team that Fred Allen coached, and later became a successful All Black coach himself.

One of the greatest things Fred Allen ever said to me was that whatever I did on the paddock, he would support. He meant in front of the team he would totally support whatever I did on the paddock. We discussed tactics and practised them before a game and we had alternatives when I wanted to change the way we were playing. I knew I had his confidence and for a captain that is amazingly powerful. It was something I used a lot in my coaching career.

Sid Going
made his test debut in 1967, when Fred Allen was the All Black coach.

The 1967 All Blacks had tremendous forward power. Our forwards were the dominating force in world rugby. They were big men for the time and within the rules of the time, got things sorted out pretty early in games. Fred Allen, our coach, wanted to play 15-man rugby, with backs and forwards all a part of the game. That was tremendous for me. Fred was very hard on centres at training. As soon as they passed the ball, they had to get around and support. Fred stressed that all the time, backing up, backing up.

Colin Meads
was a senior player throughout Fred Allen's tenure as All Black coach.

It was the Wednesday before the fourth test against the Lions in 1966. The team meeting was at ten o'clock, before training. I was sitting at the back of the lounge. I suppose, to be truthful, I wasn't paying enough attention and I yawned. Fred [Allen] nearly jumped across the table and the whole team were aghast… Colin Meads getting told off like this. He told me I could catch the next bus home if I wasn't interested and this sort of thing. He laid it on. You know, "Are you interested?" I had to say, "Yes, Fred, I'm interested." I thought, "You just wait until we get to training." Fred was always the boss and we were scared of him.

He was a great coach. He picked everyone's brains. After the second game in Britain in 1967, he went around talking to everyone that evening. He just felt something was wrong. I told him the trouble was that we'd come from harder grounds in New Zealand and the boys were all wearing little sprigs. They couldn't get a footing. He asked me what sprigs I had and I said I had both. I had two pairs of boots, one with long and one with short sprigs. So it comes to the next team talk and Fred turns it right around. He says, "There's one bugger in this team who's been here before and knows all about this sprig problem, but hasn't told anyone." I had actually, but Fred went around the whole team and asked them what sort of sprigs they had, then blamed me. That's the sort of coach he was; he put the pressure on. The Sam Strahans and the rest of them thought old Colin Meads getting told off by Fred Allen was pretty good. I'd told Sam to put on big sprigs, but it was all turned around on me. Fred coached with a bit of fear. He was cruel and hard, but fair.

I can recall him saying to the wingers who were throwing into the lineouts, "Another crooked one and you won't be playing on Saturday." And he duly didn't pick one of them. He told him to shoot off and come back when he could throw properly, only I don't think he used the word "shoot". Fred was a perfectionist.

The only bloke who beat Fred was Alister Hopkinson. We were running round a park in Suva one day – Fred was a great one for laps. They had huge goal-posts there and Hoppy hid behind a post. As we came round again, Hoppy joined in. Fred never knew. If he had, Hoppy wouldn't have played the next game.

Laurie [Mains] used to like to have secret training sessions and I'd be his manager, running round the park, chasing people away. But Fred was the opposite.

The Coaches – The Quinn Tapes

He loved the crowds, especially in France, where thousands of people would come to watch you train. Jazz Muller didn't like it because the bigger the crowd, the harder we trained. Jazz would take one look at the crowd and shudder.

When Ivan Vodanovich took over from Fred, Ivan was a hard task-master at training. Jazz used to say that as long as he could get through training, he'd be okay in the game. Jazz never said too much, but he was one of the characters of New Zealand rugby.

Fergie McCormick
was chosen by Fred Allen as the All Black fullback for the 1967 tour of Great Britain.

Fred Allen, even at his age now, would handle the professional scene. These days they have these people who analyse people's minds, but Fred was doing that in the 1960s. Fred would have you at training for a couple of days and he'd have worked out your personality – whether you were sulky or outgoing or needed a boot in the backside or a pat on the head. Without wanting to criticise today's coaches, I think some of them need to go back to the way Fred did things. They should learn to read their side themselves without outside help.

Fred Allen
became All Black coach in 1966, after a hugely successful term as Auckland coach. He coached New Zealand in 37 matches and lost none.

The big word in my coaching dictionary was discipline. I'd been in the war for five and a half years, and been ▶

Ian Kirkpatrick
was an All Black from 1967-77. His first All Black coach was Fred Allen.

What an introduction, Fred Allen as coach and Charlie Saxton as manager. They both had that army discipline background. You were late once and you were never late again. Also, on the training paddock, if you thought you were training okay, Fred probably had other ideas and let you know. But he was brilliant. His main attribute was that he had the knack of getting good players to play well all the time. He didn't get too strategic or complicated.

Fred was also very emotional and gave some inspiring team talks. He didn't barrel all the players. He'd lift some and push down others, if he thought they were a bit too cocky. He had skills that no other coach I encountered had.

Ian Kirkpatrick... 'Fred was brilliant.'

Legends of the All Blacks

The Needle

wounded a couple of times. You learn a lot in those sort of situations and it sticks with you forever. To me discipline is so important. It teaches you respect. One of the most important things in coaching is the team work and team spirit. The rest comes into skills which you can teach the players if you know anything about it. But you build your side around discipline and that can lift players, make them believe in themselves. Nowadays they have psychologists and head-shrinkers and doctors. We didn't have them. But we did the same job. A lot of it is common-sense. You stick to the basics of position, possession and pace – there's no difference in that since the days when Vic Cavanagh and Charlie Saxton were coaching.

•

I coached by repetition. They hated it, especially some of the old hands. I'd make them walk the field and pass the ball, keep them moving onto the ball. We'd get the backline in staircase formation, not too deep, but just deep enough. Then we'd do it quicker and quicker until we could do the moves at speed. They knew exactly what was happening. If we had four or five moves, we'd go over them, not two or three times, but ten or eleven. The players would be bleating within themselves, but that's when self-discipline comes into it. By the end, the moves became instinctive and automatic and they didn't drop the ball. You only need four or five good moves. There are too many these days. The moves you do use have to be perfect. That's where the repetition at practice comes in.

•

Sometimes I'd wake up in the night and think about the team talk I was going to give the next day. I'd go through the players individually. You had to be able to lift them, make them believe. You don't read notes, you do it off the cuff. The players won't get bored if it's common-sense and factual.

But I'd tell all sorts of stories to lift the players. One time when I was coaching Auckland, the Ranfurly Shield wasn't in the room. We used to have our team talk in the commercial room in the old Station Hotel.

Even Colin Meads wasn't immune from a Fred Allen tongue-lashing.

We always used to have the Shield there for our final team talk. Barry Thomas asked me where it was and I said I'd lent it to Canterbury because they wanted a photograph of it with their team so they could have it ready for the Christchurch players first thing next morning. After that you didn't really need a team talk. The players were steaming to get out there.

You used any trick you could to grab their attention. Colin Meads, Pinetree, was one of the greatest forwards I ever saw. I had two young fellows in one of my All Black teams and I was looking for a way of getting to them without them being too upset or excited. We're having our team talk in the Clarendon Hotel and everyone's around, very attentive. Then old Pinetree lifts his head and yawns. I said, "Am I boring you, Meads?" Poor old Pinetree jumped up. "No, no," he said. Well, if you'd seen these young kids – that was just the lift they needed. They thought, "God, if Meads is copping it, what will I get?"

•

By 1968, when I took the team to Australia, I felt there was a little bit of jealousy creeping in. I probably wasn't an easy person to get on with. I'm sure it never went to

The Coaches – The Quinn Tapes

Ivan Vodanovich (left) succeeded Fred Allen as All Black coach.

my head, but there were some little incidents. I was tuning up Kirton and Thorne. We were beating New South Wales, giving them a decent hiding. Then they decided to kick the ball, and that was the start of it.

Then I let one of the reporters, Alex Veysey, into a team talk. I'd let Ronnie Dawson in in 1967. There was nothing said about that. They were going to Africa and asked Charlie if Ronnie Dawson could sit in and I said it was fine with me. There was nothing to hide. If you do your skills correctly, better than the next bloke, you'll be okay. So if you're winding up individuals, it's just to get them ready for the game. You must win. I didn't see anything wrong in allowing Alex Veysey in, but it didn't go down well with the Rugby Union.

There were a few whispers behind the scenes. I sensed they were not going to let me take the team to Africa in 1970. I'd love to have gone, but there was too much pin-pricking. The Rugby Union were waiting for me to lose a game. I'd gone 30-odd games and never had a loss and they probably felt they couldn't get rid of me if I didn't lose a game. Maybe they thought I was a bit arrogant. I didn't think I was. There might have been a bit of jealousy. The side was going like a machine by 1969 against the Welsh. They murdered them. I went over there to South Africa in 1970 and they were going well there, too. How they lost those tests, I don't know.

Legends of the All Blacks

JJ Stewart
All Black coach 1974-76.

I never felt that coaching at any level was a matter of motivation. I'm not a great believer in that because, quite frankly, I can't swallow my own bullshit and I don't like submitting players to the high-powered yelling and screaming stuff. But you do have to look at the player and see if he's got any problems that you can help diagnose. For instance, if a player is not tackling very well, you don't help him by telling him he's a bad tackler and is costing his team points. You have to explain what he is doing wrong – he is trying to grab the guy too far out, or he is not getting his hands or his arms working, or his shoulder into the guy, or he's not looking, or whatever. Very often it just requires a quiet talk over a beer.

Coach JJ Stewart with fullback Laurie Mains, South Africa, 1976.

Andy Leslie
was captain of the All Blacks from 1974-76. JJ Stewart was the All Black coach during that period.

JJ Stewart brought a lot of fun to training. We'd do the hide-the-ball-up-the-jersey trick in training, though we never did it in a game. And we'd have moves where we threw backs over a scrum to score tries. Or we'd have a situation where the backline would stand facing the wrong way and run the wrong way. The Australian coaches came to watch us one day and couldn't believe what they were seeing. JJ was miles ahead of his time. He was an absolutely superb coach in the sense of getting the best out of people. He wouldn't hinder players by trying to impose his style, but would develop what skills they had.

Ron Palenski
New Zealand journalist.

The foundations for the relationship between coach Jack Gleeson and captain Graham Mourie were laid in Argentina in 1976 when they took away what was really a third-string All Black team. What developed in Britain in 1978 began in Argentina and continued in France in 1977. It was the bringing together of like minds to play rugby in a way they wanted, regardless of the strengths of the opposition. They wanted to play a fast, entertaining game and wanted the players to think. They wanted to play for eighty minutes, not get ten points up then stop playing.

Graham Mourie
captained the All Blacks virtually throughout the Jack Gleeson era.

KQ: Wasn't the second test against France at Paris in 1977 a triumph of planning, after the hammering the All Blacks received in the first test at Toulouse just a week earlier?

Well, before that test Jack Gleeson and I did our analysis and felt that to beat them we had to use our

The Coaches – The Quinn Tapes

mobility. We made a conscious effort not to try to match them up front, but to concentrate on playing the game very, very quickly. It worked for us. We played to our strengths and away from theirs and ended up with a pretty total victory.

Bruce Robertson
played under Jack Gleeson in the All Blacks in 1972 and in 1977-78.

Jack Gleeson was a coach who was able to use all the players' strengths. It wasn't a case of Jack telling everyone to do it his way. He utilised the guys and said, "What do you thing of this? How do you think we should approach this?" He used the players' ideas, but he'd come up with the final, "Yes this is the way we'll do it." With Jack, though, the players felt they'd contributed and because of that they were more likely to get in behind the whole flow of the game.

David Kirk
made his All Black test debut in 1985.

My first test was against England at Lancaster Park and it was such a let-down. I'd waited two years to play a test and it was a shocker, one of those awful mistake-ridden games. They scored two tries and we kicked six penalties and we won. So Brian Lochore, our coach, basically put the whole team on very explicit notice. "Another one of those and there'll be significant changes." So we went to Athletic Park and played really well on a very windy day. We played tight driving football in the first half into the wind, then opened it up in the second half and won 42-15.

Wayne Shelford
made his All Black debut in 1985.

Brian Lochore was the type of coach I loved. He didn't say much, but when he said things, they were true and correct and you could get on with the job.

Brian Lochore drinks from the Webb Ellis Trophy after New Zealand's World Cup triumph in 1987.

Legends of the All Blacks

HART v WYLLIE

John Hart
became an All Black selector in 1987, and after several attempts, was finally named All Black coach in 1995.

I was disappointed but realistic when I didn't get the coach's job for 1988. I'd taken the All Blacks to Japan in 1987, with Alex as the assistant. But I had huge respect for Alex as a coach. We'd come through the same period – me with Auckland, Alex with Canterbury – and had some great battles. It didn't surprise me he got the job. For one thing, he'd been an All Black and I hadn't.

John Hart

I was more shattered missing out in 1992. By then my record with the New Zealand Colts was without blemish and I'd coached the New Zealand XV. I thought I'd done what I'd been asked to do at the 1991 World Cup. So I was devastated when Laurie Mains was awarded the job because his record wasn't comparable with mine at that stage. That contrasted to the situation in 1987, when Alex and I had comparable records.

Alex Wyllie
coached New Zealand from 1988-91. In 1987 he and John Hart were coach Brian Lochore's fellow All Black selectors and vied for the coach's job when it became vacant.

John Hart wanted to be No 1 and as I said it was a surprise to me when I got the job. I would have been quite happy to wait if he wanted it that badly.

KQ: How do you think history will judge Alex Wyllie as an All Black coach?

I suppose the pity of it is that that period will go down as a bit of a front-on between two coaches. I just hope history notes that I tried to do my best for the game because that's all I ever tried to do.

KQ: During the 1991 World Cup, there were charges that under the stresses of being All Black coach, you had late nights and that maybe your own concentration wavered. Were such accusations true?

Well, that might go back to the French tour in 1990. I was told some time afterwards that I hadn't been able to make a training run. Absolutely ridiculous! That was the sort of talk going on behind my back, stories that were totally untrue. If you talk about late nights, I think you'd be talking of just a couple of players who were in the same position. I was in the same position in South Africa once when I was a player [in 1970], having a late night. I came out the next morning and the two players who were meant to be on standby couldn't play. One had a bad knee and the other was sick. I'd had the night out because I wasn't even going to be on the bench.

I'm one hundred per cent confident that I didn't have any late nights or do any drinking during the World Cup that detracted in any way from the players. Perhaps there might have been times when I went out, but those occasions never took away anything I was doing with the team.

Wayne Shelford

Alex Wyllie was limited as a coach. He didn't talk to the players a lot, but I got on really well with him.

KQ: There have been suggestions that Alex Wyllie drank too much and that it affected his ability to coach the All Blacks. How did you gauge the situation?

Sure, Alex drinks a lot, just like we all do, and he'd get

The Coaches – The Quinn Tapes

pretty full at times. But that was Alex and I accepted him for that.

It wasn't up to me to monitor his drinking. That was for the hierarchy of the New Zealand union. If anything, the weakness was in the New Zealand union not spotting it. A lot of people in high-risk jobs, under a lot of stress and strain, drink after work. That's their outlet. That was Grizz. In my time, I never saw him come to training drunk. Ever. You're talking about a person who probably smells of grog after a night. Fair enough. It doesn't mean to say he's been drinking that morning.

Gary Whetton
captained the All Blacks from 1990-91.

Grizz was a fantastic coach in his early days. He had a great era with Canterbury and then we had a great run with the All Blacks in 1988-89, some happy years. In 1990 the wheels started to fall off.

In France in 1990, I took it on myself, really, to prepare the team in lots of ways. Grizz was under pressure. We'd have lots of discussions about what the team should be. I never selected a team, didn't want to. But he'd always ask me my thoughts. Well, we got to the training ground [before the first test] and the press were waiting for the test team. He couldn't make up his mind between Mike Brewer and Zinzan Brooke at No 8. He said, "What do you think, Gary?" and I said, "Grizz, it has to be your call. One plays this way and one plays that. I'm not sure. That's your job, mate."

Alex Wyllie

So he gave the team to John Sturgeon [the manager] and he had bracketed Brewer and Brooke. He hadn't made up his mind. Then he said, "Right, forwards, to the scrum machine. Let's get that pack down." The forwards and reserves went over and he said, "Right, test team, in you go."

So we all went in except the two No 8s. They stood there together, not knowing who had priority. Then Mike Brewer, who's always been a bit quicker, looked round, realised what was going on and put his head in for the first scrum. He was announcing that he was the No 8. After a while he went up to Grizz and said, "Grizz, my ankle is sore. I'll sit out the next two training runs, and I'll be right for the test." And he sat down again. So Zinzan did the training runs for the whole week and Mike Brewer started the game, played till half-time or just after, then came off. An interesting story.

Wayne Shelford

Having Alex Wyllie and John Hart as co-coaches at the 1991 World Cup was never going to work. Never. The New Zealand union at that time was pretty vulnerable. It was being hounded by the Auckland consortium and the South Island consortium and in the end it compromised. It was not big enough to say, "You're the man. Now go and do it." Instead they put two people in charge and they both got ripped off; they both got stood down, and Laurie [Mains] was outside laughing all the way to the bank. What the union did was get rid of two very good coaches."

Legends of the All Blacks

Mains in Charge

Laurie Mains
of Otago took over from Alex Wyllie as the All Black coach in 1992

I often say to my teams there's only room for one prick in a rugby team. The players have to totally support each other and never be critical of each other. I'm the only one who'll fire the shots.

One time we were at a training camp in Taupo. Now Craig Dowd had broken his leg the end of the previous season and we were finishing what had been an absolutely gruelling day. Ross Cooper referred to it as being barbaric. I was giving the guys their 150s at the end and Craig Dowd was in so much pain that I was starting to hurt. I said to him, "Dowdy, pull out if it's hurting." He wouldn't. He just refused. He went on and on and in the end I had to order him off. I just couldn't put up with the pain any more!

But then Robin Brooke developed a problem with one of his boots and he pulled out and missed two of the 150s. At the end they did twenty-five 150s. These were as physically demanding as I've ever seen a team go through and Robin had missed two. I said, "Righto, Robin, you've got two to catch up." And Fitzy says, "I'm going with him." Then the rest of the forwards said, "We're all going." And then Frank Bunce says, "Well, if the forwards are going, I'm going too." Three players objected and I saw it in the body language. They were not terribly happy about the whole situation. So anyhow, they went ahead and did it and supported Robin.

It's ironic – there's a message there. We talk about the last ten or twenty minutes of a really tough test when they really have to pull out all the stops. You know the guys who will come through and these sort of things tell you the ones who won't. In the end those three players never made the World Cup. The selection was done on performance, of course, but those things come into it. You have to look at the players' attitude as well as performance.

Grant Fox
played test rugby from 1984-93 under five All Black coaches.

I was disappointed to get dropped in 1992, because I desperately wanted to play for the All Blacks. But being stood down was a good thing. I also helped myself by talking to the three selectors before the trial in Napier. I wanted to know what they wanted out of their first five-eighth. Then, hopefully, I could go away and work on delivering what they were looking for. Laurie Mains kept me informed all the way through. He told me when they weren't going to pick me, so it wasn't an outright shock when the team was read out. There were four tests in a row I didn't play. I recall when we went to Athletic Park to play Ireland in the second test before the tour of Australia, I was in the reserves and went to tell Laurie that I wasn't available to tour Australia. I didn't think that going on a tour to Australia if I wasn't the No 1 first five-eighth was the right thing for the team. If the selectors thought Walter Little was such a fine player, that was their choice, but I thought they should take a younger player away to blood on a tour of Australia where you get the odd easier up-country fixture. I couldn't see the point in taking me in my late 20s if I was going to sit on the bench.

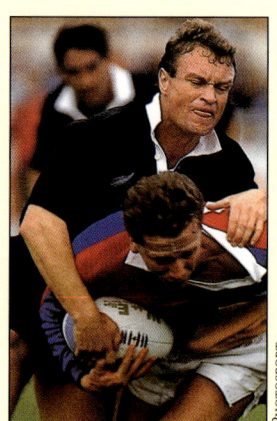

Grant Fox

So on the Friday afternoon I knocked on Laurie's door and asked him for a word. I asked him what his plans were for me and he essentially said that I would be playing in the first test against Australia at Sydney. That was certainly the inference I got, provided I was able to keep improving. So I went away dumbfounded

The Coaches – The Quinn Tapes

because I hadn't expected that at all. I told my wife Adele what Laurie had said. She asked me if I could trust him and I felt I could. The rest is history. So really he was very good to me during that period, despite the fact that some people might have thought it was a difficult time for me. It was, but he really helped me and had a master plan in place.

Earle Kirton
a former All Black first five-eighth, was a New Zealand selector for much of the time that Laurie Mains coached the All Blacks.

He's an astute coach. I would say that he was the best forward coach in the world. But why do I say only forwards because he's got a wonderful appreciation of backs, too? He is an outstanding all-round coach. If you're talking about the world stage, I can't think of anyone better. Some would be better man-managers and some coaches would have dealt slightly better with the media than Lawrence did from time to time, but that was the intensity of the man. The players enjoyed him. They liked him and wanted him. They knew he was giving them the bully and the oil, and you can't say more than that. In terms of management and organisation, then John Hart for sure, but in terms of technical ability, hands-on coaching, well, Laurie really had it.

Grant Fox
had been an All Black for eight years before Laurie Mains became New Zealand coach in 1992.

Within the team there was supreme confidence in Laurie Mains. I don't think his PR skills were particularly good and he was always suspicious of the

Part of the All Black think tank – coach Laurie Mains (left) and selector Earle Kirton.

media. But technically he knew a lot about the game and for a guy who played in the No 15 jersey, he knew a lot about forward play. He engendered a great deal of loyalty out of his players, at times creating a them and us feeling – here's our All Black camp and everyone else was the enemy.

Laurie Mains

I believed that at the end of my time I had met the responsibilities of an All Black coach. I had left All ▶

Legends of the All Blacks

Mains in Charge

Black rugby in a much stronger state than I picked it up, and I'd left my successor with a team that meant he could have gone through for at least a year or two with his eyes closed and they would still perform well. Not only were they the right players, but they had been prepared the right way and they had the right game plan. I believe anybody could have coached that team after 1995 for at least a year.

The tragedy for both Alex Wyllie and myself was that there was this great division in New Zealand about who should coach the All Blacks. Both of us had the public perception of our coaching tainted by that division. As time went on, I had a tremendous amount of supporters who could see where I was heading with the All Blacks and were very supportive. Since my retirement, I believe the public and the media have become more and more aware of just what I did achieve with the All Blacks and how good they were when I finished. The understanding of Laurie Mains as a coach has increased with time. The New Zealand public now has a much better understanding of the quality of the work I did with the All Blacks.

It is significant that with both Alex Wyllie and myself, the same person was in the background. There was a section of the media which unfortunately is very influential in New Zealand… head offices and all those sort of things are in Auckland. It's the population base. Therefore Aucklanders were supporting John Hart. Both Alex and I had difficult times because of that division. It's a sad thing for New Zealand when that sort of division is allowed to develop.

John Hart had been out of rugby for a long time and the game had changed an awful lot. I know, as one leading player said to me, the All Blacks basically did it themselves in 1996, in terms of the way they played, their pattern and the little things. For an All Black coach to get it as easy as he did in 1996 when the All Blacks were clearly the best team in the world, in playing style, cohesion and personnel…

During 1997, the pattern started to break down. All Black rugby didn't move forward as it needed to. If you are going to retain your edge, you need to move forward in your tactics and many of the techniques that you use. Some of the leading players, like Zinzan Brooke, Frank Bunce and Sean Fitzpatrick, who called the shots and had played a big part in keeping the pattern together, retired. In the absence of leadership from the top, it all started to fall apart and during the 1998 season we saw the consequences of resting on your laurels.

Sean Fitzpatrick
was the All Black captain in 1992 and gradually built up a rapport with Laurie Mains.

Laurie and I took a while to gain a mutual respect for each other. He had his doubts early on, but by the end we felt very comfortable working together. In terms of his coaching Otago, no-one rated Laurie that highly and it took a while to have belief in him. In Laurie's early years, he was a dictator. He didn't want to involve the whole team. There was his way or we didn't do it.

Laurie developed as a coach and probably didn't reach his potential until the end of 1994, going into 1995. But he was under extreme pressure like no other coach before, similar to what John Hart went through in 1998, except Laurie had it for four years. I think that reflected some of the moods that Laurie brought into the team. He had a problem with the media, and that was a problem in terms of the way our team was perceived. He became very insular and was worried about the media the whole time. He trusted no-one and that had a follow-on effect to the team.

He was the best forward coach I've ever had. He had a real passion for the game and for the All Blacks. He did a huge amount of work. The way he prepared for the 1995 World Cup was the best I've ever seen any coach prepare.

The Coaches – The Quinn Tapes

HART GETS HIS CHANCE

Sean Fitzpatrick

In the two years I was there, John Hart had a dream run. There was a huge turnaround with the media. John had the people he wanted and did a fantastic job. He pushed all the right buttons for me.

One of John's great attributes was that he had been out of the game for so long, he was as keen for as much information to be fed in from the players as possible. The players loved that.

John Hart
All Black coach 1996-99.

KQ: How hurtful is it when people say that all you've done is carry on with the team Laurie Mains built?

I hear that comment, probably more from Laurie Mains than anyone else. I know what I did with that side, how the attitudes changed when I became coach. Zinzan Brooke himself said at the end of 1996 we'd won games we wouldn't have won the year before. We weren't looking for wholesale change, but we needed to step up, continue to fine-tune our game and increase the mental toughness of players. Our whole management team in 1996 was a breath of fresh air. We created among the team an attitude that allowed them to go out and express themselves.

Wayne Shelford

John Hart is a very good coach. He manipulates a lot, but he's been very good for New Zealand over the last three years. However, he's probably had an easier road than any other coach. He has all the financial backing, he's had the people around him he wanted and he's been able to have more players on his tours. ▶

Sean Fitzpatrick

Hart Gets his Chance

John Hart

There's no one reason why we had the disastrous year in 1998. We lost a lot of good players at once – Zinzan, Sean, Michael Jones, Frank Bunce. That was a big hole in terms of leadership and experience. We struggled with injuries, we didn't kick as accurately as we had. We [selectors] made some mistakes, brought back players too soon from injury and so on. It was a hugely difficult time. My family was under pressure, talkback was going berserk and some hurtful things were said. It does dent your confidence. I did a lot of soul-searching and I think I'm better for the experience.

Andy Haden
was an All Black lock from 1972-85.

KQ: Can you sum up the coaching ability of Alex Wyllie, John Hart and Laurie Mains?

Alex Wyllie was a capable coach and he [his Canterbury teams] certainly put us [Auckland] to the sword until John Hart got us organised. His ability to get a hard-nosed attitude into his team was legendary. He wasn't as good a planner as Hart, or as good a tactician, but when you played Wyllie's teams, you knew you were in for a hard battle. He let himself down towards the end of his coaching career. You have to have standards for yourself that are higher than those you set for your team. Alex Wyllie's standards were not as high as an All Black coach's needed to be.

As a player, Mains was modest, one of the models I tried to avoid. He was a better coach than a player, but I didn't put him on the same level as Hart, who had greater ability. I watched Mains' Otago teams through ten years and they never looked very good to me, certainly didn't win the games that counted. They beat a very second-rate Auckland side to win the competition one year, but one in ten didn't stack up in my book.

John Hart is a stickler for detail, plans well. He let his guard down in 1998 and missed a few beats, but overall his coaching is always in the top drawer. He turned Auckland around in the 1980s and the great era he began has only just closed. I wasn't a John Hart supporter at the start of his coaching career, but he really won me over.

Alan Jones
Wallaby coach from 1984-87.

KQ: As we go into the 1999 international season, how do you rate John Hart's tenure as the All Black coach?

I've been very disappointed with John Hart. When he became coach, I thought it was a good thing. He presents well. But sometimes you give people authority and they go too far.

Alan Jones

Australia

Bledisloe Battles

By Lindsay Knight

Great sporting occasions and events frequently have a defining moment into which are encapsulated all of the elements and fibres which help drive their participants. Dick Tayler's win at the 1974 Christchurch Commonwealth Games is one obvious example. So too is Brian McKechnie's flinging of his bat soon after he had received the infamous underarm delivery from Trevor Chappell at the Melbourne Cricket Ground in 1981.

In All Black-Wallaby rugby one episode exceeds all others in suddenly illustrating, perhaps to New Zealanders most of all, the significance of the Bledisloe Cup. This came at the Sydney Cricket Ground in 1979 when, at the end of the one-off test played between the Wallabies and the All Blacks that year, the Australian players embraced the cup as if it were a communion chalice and, holding it aloft, did a victory circuit of the ground. The All Blacks and other New Zealanders either at the ground or watching on TV, looked on in amazement and some disdain. Surely the Australians' celebration was unduly arrogant and typically Australian in its lack of modesty. But it was somewhat deeper than that and when New Zealanders, if only in latter years, began to reflect on that victory they, too, were able to appreciate some of the reasons. Really the Australian glee was no more than a tribute to the mystique of All Black rugby, and the Wallabies' celebration in vanquishing such a redoubtable opponent was understandable.

Reverse the roles and the sports and remember how much national euphoria there was in New Zealand when at long last this country achieved its first cricket test over Australia in 1974. At the time they gained their 1979 win, Australians in rugby had endured just as much humiliation from defeat after defeat at the hands of the seemingly invincible men in black.

That victory lap made many New Zealanders aware of the fact there was even a trophy called the Bledisloe Cup. Until then, on this side of the Tasman, it had an extremely low profile. For some years after the Second World War it lay ignored, gathering dust in a Melbourne store room. Apart from 1934 and 1949, the cup had been New Zealand's almost permanently since its presentation in 1931 by New Zealand's Governor-General, Lord Bledisloe. New Zealanders would find it hard to give validity to the 1949 two-match series in this country, for at the same time virtually all of the country's best players were involved in another series in South Africa.

Legends of the All Blacks

So until the late 1970s, New Zealand rugby supremacy over Australia was pretty well taken for granted, the relationship being akin to New Zealand's inferiority to Australia in cricket.

That win at the SCG in 1979 was the Wallabies' first over the All Blacks on their home soil since 1934. The best the Wallabies had achieved after that in home series (in 1938, 1947, 1951, 1957, 1962, 1968 and 1974) had been a 16-16 draw at Brisbane in 1974. The only losses the All Blacks had sustained on those seven tours had been to New South Wales in 1947 and 1962. Occasionally the Wallabies won matches in series in New Zealand: in 1952, 1955, 1958 and 1964. But these were so infrequent as to be almost meaningless.

It was little wonder that while the Wallabies rankled over their constant failures, New Zealanders were inclined to be blasé about any threat from Australian sides. The 1979 match, however, was one of the early signs that that dominance was about to end and the All Blacks were to have a new arch-rival almost comparable to the mighty Springboks.

If the 1979 one-off test in Sydney and the Wallabies' victory lap have a certain symbolism in Bledisloe Cup rivalry, a Wallabies' tour which in all respects was a fiasco represents another significant turning point. This was the tour made by Australia to New Zealand in 1972. On this tour Australian rugby reached an absolute nadir. The Wallabies were thrashed in all three tests, won only five of their 13 tour matches and among the losses to provincial teams was one to a modest Buller-West Coast combination. New Zealand journalists accompanying the team appeared to be in some sort of competition in alliteration to think of the most insulting name to brand them. The "Woeful Wallabies" had some popularity, but the most enduring became the "Awful Aussies", which was coined by *Rugby News* editor Bob Howitt.

It wasn't as if All Black rugby was all that wonderful at that stage, either. Just a few months later the All Blacks went on the least distinguished overseas tour in New Zealand rugby history. Amazingly enough, the 1972-73 side which toured Britain and France almost achieved a Grand Slam of wins against the British countries and Ireland, missing out on that distinction only when Ireland wing Tom Grace scored a late try to force a 10-10 draw. But there were losses to the Barbarians in a virtual test, to France and in a number of other games. The tour is remembered for the ignominious fact that giant prop Keith Murdoch was expelled from the party in disgrace after the Wales international.

That was the most glaring symptom of some of the ill-discipline and poor planning which accompanied All Black rugby at that time. A correspondent on that tour, champion decathlete Roy Williams, was incredulous once when his question as to why there was no ice at training in case of injury was scoffed at by the team management. "Are we supposed to have ice here to put in their drinks?"

New Zealand rugby, the big wins of 1972 over the "Awful Aussies"

Australia

The turning point – Peter Carson (left) and Stan Pilecki celebrate the Wallabies' 1979 victory over the All Blacks in Sydney.

notwithstanding, was extremely amateurish in those years. Before the second test Wellington first five-eighth John Dougan pulled out after the All Blacks' Thursday training session with an injured knee. Otago's Lyn Jaffray was summoned from Dunedin for his first cap. All he had for his preparation was one training run on the Friday, barely 24 hours before the match. Moreover, he was teamed in the inside backs with Northlander Sid Going, a notoriously difficult halfback for any first-five to play outside. For Jaffray it was especially so, for in the two backline positions, more interlocked than others, he was playing with a man with whom he had never played previously or even met. Yet against an All Black team utterly lacking in organisation, the Wallabies received three consecutive hidings.

So dismal were the Wallabies there was even a call for them to be taken off the All Blacks' playing schedule. This came in a front page story in *Rugby News* on the eve of the third test at Eden Park on September 16 and was penned under the byline of Phil Allan, who was none other than the distinguished TP (later Sir Terry) McLean who moonlighted under that name out of deference to his primary employer, the *New Zealand Herald*. Wrote an impassioned TP: "If nothing else, the harrowing tour by the Australian Wallabies has demonstrated that the New Zealand Rugby Union must rethink its international programme… The latest edition of Australian rugby has been so dismally incompetent that it wouldn't be safe for the Enzed council to look upon their old partner as the safest and best of backstops." McLean compared the Wallabies unfavourably with a California Grizzlies team which had toured a few weeks earlier in 1972 and urged the New Zealand union to replace Wallaby tours with the likes of Argentina and Japan.

Sometimes a disaster is needed before much-needed remedies are applied. Wretched as were the results and much of the rugby played by the Wallabies during 1972, the "Awful Aussies" tour has become an important event in reviving the trans-Tasman rugby bond. The manager and coach of the poorly-performed Wallabies were Joe French and Bob Templeton respectively. Both were shattered by the events of that tour, but to their credit they learned from their mistakes and took a full part in the exhaustive post mortem which was conducted to the highest levels of Australian rugby over the next year. Significantly, too, both men were Queenslanders and it was to be that state which was to take a leading role in the revival of Australian rugby from the mid-1970s.

At the start of the 1972 tour in Dunedin, French had been scathing in his criticism of the irregular contacts between the All Blacks and the Wallabies. The two countries, despite being such close neighbours, had last played each other in 1968 when the All Blacks had toured Australia. And before 1968, the only match since the Wallabies' 1964 tour had been the one-off New Zealand union Jubilee test at Athletic Park in 1967. It all seems somewhat bizarre when compared to the modern era when from 1982-98 not a season passed without at least one Bledisloe Cup test and in those 17 seasons there were 37 tests.

After the 1972 fiasco the Australians realised that if they were to compete on even terms with New Zealand rugby, they needed to increase contacts and not rely solely on a couple of matches a year between Queensland and New South Wales. And the contacts had to be not just at international level, but among provinces. Accordingly, New South Wales and especially Queensland from the mid-1970s began a regular interchange of matches with the top New Zealand provincial sides.

The transformation in Queensland was especially dramatic. For many years, even into the '70s, they had been very much New South Wales' junior partner, generally having no more than two or three places in a Wallaby test side. Their games against touring teams were often midweek and invariably ended in heavy defeats. But by the end of the decade Queensland sides were regularly thrashing NSW (a momentous 42-6 win in 1976) and in 1980 they beat the All Blacks. From then on they provided a stack of players for Wallaby test sides.

A Queenslander from this period who went on to become a Wallaby was Chris Handy, the celebrated "Buddha" who is now a popular television comments man. He says: "What really changed the quality of Australian rugby was playing often against the All Blacks at international level and against the best of their provincial sides. Being matched against these great teams provided us with the opportunity to learn and subsequently to develop the things we discovered from them to a level where we were able to match and ultimately to conquer them."

The disparity which existed between New Zealand and Australian rugby until the late 1970s – that day at the SCG when the celebrating Wallabies drew attention to a trophy in danger of being forgotten – goes back to the origins of the game in each country.

From pioneering days rugby thrived in New Zealand virtually without opposition. It was always the game for all classes, working people, the more affluent, those in towns and those in the country. In Australia, because of

Australia

Michael O'Connor, one of the great Wallabies lost by rugby.

social and religious factors, it was a little different. Rugby in Australia always faced opposition from other football codes and in some years, because they were not restricted by the same amateurism regulations, that almost proved overwhelming. This was especially so from the 1950s to the 1980s. Australia no sooner found itself with a good Wallaby side than key players were whipped away by lucrative rugby league contracts. Many great players were lost, from Trevor Allan, Ken Kearney and Rex Mossop in the '40s, Arthur Summons, Dick Thornett, Phil Hawthorne in the '50s and '60s through to Ray Price, Michael O'Connor and Ricky Stuart more recently.

In Western Australia and South Australia, rugby – either union or league – was barely played. Because of the influence of Irish diggers in the Victorian goldfields, Australian rules, a game unique to Australia but akin to Gaelic football, took a firm root. In New South Wales and Queensland, rugby remained the preference but increasingly from the turn of the century it was league which was the more popular variety. To a large degree this was also because of the Irish influence.

During the First World War, league continued in both NSW and Queensland, whereas rugby ceased. The effect in Queensland was such that throughout the 1920s no Australian national team was fielded and any internationals played during the decade were by the New South Wales Waratahs. In recent times, some of the New South Wales matches have been reclassified as official tests and caps awarded retrospectively. In the many Catholic schools in Sydney, league became ingrained and the code also became intertwined at socio-economic and political levels with the Labour party and trade union movement in Australia.

Rugby – or union, oddly enough called that despite league's stronger working class links – became very much the game of the privileged Greater Public Schools. As a result, for many years the Wallabies were studded with very much middle class products, having even into recent years a higher ratio of lawyers, accountants and stockbrokers in their ranks than the more proletarian All Blacks. Many Australians, and New Zealanders who've lived across the Tasman, such as Grant Batty, the All Black wing of the 1970s, believe this component has always been one reason for New Zealand's traditional rugby dominance. "There haven't always been enough mongrels in the Wallaby teams," Batty says. "They haven't had the same hunger."

Legends of the All Blacks

The differences in socio-economic backgrounds are sometimes reflected in the media responses from Australian players in the respective codes. Wallaby players generally speak better than their league counterparts and until recent years have been noticeably more articulate than most All Blacks.

Even allowing for the gap between New Zealand and Australian rugby, the crevasse into which the 1972 Wallabies plunged was something of an aberration. Generally games between the Wallabies and the All Blacks were not as one-sided as were that year's three tests. But until the 1979 watershed test the general dominance of the All Blacks was as inarguable as that of the Aussies in practically every other sport – cricket, tennis, league, swimming, netball and most track and field events.

The pattern of All Black superiority was set in the first test between the two countries – at Sydney in 1903 – when the All Blacks won 22-3. It was not till 1910 and the seventh game that Australia scored its first victory, 11-0 in Sydney.

Of the 67 tests played between the countries between 1903 and 1978 the All Blacks won 49, the Wallabies 14 and there were four draws. In the 41 tests played between 1979 and 1998, the All Blacks won 24, the Wallabies 16 and there was one draw.

Until the 1979 victory in the one-off game at the SCG, the Wallabies had won only three test series, in 1929, 1934 and 1949, and two of those contained heavy qualifications.

In 1929, the Wallabies achieved the first of their two 3-0 whitewashes: 9-8 in Sydney, 17-9 in Brisbane and 15-13 in the return in Sydney. However, this was not a strong All Black team. Many leading players were unavailable, presumably because of the time spent the previous year on the tour of South Africa. Of the team which went to Australia, only six survived from the All Blacks of 1928 who had been good enough to square a four-test series with the Springboks. The six 1928 survivors were Herb Lilburne, Bert Grenside, Syd Carlton, Bill Dalley, Rube McWilliams and Eric Snow. Among those who didn't go to Australia were key players in South Africa such as Maurice Brownlie, Mark Nicholls, Ron Stewart, Ian Harvey, Alan Robilliard, Fred Lucas, Archie Strang, Bill Hazlett and Bunny Finlayson. And Bert Cooke, the most gifted back of his generation, was again unavailable. No fewer than 12 new All Blacks were introduced for the 1929 tour. The tourists were further weakened when such experienced players as the great fullback George Nepia, Dalley and the captain Cliff Porter suffered injuries. Neither Porter nor Dalley, the vice captain, could play in the first test and so Lilburne, at 21, became, as he remains today, the youngest All Black test captain. Porter's absence meant that Lew Hook, normally a centre and only 10st in weight, played at wing forward.

In 1949, the Wallabies won both tests – in Wellington and Auckland – and, as with their predecessors 20 years before, were clearly the better side. But both tests were played while the All Blacks were touring South Africa. Still,

Australia

George Nepia (left) and Cliff Porter – two legendary All Blacks who suffered injuries and missed some of the tour to Australia in 1929.

there were some fine players in the tests against the Wallabies. Great lock Tiny White played the first of his 23 tests and the centre was the celebrated Johnny Smith who, but for his Maori ancestry, would have been with the side in South Africa. Today, of course, simultaneous test series against opponents like the Wallabies and the Springboks wouldn't be contemplated. Such a second selection – in reality the equivalent of the modern day New Zealand A side – would certainly not receive full All Black status.

There could not be the same reservations of the win by the Wallabies in 1934 – the first time they had held the Bledisloe Cup. They outplayed the All Blacks decisively in the first test, winning 25-11, and clinched the series with a 3-3 draw. The 1930s were a notable decade in Australia and three backs, fullback Alec Ross, centre Cyril Towers and halfback Syd Malcolm, were rated among the finest produced in any generation.

In 1931 the All Blacks claimed the Bledisloe Cup, winning 20-13 at Eden Park. The fullback in this match for the All Blacks was Ron Bush who, though he contributed 14 points, never appeared again. It's clear, too, that only scant attention was paid to the fact that the cup was at stake. Historians Neville McMillan and Rod Chester produced some monumental research on All Black test rugby. But in neither of their two thorough reference books, *Men in Black* and *Centenary*, is there even a passing mention of the cup being at stake in their accounts of the 1931 match.

After 1934 the All Blacks were rarely challenged by the Wallabies. The 1930s, the decade of the world's great economic depression, weren't all that kind to New Zealand rugby, either. The series defeat in 1934 was accompanied by a lacklustre tour of Britain in 1935-36 in which the internationals to Wales and England were lost, and a 2-1 series defeat to the Springboks in 1937. But the decade at least finished on a bright note before the careers and sometimes lives of many fine players were abruptly ended

Legends of the All Blacks

by the antics of one, to whom rugby meant little, A Hitler. The outbreak of the Second World War also meant the cancellation of the scheduled All Black tour of South Africa in 1940.

The All Blacks toured Australia in 1938 and enjoyed such success it's diverting to wonder, the brilliance of the 1937 Springboks notwithstanding, how they may have fared on the South African tour had it proceeded. All nine matches on the Australian tour were won and all three tests, the first (24-9) and the third (14-6) with reasonable comfort. But in the second a competent Wallabies side shared the tries at three apiece though losing 20-14.

In New Zealand's first test after the war, the All Blacks whipped the Wallabies 31-8 in Dunedin in 1946. The match makes an ideal test for trivia buffs. Because of the war and injuries to the two in the Wallaby side who'd been there in the 1930s every player who appeared in that game was making his test debut. The All Black side included some who were to become legends, notably Bob Scott, Johnny Smith and Fred Allen. By a much more slender margin the All Blacks won the second test in Auckland.

There was another 2-0 result when the All Blacks crossed the Tasman the following year. The second test in Sydney, won by the All Blacks 27-14, was notable for some phenomenal goal-kicking, firstly by Scott, who had a faultless record of three penalties and three conversions, and even more remarkably by the No. 8 Neville Thornton. Late in the match Scott, because of a slight groin strain, was reluctant when Allen asked him about an attempt at a penalty goal from halfway. Up stepped Thornton who carried the nickname "Nutcracker" because of his distinctive facial features. "Give me the ball, Punch," he said to Allen. "I'll kick a goal." And so he did. It was no fluke, either, for in 1948 Thornton added to his halfway penalty by potting a 40-metre goal to give Auckland a narrow win in their annual match against Waikato.

With the exception of 1949, Bledisloe Cup matches through to 1979 followed a uniform pattern. The All Blacks on their tours to Australia were generally unbeaten or dropped just the one to New South Wales, as was the case in 1947 and 1962. And in the years before the resurgence of Queensland, New South Wales sides didn't vary a great deal from the Wallabies. In the other tours, in 1951, 1957, 1968 and 1974, the All Blacks were unbeaten.

Some of the games against country composite teams or lesser states like South Australia were won by huge scores, which inevitably raised questions as to whether the exercises had much point or value. In some of the games there were some extraordinary individual achievements. Ron Jarden, the flying wing who was the star of the 1951 tour, scored 38 points in a game at Parkes from six tries (they counted for only three points) and 10 conversions. In 1957, another wing, Russell Watt, scored seven tries in one game and in 1962 former national sprint champion Rod Heeps scored eight. In 1974, fullback Joe Karam collected 41 points against South Australia.

For 45 years between 1934 and 1979 the All Blacks didn't lose a test on

Australian soil. But during those Australian tours there were some narrow escapes. In 1968 there was the penalty try incident at Brisbane which denied the Wallabies, who had been leading 18-14 into the final minutes, a famous, unexpected victory. The All Blacks, who just a few months before had swept all before them on a tour of Britain and France, were overwhelming favourites. But the loss of key forwards Brian Lochore and Ken Gray to injuries and an inability to adapt to the Wallabies' unorthodox tactics caused the All Blacks to struggle. Wallaby coach Des Connor (a halfback who'd played for each country) had his pack repeatedly use shortened lineouts, leaving the other forwards free to stifle backline attacks.

And the penalty try called by a local referee Kevin Crowe? To this day there is confusion over the reasons, possibly because some years later Crowe revised the explanation which he or someone on his behalf had given immediately after the match. The first version was that the call had

Des Connor (second from left) leaves the field after helping New Zealand beat Australia 14-5 at Sydney, 1962.

been made against the Wallaby centre Barry Honan for a late tackle on his All Black opposite, Bill Davis. Even to New Zealanders Honan's offence appeared only borderline. But in the same movement the All Black wing Grahame Thorne was clearly obstructed by his marker, Alan Cardy, and years later it was this offence that Crowe claimed had led to the penalty try.

When Fred Allen, the All Black coach, had coached Auckland in their successful 1960-63 Ranfurly Shield era one of his mainstays had been Connor. Despite this, there was a frosty exchange when the All Black management accused Connor of having the Wallabies use negative tactics. Connor replied: "I personally was disappointed that they never countered our play. Rather than seek answers to it, they preferred to whinge. I concede the test was an awful

Legends of the All Blacks

spectacle but we almost succeeded in lowering the mighty All Blacks."

Six years later – in 1974 – Ballymore was the scene of another cliff-hanger. Andy Leslie's All Blacks saved their unbeaten tour record with a 16-16 draw in the second test at Ballymore.

That was the only blemish on the 1974 All Blacks' record. Largely through the efforts of the mighty loose forward Ian Kirkpatrick, New Zealand won each of the tests played that year in Sydney. Both were worthy efforts, for on each occasion, the All Blacks had to overcome refereeing by Dr Roger Vanderfield that in all charity was at best indifferent. His penalty count in the second half of the final test was 10-0 in favour of the Wallabies, prompting the All Black coach JJ Stewart to congratulate the Wallabies on their perfect knowledge of rugby laws. And the weather conditions for the first were the most vile imaginable. Rain and wind lashed Sydney and once when Karam was attempting a goal, Leslie had to sweep away water with his arms to enable him to make a mark.

Kirkpatrick's performances were especially heroic, for he made that tour under some personal difficulty. Stewart had taken a selectorial axe to the All Blacks in the wake of the traumatic tour of Britain in 1972-73 and subsequent disastrous results in the 1973 domestic season when matches were lost to England, a President's XV led by an ageing Colin Meads and, most remarkably, to an under-23 selection. Several leading players were left out of the 1974 side, notably Sid Going, and no fewer than 15 of the 25 players were new All Blacks, one of whom, Leslie, was elevated to the captaincy. Kirkpatrick, who learned of his dumping along with everyone else underneath Athletic Park's grandstand when the team was announced, assured Leslie of his full support. He was as good as his word, his displays in the two Sydney tests being inspirational.

Ian Kirkpatrick – heroic performances in 1974.

Just as the All Black tours to Australia seemed to have an immutable pattern, so also did those made by the Wallabies to New Zealand before the 1980s. The 1972 tour was an exception,

Australia

but generally the Wallabies competed well. They were usually outgunned in the forwards but praised for their gallantry, and their backs were always admired for their flair and enterprise. The Wallabies in particular seemed to have a knack of producing outstanding halfbacks… Cyril Burke and Brian Cox in the early '50s, Des Connor in the late '50s, Ken Catchpole in the '60s, John Hipwell in the '70s and Nick Farr-Jones in the '80s. Though they didn't win a series in New Zealand until 1986, these ingredients made the Wallabies a dangerous opponent and few rubbers went by when they didn't pick up at least one test win.

In each of their tours of 1952, 1955, 1958, 1964 and 1978 the Wallabies had the consolation of a significant win. In 1962 there was a 9-9 draw in Wellington, the All Blacks being saved from defeat by a late Don Clarke penalty, and a 3-0 All Black win in Dunedin, Clarke's boot providing the only score. Both the 1952 and 1958 wins were at Christchurch's Lancaster Park and each placed the Wallabies in what then was the rare position of being able to win a series in New Zealand. But after losing the first of the two tests 14-9 in 1952, the All Blacks recovered a week later in Wellington to win 15-8 and so retain the Bledisloe Cup.

The Australian win six years later was the more celebrated for it was against all predictions and ranked among the major upsets in international rugby. New Zealand, captained for the first time by Wilson Whineray, had won the first test 25-3, seven tries to one. It was an extremely young Wallaby side with Australian rugby in one of its frequent rebuilding phases after a disastrous 1957-58 tour of Britain and France when only 16 of the 34 matches were won and all five internationals were lost.

Yet at Lancaster Park, though the margin was only 6-3 and there was a try apiece, the visitors thoroughly deserved to win. The backline stars were Des Connor, soon to move to New Zealand, young fullback Terry Curley, who at 20 quit test rugby to become a Marist brother, and first five-eighth Arthur Summons, who subsequently switched to league. He became a captain and coach of the Kangaroos and is one of the mud-caked figures in a 1960s Sydney grand final shot which has become one of the most reproduced photos of Australian sports journalism. But the main hero was wing Alan Morton, who in the second spell raced 40 metres past some ineffectual tackles for the winning try.

The 1955, 1964 and 1978 Wallaby wins came when each series had been decided in the All Blacks' favour. But they were no less significant for that and, indeed, had as much benefit for the All Blacks as they did for Australian rugby. The All Blacks played only moderately to win the 1955 series and the 8-3 defeat in the final test at Eden Park helped pinpoint a lack of fitness among the New Zealand players. This was something remedied over the summer months and after a "get fit" directive from selection convener Tom Morrison, the All Blacks were in much better shape for the epic series against the Springboks the following year.

Legends of the All Blacks

By coincidence, the All Blacks' 20-5 defeat at Athletic Park in 1964, still one of the All Blacks' heaviest, also preceded a Springbok tour the following year and again had the effect of ironing out any complacency. The loss, in fact, was the All Blacks' first in tests for four years and broke a sequence of 17 matches without defeat. Loose forwards Greg Davis and Jules Guerrassimoff were outstanding for the Wallabies in the 1964 match. By modern standards both were comparatively small, but they were as swift and relentless as terriers in their aggressive defence. Davis, a New Zealander, moved to Australia and became a star of the 1963 tour of South Africa. He had previously played for Auckland, Thames Valley and Bay of Plenty. After the Athletic Park match he was approached by the president of the New Zealand union, the forthright Tom Pearce. "How on earth did we ever let you go?" exclaimed Pearce.

Greg Davis

Remarkably, it was to be 14 years before the Wallabies could boast another win over the All Blacks. And though it, too, came with the rubber dead, it was another stirring, even heroic triumph.

The heroism derived not merely from recovering for the loss of the first two tests, even if the first at Athletic Park was by only 13-12, but from a more personal cause. Just before the third test the Wallabies lost their coach Daryl Haberecht, one of the most original and innovative thinkers rugby has known, to a heart attack for which he was admitted to hospital. With the help of manager Ross Turnbull, the Wallaby players were largely responsible for their own third test preparation. One of the players brought into the team was the genial, squarely-built prop Chris Handy who just before kick-off showed some of the wit which has made him a popular TV comments man and raconteur. Turnbull made Handy his special target in his pre-match address. "We've got to stop Andy Haden in the lineouts and Buddha, you're the man to do it." Handy, of course, is as wide as he is tall and at little more than 1.78m, was several centimetres shorter than the towering Haden. "Well," said Handy, "you'd better find me a stepladder."

The Wallabies produced some brilliant running rugby to win 30-16, the game being forever associated with the loose forward Greg Cornelsen. He had one of those days few players even dream about. The ball seemed to follow him and with inspired opportunism he scored four of the Wallabies' five tries.

The 1979 match signalled the beginning of the modern Bledisloe Cup era in which the Wallabies have forged an arch-rivalry with the All Blacks almost equal to that between New Zealand and the Springboks. In 1980 the All Blacks toured Australia and, suffering from self-imposed handicaps, notably the inexplicable omission of the great centre Bruce Robertson, deservedly lost the series 2-1.

Australia

Four-try wonder Greg Cornelsen has support from John Hipwell (left) at Auckland, 1978.

The Wallabies' most enduring feat that year was to revive the art of scintillating back play. Mark Ella, Michael Hawker, Michael O'Connor, Brendan Moon and Roger Gould were a class above the All Blacks. Not even an outbreak of food poisoning among the All Blacks on the eve of the third test could be offered as a valid excuse for the All Blacks' inferiority. The one bright New Zealand note came in the second test in Brisbane when Robertson, taken over as a replacement when the selectors finally came to their senses, inspired a marvellous try to hooker Hika Reid to provide a 12-9 win.

In 1982, the All Blacks recaptured the cup when the Wallabies toured New Zealand. But this was a series where Australia won much of the glory. They were minus 10 first-choice players, partly for financial reasons and partly from what suspicions Queenslanders perceived as New South Wales

165

Legends of the All Blacks

bias in the selections of new coach Bob Dwyer. Yet the Wallabies, captained by Mark Ella and with an exciting teenager named David Campese on the wing, provided a spirited contest with an experienced, competent All Black side. Campese was sensational, outplaying the deeply-respected Stu Wilson and producing his dazzling trademark "goosestep". The Wallabies won the second test 19-16 at Athletic Park and may have won the third at Eden Park after starting in style with an early try by fullback Gould. But the All Blacks rallied under the leadership for the last time of Graham Mourie and with fullback Allan Hewson scoring a record 26 points for a test, won 33-18.

Between 1984 and 1986, there were some intensely-fought tests between the All Blacks and the Wallabies, best illustrated by the fact that four consecutive matches, the 1984 third test in Sydney, the one-off match at Eden Park in 1985 and the first two of the 1986 series in New Zealand were decided by a single point.

Alan Jones had taken over the Wallaby coaching from Dwyer for the 1984 series and he was to become a tempestuous, controversial figure disliked by many New Zealanders and more than a few Australians. But despite his divisive nature, he enjoyed a large measure of success, especially in his early years, coaching the 1984 Wallabies to their first Grand Slam in Britain and to a series win in New Zealand in 1986. Jones was quick to proclaim the latter as an acme of international success after the Wallabies had won the third and deciding test at Eden Park 22-9.

"Quo vadis?" he asked, a Latin reference which effectively means: what can we do now to better this? No question that the Wallabies deserved to win in 1986 for it might well have been a clean sweep. The All Blacks won 13-12 in Dunedin, but were lucky to do so because Welsh referee Derek Bevan erred in not awarding a clear try to the Wallaby No. 8 Steve Tuynman.

Yet for all the merits of the series victory, Jones misread some of the factors contributing to the Wallabies' win. The All Blacks were hopelessly divided by the Cavaliers-Baby Blacks issue and much ill-feeling existed when, after running the Wallabies so close in the first test in Wellington, many of the Baby Blacks were axed for Cavaliers returning from their test suspensions.

A more accurate picture of the respective strengths of the two countries came in 1987 in the inaugural World Cup.

The All Blacks refound unity under coach Brian Lochore and his new assistants, Alex Wyllie and John Hart, and swept all before them to comfortably win the World Cup. The Wallabies, by contrast, failed to live up to their tag of favouritism and despite participating in a semi-final thriller with France, didn't make the final.

New Zealand and Australia didn't meet in the tournament, but clashed a few weeks later in the one-off Bledisloe Cup test at Concord Oval. In another thriller, the All Blacks won 30-16, Sean Fitzpatrick confirming himself as a hooker in stellar class with two tries. In view of all that had

Australia

happened during 1986, it's little wonder the All Blacks saw that Sydney win as nearly as pleasurable as winning the World Cup.

From 1988-90, the All Blacks maintained their edge, touring Australia without defeat in 1988 and winning the first and third tests at Concord Oval with the sort of displays which made Kiwi spines shudder. Wayne Shelford's leadership by example was typified by the blood which streamed from his cut face after the third test as he held aloft the Bledisloe Cup. But the enduring image of this test was Michael Jones' surge from a ruck near his own 22 to send away John Kirwan, the master of Campese in this test series, for a stirring try.

But by 1990, when the Wallabies – boasting their "big three" of halfback Nick Farr-Jones, first-five and kicker Michael Lynagh and winger-fullback David Campese – turned up at Athletic Park and ended New Zealand's 50-match, 23-test sequence without defeat, the All Blacks' edge was waning.

Champion Wallaby first five-eighth and goal-kicker Michael Lynagh.

Legends of the All Blacks

Phil Kearns scored the winning try at Wellington and the mouthing and the two-fingered barbecue invitation he gave his great rival Fitzpatrick soon took on a symbolic aspect.

Attention turned in 1991 to the second World Cup. Australia and New Zealand split tests during the season, then travelled north. That World Cup final may have been at Twickenham when the Wallabies beat England, but the decider was the semi-final at Dublin.

Inspired by the genius of Campese, the Wallabies deservedly won the only test between them and the All Blacks played in a neutral country. Their 16-6 triumph at Dublin confirmed the rise of a new power in world rugby.

As befitting their new status as world champions, the Wallabies won the Bledisloe Cup series in Australia the following year. But apart from an incident involving Richard Loe and Paul Carozza, when the latter had his nose broken, there was little disgrace in the defeat for the All Blacks. A remarkable series produced yet another statistical oddity to underline the closeness now in the trans-Tasman rugby rivalry. After three tests the teams finished with the same number of points (58) and the same number of tries (6).

From 1993-97, the All Blacks generally dominated, the only interruption in a winning sequence being in 1994 in the first night test between the two countries. An All Black fightback in the second spell failed to end in victory only when a diving Jeff Wilson had the ball jolted from his arms in a tackle by George Gregan as he was about to score the winning try.

In 1995 the 100th All Black-Wallaby test was played at the Sydney Football Stadium and resulted in an All Black win. It was a stunning display with Jonah Lomu as dynamic as he had been a few weeks previously during the World Cup. But overshadowing everything on this occasion was the coincidental climax of the proposed WRC breakaway. At that point it appeared a reality and many watched the 1995 game fearful it was the end of test rugby as it had been known for more than a century.

There was a new dimension to Bledisloe Cup tests from 1996, for professionalism had become official and the matches became part of the new Tri-Nations competition in which South Africa were also a part. The All Blacks were supreme in the first two years of the Tri-Nations, their 1996 matches against the Wallabies taking their place among the classics. At Athletic Park they played near-perfect rugby in vile conditions to win by a record 43-6. They were much more human a few weeks later in Brisbane, trailing 25-9 only to escape with a 32-25 win when Andrew Mehrtens engineered a backline move which brought Frank Bunce a last-minute try.

Though there was an All Black 3-0 clean sweep in 1997, there were signs of another downward cycle looming. In the last match, in Dunedin, the All Blacks led 36-0 at half-time, only to stay scoreless in the second spell while the Wallabies replied with 24 points. The Carisbrook second half was the harbinger of what for the All Blacks was a 1998 season from hell. Of five successive matches lost, three were to the Wallabies.

Australia – The Quinn Tapes

Fred Allen
led the All Blacks in series against Australia in 1946 and 1947.

After the war the All Black side to play Australia was chosen. Charlie Saxton would have been the captain without any shadow of doubt, but he had a bad shoulder and had to pull out. So I was named captain. I got the shock of my life, not only getting in the side, but being made captain.

The Aussies were pretty good to play against. In those days they didn't have the forward power they do now, but they had some brilliant backs. We played them in two tests. We beat them 31-8 in Dunedin and then had a hard game in Auckland. Charlie Eastes scored a couple of good tries for them. I tried to get Jimmy Haig to go off. He was hurt, but there was no way he would go off. I wanted Doc Paewai to get onto the field and get an All Black blazer. Paewai was a brilliant footballer, but never did become an All Black because I couldn't get Haig off the park that day.

Fred Allen leads the All Blacks on to Eden Park for the second test of the 1946 series against Australia.

Ross Brown
All Black five-eighth from 1955-62.

I played the last test against Australia in 1955. I was very raw. The Aussies had some very quick loose forwards and they played us up front. The night before the game, Tom Morrison had us training until it was dark. The poor forwards were leaden-footed and they got beaten and deservedly so.

Colin Meads
made his test debut in Australia in 1957. He played as a side row forward during that series, except for a memorable few minutes in the second test.

In the second test, Frank McMullen got hurt early in the piece and I had to go onto the wing – there were no replacements in those days. I scored my first test try as a winger. I had to mark an Australian Empire Games sprinter named Morton, and Pat Walsh came over to me from where he was at centre and said, "Whatever happens, don't let him come inside you. I'll catch him if he goes round you, but if he comes inside, we're gone. So I made sure he never got inside me.

He went round a couple of times and Pat caught him. Then Pat said, "When you get the ball, don't try to beat him. You run straight at him. I found out he could run faster backwards than I could forwards! Pat gave me the ball about 20 yards out and I ran straight at the goal-line and scored. It was a great experience, but I don't think the selectors ever saw me as a winger."

Legends of the All Blacks

Colin Meads
was not often dropped from the test team, but it happened in 1962.

KQ: Colin, the story goes that after you were dropped against Australia in 1962, you gave the coach the cold shoulder when you got back in. Is there any truth in that?

Well, Kel and I were dropped for the second test, which we only just won 3-0. I came back for the third test but Kel had to wait until next year. Keith Nelson had taken his place. So we're there and the selectors are asking me, "What about this?" and "What about that?" and I'm just grunting. I said I was there to do a bloody job and was going to prove something to them. I remember Neil McPhail [the coach] standing at the back of the lineout during training and we were driving around. I had great delight in running into him and bowling him over. There was no talking; it was an angry Colin Meads. I was going to show the selectors that if they dropped me, I'd come back and play better than before.

Brian Lochore
captained the 1968 All Blacks to Australia.

Back in 1968, the strength of Australian rugby was really New South Wales. Queensland was just a fledging union. So on tour you played a lot of easy games, and could get into bad habits, and then hit New South Wales, then the tests. We were lucky to win the third test in Sydney and from my point of view it was disappointing because I broke my thumb. I stayed on for a little while, and then I got a twinge in my hamstring. I thought there was no point in staying on. Then they brought in short lineouts, which we'd never had before. It was a ploy to upset us. So I got that sorted out, then departed. Ian Kirkpatrick came in and made his mark by scoring three tries. It was great for Kirky. He'd been a great tourist in 1967, even though he played in only one of the tests.

More fields to conquer – Colin Meads (left), Ken Gray, Kel Tremain and Brian Lochore head overseas.

Australia – The Quinn Tapes

The 'Catchpole Test'

Colin Meads
was involved in some controversial moments during his long career, few more so than the incident involving Australian halfback Ken Catchpole at Sydney in 1968.

I received a lot of criticism for the Ken Catchpole incident over there in 1968. Catchy had been cutting back in towards the forwards and at half-time we spoke about how we had to put him on the ground so that he wouldn't be so keen on being in with the forwards.

The incident happened soon after half-time. He ducked back in there and I grabbed one leg. I thought I'd put him on the ground – tip him up – so he could then have some good New Zealand rucking done to him. But I didn't know his other leg was pinned. He did the splits, and of course was badly injured. He was an Australian rugby hero, so I wasn't very popular. It's one of those things really. You did it, you're not very proud of it, but there wasn't any malice in it.

While the injury was a serious one, he was coming to the end of his career and he did play afterwards. I played some festival games in Tonga a few years later with Catchy and we discussed it then. The whole thing obviously hurt him quite deeply.

Des Connor
who played test rugby for Australia and New Zealand, coached Australia against the All Blacks in 1968.

In the first test [in 1968] we got a thrashing. We had good forwards, but they were young and didn't have a lot of knowledge or height. Meads and the rest of them had a field day. But one thing about the All Blacks then was that they were very predictable. I thought we had to try to upset them. So we worked out the two and three-man lineouts and played five-man hit-and-run scrums, purely to disrupt them.

For the first twenty minutes the All Blacks didn't know what was going on. They'd arrive at a lineout and we'd only have two there and they'd be going backwards and forwards. And we bloody near won the thing, but for that penalty try at the end.

Afterwards Duncan Ross, the All Black manager, wouldn't talk to me. He said you just didn't do that sort of thing, which gave me great pleasure. But Fred Allen, the coach, was very gracious and said to me, "Wallaby – that was my nickname – you bloody near won that. We were lucky to get out of it." He appreciated what we were about and knew what I was up against.

Ken Catchpole
Wallaby test halfback from 1961-68.

Colin Meads went around and grabbed one of my legs and pulled it up, more in frustration than anything else. I was held at the top and he held my leg at the back. The ruck collapsed. That's when the injury occurred. Rather than letting go my leg immediately, Colin kept pulling, which I thought was pretty stupid, and it gave the crowd the impression he was intentionally trying to injure me. I don't believe he was. I believe it was mostly an accident, but that he was a bit foolish doing what he did.

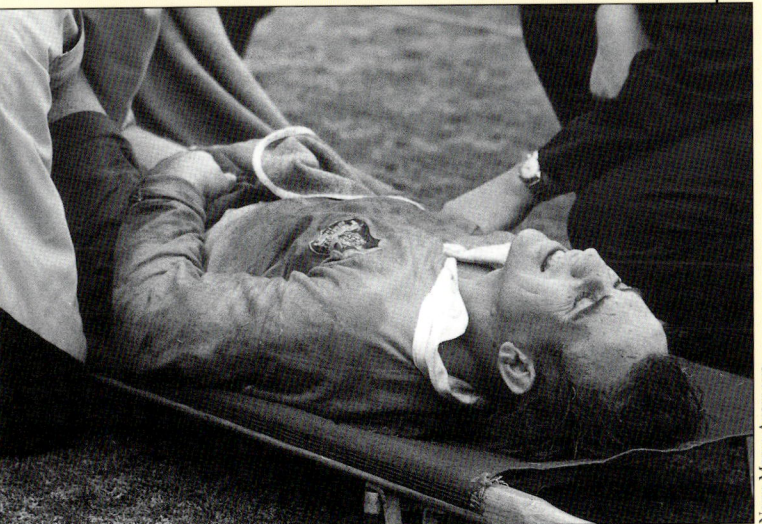

Ken Catchpole's test career ends in unhappy circumstances, Sydney, 1968.

Legends of the All Blacks

Ian Kirkpatrick
All Black loose forward from 1967-77.

Australia always seemed to produce outstanding backs, but they would get picked off by league. So the Aussies would have to start again with another young guy. Their teams lacked continuity because they kept getting disrupted.

Andy Leslie
captained the 1974 All Blacks to Australia.

We played very well in Australia in 1974, but only drew the second test. A couple of nights before that game we had a function and Mr Burnett, who was to be our referee, was there. He came up to me and said, "Andy, if there are any problems during the game, you just let me know and we'll talk it through." Well, after the first lineout of the test, Kenny Stewart was penalised and before we knew it we were 3-0 down. As we were running back towards halfway, I turned to the ref and asked him about the penalty. I felt he'd made an incorrect ruling. He turned to me and said: "Bugger off! It's got nothing to do with you. I'm refereeing this bloody game!" So that was Mr Burnett.

Bob Templeton
coached the Wallabies through much of the 1970s.

Australian rugby in the 1970s was never as consistent as it should have been. We'd have a good win, and then suffer three or four losses. But that's changed now, with the development of rugby, particularly coaching, and the regular competition over the years with strong New Zealand provinces like Canterbury, Wellington, North Auckland and so on.

Ross Turnbull
managed the 1978 Australian team to New Zealand.

It was a tough tour and then after the second test our coach, Daryl Haberecht, who had done a magnificent job, suffered a heart attack. We had to regroup. I called a meeting of the senior players and we decided we wouldn't seek the [fulltime] assistance of an outside coach. We decided to stick together and not to lose another match. JJ Stewart took us for a training session for a couple of hours and said some very significant things to our boys about not taking backward steps and about being positive. We went through the balance of the tour and didn't lose another game. The last test in Auckland was remarkable, with Greg Cornelsen scoring four tries.

Bob Templeton

When we won the Bledisloe Cup series in 1980, it was a dream realised. We'd won a one-off test in 1979, but to come back and play very good rugby with Mark Ella, Michael Hawker, Michael O'Connor – all those boys

Spiro Zavos
New Zealand journalist.

New Zealand saved the game of rugby in Australia. If they hadn't, rugby would have become another of the sports that died out, like professional sculling and professional wrestling. New Zealand rugby saved Australian rugby not only in the 1920s and '30s, but also in the 1960s and '70s. There was a game played between New South Wales and Queensland at the North Sydney Oval and only a couple of thousand people turned up. The New South Wales union treasurer, a man named John Howard, and Norbert Byrne, a famous Queensland administrator, called an urgent conference. This was in 1972. Colin Meads, Brian Lochore, Wilson Whineray – a lot of New Zealanders – went across and formed a plan to save the game in Australia. It involved sending schoolboy teams and looking after rugby from the grassroots up.

Australia – The Quinn Tapes

from the great schoolboy rugby sides – was fantastic. We won the first test, lost the second narrowly, then beat New Zealand in the third, albeit they claimed they were suffering from food poisoning.

One of the things I said to the boys at that stage was, "We will not be intimidated. Don't take a backward step." And they didn't.

Mark Ella
played for the Wallabies from 1980-84.

KQ: *What is your recollection of that third test in 1980 when you won the Bledisloe Cup?*

We were a young side. We couldn't compete with the All Blacks up front, but we thought they had a weakness out wide, so we moved the ball. And we had no inhibitions. We opened it up and won 26-10. We ran at them at every opportunity, and I don't think they were prepared for that.

•

We always used New Zealand as a measuring stick. If we were going to be respected in world rugby, we had to beat New Zealand. In the initial years we worked hard and many times got battered and bruised. But we learned and finally we were able to look at New Zealand and say, "Hey, we're as good as you guys." But without the continual losses, the humiliations that we went through, we wouldn't have worked hard enough to drag ourselves to where we are now.

Jock Hobbs
played for the All Blacks from 1983-86, captaining them in four tests.

We certainly didn't regard Australia as easy-beats by 1983-84. They had a strong side in 1984 and the series was a real struggle. Aussies always bring certain qualities into matches against the All Blacks. They have confidence, athleticism, aggression. They like to win and they are always hard to beat.

Nick Farr-Jones
played for Australia from 1984-93 and captained the team from 1988-92.

If we'd lost the third test at Wellington in 1990, Bob Dwyer would have been gone. Queensland were after him. We'd been cleaned out in Christchurch and Auckland and had John Connolly come in as coach, he would have picked someone like Bill Campbell to captain the side. So I'd have lost my job, too. Peter Slattery, a terrific halfback, could have taken the halfback's job. So that match was crucial to us. I remember saying to Dwyer beforehand that I owed him a captain's knock.

We trailed by three points at halftime, running into a really strong breeze. Then Kearnsy [Phil Kearns] got his try shortly after halftime and basically that was it.

Mark Ella

Legends of the All Blacks

He invited his mate, Sean Fitzpatrick, to a couple of barbecues after he scored the try, and that epitomised the way we felt. We'd been kicked around by New Zealand for a couple of years, feeding on scraps. Now we'd stood up and delivered.

Phil Kearns
a hooker, first represented Australia in 1989 and by 1999 had played 61 tests.

I'm not a sledger at all on the field. That thing with Fitzy was just a culmination of having him on my back for four tests in a row and was a little way of getting back. I regret it in a way now, but it certainly achieved some degree of infamy.

•

The best test series I've ever been involved in was in 1992 when Australia played New Zealand and over three weeks we scored exactly the same number of points and tries. We won the series two tests to one.

John Eales
first played for Australia in 1991 and by 1999 had played 64 tests.

When George Gregan tackled Jeff Wilson in the last moment of that test [at Sydney in 1994] it was one of the most famous moments in the history of the Bledisloe Cup. We'd had a great start and built up a very big lead. But then we played to hang on and New Zealand attacked us so strongly that we were totally run off our feet. Everyone was absolutely stuffed. New Zealand made that last break and it looked for all the world like a try. Jeff Wilson had beaten a couple of defenders before George came through with his tackle. I don't think anyone who was out on the field at the time realised just how good an effort it was from George.

Wallaby coach Bob Dwyer and captain Nick Farr-Jones ponder another Bledisloe Cup clash with New Zealand.

Australia – The Quinn Tapes

That Tackle!

George Gregan makes the match-saving tackle on Jeff Wilson at Sydney, 1994.

George Gregan
a halfback, first played for Australia in 1994.

It just happened in a blur. It was one of those things where you're trying to have a go at someone and luckily for me, it came off. I didn't have much time to think about it. You dive in high and try to tackle the ball into orbit. It's a desperate situation and if it comes off, it comes off. If I did it a hundred thousand times, it probably wouldn't happen again.

Jeff and I have a lot of respect for each other. People who bring up that tackle should ask how many times he has stepped or run around me. I think he's probably got me in that regard.

Jeff Wilson
first played for New Zealand in 1993 and by 1999 had played 42 tests.

I never saw it coming and as soon as it happened, I knew what had happened.

It's hard to come to terms with. I was shell-shocked. For the next summer I had to live with it and deal with it. It wasn't easy. I was devastated for a long time.

I'd sat on the bench for the All Blacks for a whole year, then to finally get my chance and blow it was hard to take. You would never want to put anyone in that position.

Legends of the All Blacks

Laurie Mains
coached the All Blacks from 1992-95.

Jonah [Lomu] never played better than against Australia at Sydney after the 1995 World Cup. Before it, I'd given him a little bit of a jab about Joe Roff, Australia's new Jonah sort of thing. We had a new move for him to do and he was excited about his training and about playing.

I'll never forget coming into the All Black team talk, where everything is usually so formal. I walked into the room and cast my eyes around. I could see Fitzpatrick with a wry sort of grin on his face. I caught Brewer looking back over his right shoulder a little bit, and I saw Zinny, extremely apprehensive. I followed their eyes and what did I see? Jonah sitting in Laurie Mains' team talk with a pair of dark glasses on. What do I do? The whole team was waiting in tense anticipation to see. Fortunately my split-second decision was the right one. I said nothing, showed no reaction except to give a wink to the big three. When I just carried on I could feel a huge release of tension.

Jonah had an incredible game. Afterwards something different happened in the dressing room. Traditionally the Brown Brothers had the guitars out and played the tunes and sang the songs that had been made popular on tours. This time the guitars stayed in the corner. Jonah had a second training bag there. Out it comes and it's his radio and speakers and up they go on the lockers. Jonah's choice in music is not the same as mine, and it's pretty heavy. I looked at Brewer and asked, "What's going on here?". Then this music strikes up and Jonah puts on his jacket, not his blazer. Suddenly he's dancing. Then Glen Osborne joins in and soon everybody ends up having a go.

Afterwards Jonah said that after the World Cup and everything else he finally felt as though he was an All Black. His big arm was around me just about driving me through the concrete floor. He made three significant statements that day. He wore his sunglasses, played a huge game and then had an influence on what happened in the dressing room.

John Eales

I'll always remember 1998 as a great year for us. We won the Bledisloe Cup series 3-0 and that had happened only once before. We'd lost all three the year before, but we knew we had it in us to play a lot better. We definitely wanted to win one game. Then we won at Melbourne and weren't satisfied with that. People commented on the pride and passion we showed, but really the big thing was that we cut down our mistakes. In Christchurch we scored a try after eighteen phases. In the past, that movement would have broken down much earlier.

Bob Templeton

KQ: What is needed to beat the All Blacks?

You've got to have parity up front and you've got to play pretty smart. The All Blacks are always a good defensive side, very basic. The All Blacks always have great confidence in their ability. They'll keep grinding away, grinding away. They don't panic. They've got faith and you have to have that same intensity to apply the pressure back to them.

Alan Jones

We rubbish the tripe out of New Zealanders, but Australians love New Zealanders. If push turns to shove, we'd fight for New Zealand and at the Olympic Games if we can't win a medal, we love New Zealand winning.

To beat New Zealand, the first thing you need is territory, because they have lethal goal-kickers. Then you've got to take them on half an inch at a time in the scrum. And when you get half an inch, get an inch. and when you've got an inch, get an inch and a half. Then they'll start to whinge, because someone will say, "Geez, what's happening back there?" Then you know you've got them. You've got to control the set pieces and be very, very jealous of the ball you get.

Pro Rugby

Money, Money, Money

By Phil Gifford

The Battle for the Blacks

An Air New Zealand flight out of Dunedin on August 10, 1995. On board are two young men who, against their every wish, seem to hold the future of All Black rugby in their hands.

Josh Kronfeld and Jeff Wilson are deciding whether they will be the first All Blacks to sign a professional contract with the New Zealand Rugby Union. They have to decide whether to break ranks with fellow All Blacks, who are still committed to a multi-million dollar scheme for a world championship, to be organised by the World Rugby Corporation, which claims the backing of Australian media giant Kerry Packer.

Kronfeld has played just seven tests for the All Blacks, Wilson 11. They are on the verge of glittering careers. But already they're stars. Wilson scored three tries in his first test, against Scotland, and Kronfeld blazed onto the international stage at the World Cup in South Africa.

On the Boeing 737, which will land at Wellington airport before the Otago team goes on to Te Kuiti for an NPC game against King Country, they're not reading the in-flight magazines. They're studying, yet again, the contracts the New Zealand union has offered them. While they're in the air, former All Black captain Jock Hobbs is sitting in the St Paul's Anglican Church, near his law firm, before he heads to the airport to cement the deal with Kronfeld and Wilson.

Hobbs is delighted, and no wonder. For three days he had been on an almost crazy whistlestop tour of the country signing provincial players. WRC is not the only outfit offering big money. The phrase Hobbs keeps hammering when he makes his pitch on behalf of the New Zealand union is that "the ding's on the table". As it happens, that ding is from another incredibly rich Australian media organisation, Rupert Murdoch's News Ltd.

On the day before the World Cup final, a deal was announced that News Corp would pay $US555 million over 10 years for the television rights to two new international contests – the Super 12 and the Tri-Nations series. The message was relayed by Dr Louis Luyt, the man New Zealanders love to hate, now deposed as the head of South African rugby, but in 1995 very much the lord of all he surveyed. Luyt isn't big on charm. At the dinner after the World Cup final, he suggested with rather misplaced humour that the South Africans were the first real World Cup winners, the 1987 and 1991 World Cups were not real world championships because South Africa hadn't been there.

But it was Luyt who was in charge of the sharp end of negotiations when South Africa, New Zealand and Australia sealed the contract with News Corp to change rugby forever. Luyt may not be big on diplomacy, but he's a seriously rich man, who rose from selling fertiliser to Afrikaner farmers to running a business empire which, among other things, owns and runs Ellis Park in Johannesburg.

Oddly enough, it was the threat from a Rupert Murdoch scheme, Super League, that drove southern hemisphere unions to open professionalism, and into Murdoch's arms. Super League, a bid by Murdoch to rob rival Kerry Packer of rugby league television rights in Australia, began with so much money rugby officials were spooked. But they didn't mess around for long. Within eight days of Super League being announced on March 31, 1995, there was a meeting of New Zealand and Australian rugby officials in Sydney to plan a new southern hemisphere competition. Within six weeks, Luyt and South Africa were on board, and, with Luyt negotiating the last details, the ding from Murdoch's company was available just before the World Cup final.

It was one of the most closely-guarded secrets in world sport. No journalists had any idea what was going on when they were summoned to Ellis Park for a special press conference. They were stunned when the deal was announced. After years of northern hemisphere rugby leaders acting and behaving as though they owned the game, the unilateral declaration of professionalism was as amazing as would an announcement today be that New Zealand is to become a state of Australia.

But that was only half the story.

Cloak and dagger time had arrived for All Black rugby. The very night that the Murdoch deal had been announced by Louis Luyt, the All Blacks were meeting in a room at their hotel in Johannesburg, where Mike Brewer and Eric Rush would tell them of another offer, from the WRC. As Ian Jones says, "Not only were we about to turn professional, but here were people bidding for our services! We were all impressed by the WRC concept. It sounded really good, and fair. What's more the money was, frankly, seductive. There really wasn't a lot of fuss about it from our point of view: this was great!"

How close did the All Blacks come to being owned by an Australian corporation? Very close, indeed. Many of the older players liked the WRC scheme for the game, and they liked the cash too, with a three-tier payment

Pro Rugby

system. Jonah Lomu would get $US1.5 million over three years. A handful of All Blacks would get $US725,000 over three years, and the rest between $US200,000 and $US300,000.

By the time the All Blacks got to the Sydney Football Stadium on July 29, 1995, where they scored a superb 34-23 win over the Wallabies, there were hidden messages everywhere. Wallabies captain Phil Kearns, a leader in the move to the WRC in Australia, stepped up to the microphone after the game and said, poignantly, "To all the Australian supporters here today, we thank you. It's been terrific, your support. And whatever happens in the future we hope you and the union support us. We thank you."

On the surface it was just another after match-speech. But bubbling underneath was the greatest crisis to face the All Blacks. The unthinkable was about to happen. The All Blacks, like the Wallabies, and the South Africans, were about to sign private professional contracts that would put them in direct opposition with their own rugby unions.

The All Blacks did not go straight to the test dinner at Sydney's Hordern Pavilion that night. Instead they stopped their bus at the luxurious Vaucluse home of Brian Power, a top executive of media multi-millionaire Kerry Packer. There all but a few players signed contracts that bound them to the World Rugby Corporation. The WRC planned to start a world competition in four months, on November 22. Packer's media empire, the All Blacks were told, was backing it. Not all the All Black party went into the house. Manager Colin Meads and coach Laurie Mains stayed on the bus and Mains eventually had to get them to leave to go to the dinner.

Phil Kearns, who made a dramatic speech to the Sydney crowd after the 1995 Bledisloe Cup match.

The test dinner in Sydney was fraught. WRC rumours were now everywhere. The New Zealand union had got Brian Lochore to deliver a letter with the union's offer, penned by Jock Hobbs and Rob Fisher, to the All Blacks' hotel. In 1995 Rob Fisher was the deputy chairman of the New Zealand union. He recalls, "[At the dinner] the players didn't exactly come up and say, 'Fantastic letter Rob, where do we sign?' It seemed to have sunk without trace, and we were pretty deflated. I certainly didn't feel like eating anything."

Fisher began in rugby with the Auckland University club, the club of All Black captain Sean Fitzpatrick. Fisher had managed the under-21 side when Fitzpatrick played in it. Their wives are friends, too. In conversation at the dinner in Sydney Fitzpatrick said he hoped they could all be friends, whatever happened. "I appreciated that, but it was a bad sign in terms of the negotiations."

The battle for the players, with Jock Hobbs the frontline trooper, assisted by the legendary Brian Lochore, was about to start. There was pressure from all sides. One former All Black stated, "These guys have to remember they don't own the bloody All Black jersey, they just have the right to wear it for a while."

The first real sign that the WRC idea was about to crumble came for the players on August 3, in a private televised linkup. In his book, *The Rugby War*, Peter FitzSimons detailed some highlights.

Sean Fitzpatrick, from the Auckland end of the line, said, "We are pleased to say that, in terms of the New Zealand position, we have 64 players signed up, which includes 23 of the World Cup squad that went to South Africa. It's not just the dollars that are enticing us… it is the whole concept of the WRC proposal which we like. Our position now is we've rolled our dice. We have said that we are into this and we are totally behind it, so at the moment we are feeling the pressure, probably as much as you guys are, but we want to make it work. One of our concerns is obviously the South Africans' position, and it was nice to speak to you on Monday Hennie [Le Roux], and be reassured. And I spoke to Francois [Pienaar] after I spoke to you, and he once again reassured me that you guys are totally behind it, which was nice to hear."

Phil Kearns said that the Australians had 60 players signed, sealed and delivered. He emphasised the players had to make sure that they stuck together.

In South Africa Le Roux apologised for Pienaar not being there. He told the New Zealand and Australians that Pienaar was under immense pressure, and was getting ready to face a couple of law suits. Le Roux said that the best contract on the day would be signed. Fitzpatrick asked if the South Africans had actually signed a contract. Le Roux replied that in principle they had signed. But it became increasingly obvious to the Australians and New Zealanders that Pienaar had backed down.

Within weeks of backing down from the WRC deal, Pienaar was driving a Ferrari, and it has been suggested by Luyt that Pienaar was given a million rand to backtrack and sign with the South African union. Within a week of the video conference, Kronfeld and Wilson had signed. But their battle was to do with their consciences rather than their bank balances.

Nevertheless, if Kronfeld and Wilson were the heroes of the day, not every veteran All Black was thrilled by it all. Zinzan Brooke said some months afterwards that he would think twice about helping out Wilson if he was at the bottom of a ruck. Brooke went into damage control later and said he had been just joking, but the rifts were not fully healed until the All Blacks won the test series in South Africa the following year.

Pro Rugby

Not Just Free Jerseys

The amateur days of the All Blacks were marked by some severe double standards.

Waka Nathan, one of the great All Black loose forwards, recalls the day his Auckland team set a Ranfurly Shield record in 1963. "We'd never got anything, but on that day Tom Pearce, who was the president of the Auckland union, came into the changing shed at Eden Park. He said how proud he was of us, and that to mark the occasion, we could all get our match jersey out of the gear bag and keep it. We all started scrambling for a dirty, sweaty jersey. All of us, guys who had played for New Zealand, guys who had good jobs, all trying to grab a jersey, because it was the only free thing we'd ever got."

In 1977 Grant Batty announced his retirement from rugby on the Thursday before a Saturday test against the Lions at Lancaster Park. His badly damaged knee had finally given out. On his return to Tauranga he received a letter from the team's manager saying how disappointed the manager was to find on Batty's expenses at the Russley Hotel drinks "allegedly ordered by you, and a charge for a meal for an additional person described as 'Batty's guest'. If these charges were in fact incurred by you I am both surprised and disappointed". Batty would point out that the drinks were for Andy Haden, Lawrie Knight and himself, and totalled $6. The guest was the local rugby union's liaison officer, and had cost $4.

It was the sort of penny-pinching that enraged many players, yet at the same time rugby officials could slip around some regulations when it suited.

In 1927, one of the game's legends, Bert Cooke, from the 1924 Invincibles tour to Britain, moved from Napier to Masterton, to a partnership in a fabric shop. His share of the partnership, £600, was provided by the Wairarapa Rugby Union.

Because most players saw, if they were lucky, more free jerseys than cash for a business, it was remarkably easy, in 1977 for a group including Auckland broadcaster Tim Bickerstaff, former All Black Joe Karam, and promoter Lew Pryme, to sign up a group of players for a potential professional troupe.

The first man on the books was Sid Going, who with his brothers Ken and Brian, signed a $3000 contract in a Whangarei motel room. In a couple of weeks they also had in the bag Ian Kirkpatrick, Alex Wyllie, and Keith Murdoch, who had not played the game since he was sent home from the tour of Britain.

Sid Going – first man on the books back in 1977.

The idea of a professional rugby circus died when a British promoter couldn't deliver northern hemisphere players, and Danie Craven, then the king of South African rugby, dithered over a chance to beat anti-apartheid bans with professionals. Eventually Craven stuck with the status quo, and the scheme was over.

It's in the Book

In their playing days Waka Nathan or Grant Batty would never have imagined the way the 1999 All Blacks operate.

Today the All Blacks fly business class and stay in four-star hotels. They have a sponsorship manager to deal with all commercial activities. They have a public relations advisor to help them deal with the media. They have a doctor and a physiotherapist to deal with injuries and illnesses. They have a fitness expert to help with training. And they have a coach, an assistant coach and a technical advisor to deal with actually playing the game.

When they toured Britain at the end of 1997, all the players received a manual, detailing where they would be on every day during the tour, and what they would be doing. In 1998, before the Tri-Nations, the players were issued a brochure that not only listed assembly and travel times, but had a photo of every hotel they would stay in, with a description of the facilities available.

Such details are a reflection of the attitudes of All Black coach, John Hart, a former leading executive at the head office of Fletcher Challenge in Auckland, and manager Mike Banks, who runs several hotels in the Manawatu and Wanganui.

One concern, with the money and the lifestyle that goes with it, is that the All Blacks will lose sight of the traditions that make the All Blacks so special. A little publicised move in that direction is the mentor scheme. Coach Hart asked past All Blacks to make themselves available to players, who could talk with a mentor privately on whatever topic the player chose. Some players haven't bothered. But North Harbour halfback Mark Robinson keeps in regular touch with Dave Loveridge, a great All Black halfback from 15 years ago, who has spent most of the time since pig farming near Inglewood.

Also on the All Black programme have been efforts to help the players deal with having so much money at such a young age. To some, the move to professionalism has seeds of destruction in it. A new generation of players has done nothing but play football for a living, and the effects of that life on a personal level can be dangerous. David Kirk, winning All Black captain at the first World Cup, is one of many who thinks there is no reason why the modern All Black shouldn't have a job, or be studying, as well as playing rugby.

Pro Rugby

The World Cup

The All Blacks set the 1987 World Cup alight from the first game at Eden Park, when John Kirwan ran almost the length of the field to score against Italy. Their campaign culminated in the final against France, when the team not only won the title, but united the country.

Just the year before, when the rebel Cavaliers went to South Africa, they were captained by Andy Dalton. David Kirk led the All Blacks while Dalton was away. Getting the two factions together wasn't easy. Kirk recalls being reduced to tears by the attitude of some Cavaliers when they toured to France together in 1986.

Dalton was originally selected as the World Cup squad captain. But he was injured in training before the tournament started, and did not play a single game. It was Dalton, the Cavaliers kingpin, who Kirk called to join him when the Webb Ellis Trophy was handed over at Eden Park.

To get the Cup off the ground at all was a battle in which New Zealand, Australia and France fought for the tournament, Ireland and Scotland fought against it, and England and Wales floated somewhere in the middle.

In January, 1985 New Zealand's Dick Littlejohn, from Whakatane, and Australia's Sir Nicholas Shehadie, from Sydney, went to Britain to try to persuade the Home Unions and France that the World Cup would be good for the game.

When they arrived in London there was nobody from the English union to meet them at the airport, and no messages at the hotel. They called journalists, and the story was broken in the pages of the *Daily Mail*.

Andy Dalton (left) and Brian Lochore leave Rugby Union headquarters in Wellington in 1985 after learning that the All Black tour of South Africa had been called off. The cancelled tour led to the formation of the rebel Cavaliers.

At that point the secretary of the English union, Bob Weighill, got in touch, and they were off to see the Irish, the Welsh and the Scots, but not the English.

At 10.30am on March 21, 1985, in Paris, the 16 members of the International Rugby Board began discussing the World Cup. Finally, at 3.50pm they voted. Ten were in favour, and six against. The World Cup was a reality.

With just two years to get ready, Australia and New Zealand had to scramble. The sponsor, a Japanese telecommunications firm called

Legends of the All Blacks

KDD, came in at the last minute, although most fans never really knew, or cared, what KDD stood for.

But the public interest was startling, especially in New Zealand. Would people in Palmerston North turn out to see Wales play Tonga? Certainly. In fact 19,000 were at the Showgrounds for that pool game.

By the time of the final at Eden Park, the country was going wild. The All Blacks played superb rugby throughout the competition. Coach Lochore dealt with John Hart and Alex Wyllie being his assistants by having only one at a time help him with the training. And there were stars by the score – Kirwan, Michael Jones, in his first matches as an All Black, Buck Shelford, John Gallagher and Grant Fox.

The All Blacks responded to the call with world-class performances, and for the next two years were the dominant team in world rugby.

The next World Cup, in Great Britain, Ireland and France in 1991, was different. As the All Blacks stumbled during the season, it was decided by the New Zealand union's council, headed by Wellington businessman Eddie Tonks, to share the coaching duties between Wyllie and Hart. It was a decision that always seemed likely to fail.

As well as the coaches not getting on, the players had got lazy and arrogant. Money was part of the problem. The players thought that the game owned them a living, and their greed got out of control. In a hospitality tent on the day of the final at Twickenham, a senior All Black, invited in briefly for a drink, grabbed bottles of wine and stuffed them into his duffel bag.

For the All Blacks, the chance to retain the Cup ground to a halt in Dublin, when the Wallabies, who eventually won the competition, beat them with some typical David Campese genius.

The fallout from the 1991 World Cup was swift and brutal. John Hart challenged for the coach's job and was beaten by Laurie Mains. Mains immediately dumped the 1991 captain, Gary Whetton.

After three years of mixed results Mains had it all right by the time the All Blacks arrived in South Africa for the 1995 Cup. They swept through the pool games, and Jonah Lomu in three weeks became the most internationally recognised rugby player in the history of the game. His amazing game against England in the semi-final was mentioned on the front page of *The Times* in London, dominated the front of the sports section, and spurred an editorial which compared him to Pele and Muhammad Ali. There was even a story in the financial pages of that edition, speculating how much money he could earn in endorsements.

The bitter end was the final, lost to South Africa, after two-thirds of the All Blacks had been stricken with a violent stomach disorder. Some claimed they were poisoned, others said it was a virus, but the result stayed the same: a 15-12 loss after extra time. The next conflict would be over who was to sign up the brand new professionals.

Pro Rugby

John Leslie – former Otago linchpin, now strutting his stuff for Scotland.

The Rugby Planet

The captain of the Japan team in 1999 is the son of a famous All Black, a ginger-headed, freckled product of Canterbury, Andrew McCormick. He's been in Japan since 1993, one of more than 35 New Zealanders playing there. Unlike his father, Fergie, McCormick was never an All Black, but there are six players who were, and at least one, Graeme Bachop, would probably still be a first-line player if he was living in New Zealand.

New Zealand's Japanese connection won't be the only New Zealanders striving for another country at the World Cup. Some former All Blacks will be coaching. Warren Gatland is in charge of the Irish squad; John Mitchell is assistant coach of England; Graham Henry will coach Wales. Shane Howarth is playing for Wales. There will be other New Zealanders playing, the Leslie brothers and Glen Metcalfe for Scotland, Ross Nesdale for Ireland.

New Zealand rugby players and coaches have become to our export trade at the end of the century what chilled lamb was at the start of it. There was a time when our All Blacks went overseas only to play for their country, but for almost 30 years there's been a roaring trade in New Zealand players going overseas to play, and – long before open professionalism – for good money too.

The French have always had an open-minded attitude to paying players, so much so that only the Second World War saved them from being booted out of the Five Nations championship by British officials offended by breaches of amateurism.

By 1973 prop Sandy McNicol was settled into the Tarbes club, as one of the first All Blacks to play in France, having just toured with Ian

Legends of the All Blacks

Kirkpatrick's All Blacks. Another of the early players there was Murray Mexted, who went through the 1977-78 winter in Agen, driving a cheese truck and playing rugby. In his book, *Pieces of Eight*, Mexted suggested he earned $2000 a month, as well as getting all his meals and accommodation paid for.

From France it was a short step to Italy, where, like France, clubs had wealthy patrons who provided ample cash to pay for imports. Craig Green went to Italy straight after the 1987 World Cup, and stayed for six years. He adapted so well he even answered to the name Tony, because Italians struggled to pronounce Craig. Dozens of high-profile All Blacks, including John Kirwan, spent time in Italy where, it was suggested, they were not living merely to sample the pasta and red wine.

John Kirwan

The exodus to Japan began in the 1980s with Marty Brooke, Zinzan and Robin's older brother, and Steve Miln from the Bay of Plenty. New Zealand officials saw Japan as a major area of concern, especially with professionalism. There is no reason why a Japanese team could not play in the World Cup with the bulk, or even all, of the side born in New Zealand.

In Japan, players like Graeme Bachop are reputed to be on over $NZ300,000 a year for about 12 competition games a season. In Great Britain and Ireland, the best players can command the same when exchange rates come into the picture, and the level of rugby is not as demanding as the Super 12, or even first division NPC.

No wonder players are flocking there, as did Auckland coach Graham Henry during 1998. Henry's departure drew a kneejerk reaction from the New Zealand union, which passed a rule that coaches who take another national team can never coach the All Blacks. There's also a rule that players cannot be selected for the All Blacks if they're not playing and living in New Zealand. The next big step of the professional era may be a change in that law. Put very simply, there may not be enough talent in New Zealand rugby to allow top players to go away, and be lost forever to the All Blacks.

Like the Brazilian soccer team, most of whom don't play club football in their native country, to keep the All Blacks at the top of the world game may need a radical change, so that the best players are considered for selection, regardless of where they live.

Pro Rugby – The Quinn Tapes

Eric Tindill
All Black first five-eighth on the 1935-36 tour of Great Britain.

During the 1935-36 All Black tour of Britain, we players were entitled to three shillings a day, but not in cash, only vouchers that had to be spent at the hotel we were staying in. So if you didn't drink and the hotel didn't sell things like razor blades or hair oil, you were at a loss to spend the vouchers. But we didn't need much money. We were taken everywhere – on trips around the countryside and to dinners and other functions in the evenings.

Most clubs back home had done a lot of fund-raising for their players. Athletic raised about 45 pounds for me, which was a huge amount then. In fact, I bought a canteen of cutlery out of that and had plenty of money to spare. So money was no object to us. When you think of what players get today, I'm not too sure, but it's rather farcical what they get paid now.

When I toured England with the New Zealand cricket team in 1937, we got eight shillings a day in cash. And we were playing six days out of seven, Sundays off. We were playing until at least six o'clock and every third day would travel to the next venue, so there wasn't much opportunity for spending money. We didn't really need much, because we were tired. I was the only wicketkeeper in the team and, of course, I was very tired long before the tour finished.

Waka Nathan
was an All Black flanker from 1962-67.

I didn't suffer too much hardship because I wasn't married at the time. I was a freezing worker and didn't get paid, but my club, Otahuhu, raised money for me and the Otahuhu district – the soccer and rugby league clubs and so on – all came to the party for both me and Mac Herewini, who was from the same club. So it was a district thing.

Neil Thimbleby
All Black prop in South Africa in 1970.

I was working on the Napier wharf when I made the All Blacks. I used to sometimes list my occupation as "cargo-ologist". The wharfies, who were a great bunch of guys, had a collection for me and looked after me, plus they put pressure on the bosses who paid me a small but guaranteed wage while I was away. It was enough to help mother and the three kids back home.

Blair Furlong
All Black utility back in South Africa in 1970.

I was in a more fortunate position than some of my team-mates when I made the All Blacks. My employer at the time paid me while I was away, and there was other assistance as well, with fund-raising activities at the club and by various other people. There would be raffles, the Calcutta-type thing, the pig-in-a-barrow fund-raising evenings, support from the business community. We were well treated by the locals in Hawke's Bay. The local bakery gave us the bread until the bread-winner came home. And, of course, we got 1.50 Rand a day, which was much bigger money back then.

Ian MacRae
All Black second five-eighth in South Africa in 1970.

I was under financial hardship when I was in the All Blacks. A lot of us were on the breadline. There was no extra money, and if you had mortgages at home, it was pretty hard to keep up the payments.

Legends of the All Blacks

Lurks and Perks

Andy Haden
was an All Black lock from 1972-85.

I learnt over four and a half months [during the 1972-73 All Black tour of Great Britain and France] that a dollar fifty a day is not a lot to live on – 75 paltry English pence. We found we could not send a stamped envelope home, buy a beer and buy a razor blade on the same day. You had to alternate between the three and I didn't write a lot.

KQ: How did you become known as the Minister of Lurks and Perks?

During the Jack Gleeson era, we had a committee to look after the commercial side of the team. A lot of players were touring under hardship. I could see that it was terribly unfair, so we did what we could during tours – got into all sorts of mischief, writing articles for papers and putting the money in the team fund, selling guest tickets. The Lurks and Perks Committee tried to outdo the tour before, raising more money in all sorts of ingenious ways. I became involved in all that shop steward type activity. Strangely, I wasn't one of the players terribly affected by the financial situation. I used to get by quite easily, but could see team-mates having problems with families at home, and jobs and so on. There wasn't a player in the teams of those days who didn't say to me, "Get into them.". I got a huge amount of encouragement to keep going down that track.

I enjoyed needling and cajoling administrators into trying to recognise that the game was professional in everything other than its payment to players. I think the Rugby Union would dearly have loved me to break a leg and not be able to play any longer. It put pressure on me to play better to keep getting selected. I was lucky there wasn't a great depth of talent in my position, maybe three or four contenders, not like the loosies where there were thirty or forty in contention.

We tried to make ends meet by selling the small allocation of tickets we got. It was frowned on by the Rugby Union, the RFU and the IRB. One day I was delegated for a certain match to be outside the main gates selling tickets. The secretary of the Irish Rugby Union came up to me to buy a ticket for a friend. I didn't recognise him. Just before kick-off I sat in my seat, which was one removed from the secretary of the Irish Rugby Union. I looked along and winced.

Players in our team could opt out of the team fund and take their two match tickets – maybe they had family or friends joining the tour. But as there was a scarcity of tickets, they had to pay £100 a ticket if they wanted more. Eric Watson met Miss New Zealand at a function once and she asked him for two tickets. When it came time for the divvy of the fund at the end of the tour, Eric's share was less two tickets for Miss New Zealand at £100 a ticket. Eric was mortified, but they were the rules. It was a pity the pressure for tickets was applied by administrators who had rows of seats, up one side of the stand and down the other.

Andy Haden – drive for show, putt for dough.

Pro Rugby – The Quinn Tapes

Sid Going
All Black halfback from 1967-77.

I was about ready to retire in 1974. I got dropped, went from being the best to not even given a trial, and that hurt. Then JJ Stewart helped me come back into it. He wanted me to go to Ireland, which turned out to be one of my favourite tours. He got someone to come and help me on my farm while I was away by milking my cows, and by helping my wife. It wasn't easy in those days, for me, or for my wife when I was away.

Billy Bush
All Black prop from 1974-79.

Before the 1978 tour to Britain, John Ashworth and I were on the dole. Nobody wanted us. I used to think, "Here I am playing for my country and I've got no money, or even a job." I used to go diving around the Peninsula in Christchurch to collect a few mussels and sea eggs and raffle them in the pub. That's really all the money that I ever had to spend.

Graham Mourie
All Black captain 1976-82.

KQ: Did lack of money ever force you to make yourself unavailable for the All Blacks?

In 1980, Andy Dalton and I both made ourselves unavailable for the tour of Australia because we did not have enough money to tour. We had both purchased farms and couldn't afford to pay someone a couple of hundred dollars a week to look after the farm. Neither of us were offered assistance, or even had any discussions about it.

Graham Mourie

Legends of the All Blacks

The Cavaliers

Andy Dalton
captained the All Blacks from 1981-85 and was one of the organisers of the 1986 Cavaliers tour to South Africa.

The money was no motivation whatsoever for the Cavaliers tour. It was a lifelong ambition to tour South Africa. There was a good team fund and we were paid an allowance in excess of what we should have been given – there was an official donation for the tour – but the motivation was not money.

Gary Whetton
All Black lock from 1981-91.

There wasn't a lot of money involved. We weren't going for that reason. We were subsidised. We had a touring fund etc. You didn't see any guys coming back who had made it. Most of them were just covered. Most of them had to leave work. A lot gave up their careers, their jobs, just to go. The money wasn't a huge factor.

Andy Haden
Cavaliers tour organiser.

KQ: What about the financial arrangements for the tour?

There was enough money to say they weren't going to enter hardship. It was not run along the lines of previous All Black tours. This time it was better than a subsistence relationship. The South Africans had got us a sponsor and we got far more match tickets than ever before.

Financially, it was well worth the players' going on the trip. I got exactly the same as every other player. That's one of the anomalies today, where some players are paid exorbitantly large amounts more than others, and in many cases don't deserve to be. It's incorrect to say the players received a hundred thousand dollars, but there was certainly a payment made to players. The team fund mounted to maybe $50,000 a player, about four or five times what it had been on previous tours.

David Kirk
All Black halfback from 1983-87, turned down an invitation to tour with the Cavaliers.

I don't know for sure how much the Cavaliers were paid. I know I was offered about a hundred thousand dollars. I notice when they talk about how the money was structured, it was a team fund. I have no specific knowledge about the payments, but it is pretty common knowledge that a significant amount of money accrued to the players on the tour.

Louis Luyt
was president of the Transvaal Rugby Union, which was heavily involved in organising the Cavaliers tour.

Dr Craven knew about the Cavaliers tour. They [the South African board] all knew about it. They agreed to bring in the Cavaliers. They had to sanction it. You can't just bring in the All Blacks and play. They were going to play as the All Blacks and we were going to play against them on rugby fields, so somebody sanctioned it. They all knew about it.

We definitely regarded the Cavaliers as the All Blacks. Your scrumhalf, Kirk, signed to come. John Kirwan would have come but his father fell ill and he had to come back to New Zealand. So really, I couldn't think of any stronger players in New Zealand. They were a tremendous side. That was New Zealand.

We didn't pay them. We had no negotiation for payment. We treated them very well. We paid the costs like normal. I have no other idea what went on because we took over the tour. There was no payment from us; we invited auditors to come in and investigate and they couldn't find anything. We didn't pay them. That's my word of honour.

Pro Rugby – The Quinn Tapes

Playing for Keep$

Peter FitzSimons
is a former Wallaby lock who is now a Sydney-based journalist.

I had a sneaking realisation in 1989. I remember being at the Sydney Football Stadium and there were forty thousand people watching. I knew my mum and dad were there, singing the national anthem. They'd paid sixty-five dollars a pop for tickets. And as we sang *Advance Australia Fair*, I thought, "There's 2.4 million dollars worth of people here today. That's funny: I'm getting thirty-six dollars fifty a day."

Geoff Levy
a South African-born Australian, was a lawyer for WRC.

In Australia, it was well-known that there were a few players getting very large amounts to keep them out of rugby league. It was done in all kinds of circuitous ways. New Zealand was semi-professional at that stage, with all kinds of trusts and things, but there was very much a case of haves and have-nots, which created a lot of internal problems.

Louis Luyt
was president of the South African Rugby Football Union in the 1990s

Rugby was forced to go professional for several reasons. Rugby league was the greatest threat because our best players were going to league. At the time there was a terrible fight between Super League and the Australian Rugby League and they were luring great players away from union. The only way to fight this was to give some incentive to the players.

I confronted everybody at an IRB meeting. I started with England and asked if they'd ever paid their players. They said they hadn't, but that they gave money to trust funds which they admitted went to players. It went around the table. Only

Louis Luyt

Argentina didn't pay a cent. They were the only ones. So I asked who were we fooling. It turned out we were all paying under the table anyhow. I learned that Timu, the All Black fullback and wing, was on eighty or one hundred thousand dollars a year through various means. So it wasn't strange to me. Another thing: when I had the Maoris out here in 1994 to play, they asked me where the boot money was. The expression "boot money" came from England, where they used to put money in boots. I couldn't believe it when I heard the Maoris using this expression. They must have had payments somewhere because where did they learn about boot money? The Samoans were the same. So there were some payments somewhere.

Legends of the All Blacks

Playing for Keep$

Richie Guy
New Zealand Rugby Football Union council chairman from 1995-96.

Rugby should have gone professional back in the 1950s or '60s. It could then have been a gradual process, whereas really it was dragged kicking and screaming into the 20th century almost at the end.

Rugby had been under threat for a number of years. Any game that's living in the past and working in an amateur situation when the players are producing a high-quality product has to be under threat. The opportunity was there for any entrepreneur to sign up all the players, and take them away from the established game.

Eddie Tonks
chairman of the New Zealand Rugby Union from 1990-95.

The lead-up to rugby going professional took about two years prior to the SANZAR deal, and a lot of work was done by me representing New Zealand rugby at IRB level. By 1995 we'd got a lot of people on side, so we knew there was a general acceptance at IRB level for a transformation to the professional level. It had been a lot of hard, tedious work, not only by me, but by many of the other councillors as well.

The hypocrisy was what had really got to me. For the World Cup in South Africa, there were prizemonies offered by individual unions and we knew that. We did it, too! There was criticism of us by the English particularly, but they were doing it as well. They were paying our players to entice them over there.

Richie Guy

Only a couple of weeks after I was appointed chairman [of the NZRFU] in 1995, the first real threat came when Super League started up in opposition to the ARL in Australia. That immediately put extra pressure on us. We'd been living in a shamateurism era. There'd been some payment to players, but it wasn't great and the amount of money being offered by Super League put most of the All Blacks under a great deal of pressure. We were in danger of losing them, so that was really the start of the change to what we might call full professionalism. France and Japan had been there for some time, but the amount of money they were offering was nothing like the money being offered by Super League.

Sean Fitzpatrick
All Black captain from 1992-97.

I first heard about the move to professionalism before we went to the final World Cup dinner in 1995. Richie Guy told me that they'd signed a deal with Rupert Murdoch and were going to pay the players "x" amount of dollars. I thought that was great. Then Hennie le Roux asked me at the dinner if I'd heard about this new professional rugby. He said they were going to earn "x" amount a year and it was three or four times what Richie Guy had told me. I walked away not realising Hennie was talking about WRC. The next day we met Ross Turnbull [WRC organiser] and that was the start of it all – the two options.

Ross Turnbull
a Wallaby who helped design the WRC concept.

I met with several New Zealand players immediately after the World Cup and couldn't help but be impressed with the calibre of men I was dealing with, their style and character. They were highly-organised, asked the proper questions and when they were satisfied, they signed the contracts. South Africa and New Zealand were superb to deal with. Australia were difficult – they didn't have the same organisation. England were all over the shop, Scotland and Wales were great, and Ireland, well they were good guys, but they held their meetings in a pub!

Sean Fitzpatrick

When we went to play the Bledisloe Cup match in Australia, it was a very heated time. There was Phil Kearns at the ground saying that maybe that would be his last game of rugby as we knew it. Then at the dinner there was the chairman of the Australian Rugby Union bashing the traditionalists' hat on the table, so it was a strange time.

Richie Guy

The WRC surfaced at just about the time of the 1995 World Cup, about a month or so after the original Super League threat. When Super League started up, I spoke to several of the experienced players individually and asked for an idea of how much money would be needed to retain the All Blacks as an identity. They came up with roughly the same amount of money – they said $150,000 a year would keep them away from Super League. Of course, WRC then came up with much bigger numbers than that and that's what set the trend for today's salary standards.

•

Upon hearing that the players wanted $150,000 each to stay away from Super League, it became clear we had to get more money. We started to think about how to generate that income. Obviously in a country of three and a half million people it's very hard to generate sufficient funds within our shores to deal with international predators. So we looked at possible targets and obviously the major international television companies were prime targets. First we designed the competition that developed into the Super 12. There were a number of differing versions of that and the New Zealand, Australian and South African unions were in contact discussing them. We organised a meeting at Sydney, where we discussed the proposals. At the same time there were also players getting into the act, wanting to promote different competitions, too. After our meeting in Sydney we met with News Corp in Australia, seeking a meeting with Rupert Murdoch's Head of Television, Sam Chisholm. Then we went off to London prior to the World Cup to meet Chisholm.

All our meetings were taking place in camera, but no matter what we did every move was covered by the media. Everybody seemed to know what we were doing. Supposedly very few people knew we were going to meet News Corp in Australia, but it was on the television news that night in Australia. In London, the meeting with Chisholm was supposed to be top secret, but we were photographed on the footpath outside his apartment when we came out of the meeting. Everyone seemed in the know.

Sam Chisholm

•

When we first met Sam Chisholm, and put to him a proposal that has evolved into the Super 12 and Tri-Nations, he said he wished to deal with only one person, which was sensible.

Louis Luyt was the logical choice to represent us. At that time the Southern Alliance – New Zealand, Australia, Argentina and South Africa – held meetings every couple of years and the host country provided the chairman of that meeting. After meeting Chisholm in London, we travelled to South Africa, where Louis chaired the meeting. With his business skills and experience, he was the ideal person to negotiate with Sam Chisholm.

Legends of the All Blacks

Playing for Keep$

Louis Luyt

Sam Chisholm, a New Zealander who lives in Australia, wanted to show me he could call the shots. He was very high up in the Murdoch organisation. During the World Cup – the Sunday when Wales played Ireland at Ellis Park and I was the host for the game – I got a call that Murdoch was in London and wanted to do a deal. I was to be in London by Monday. So I had to make all sorts of excuses. I couldn't tell the Five Nations people where I was going. I went off that Sunday night to arrive in London on Monday morning and went straight to Sam's apartment and into negotiations. Ian Frykberg knew what we wanted and we knew what Sam Chisholm was willing to pay. Sam made me the offer and I opted for a few million more because I wanted to have the final say. He said, "Shake," and we had a deal. That same night I came straight back. No-one knew where I'd been, except I had to tell Richie Guy and Leo Williams because they were my partners in this. I told them we'd signed a deal. The Friday before the final, it was announced.

Geoff Levy

The only time we [WRC] spoke to or started to sign players was after their World Cup commitments.

•

The SANZAR deal didn't seem so great. It seemed like they'd sold out rugby very cheaply, based on what we'd worked out to be the value of the amounts that could be made from television. It seems that the Murdoch organisation has more than recouped its investment by on-selling the coverage in various countries.

Richie Guy

We were very nervous because although News Corp possibly didn't know it, there weren't any other bidders, so we were dealing with one company that was really interested in the product. We had to deal with News Corp the best we could, providing the deal was satisfactory. So it was a nervous time for us, especially when Louis Luyt went back to London to negotiate with Sam Chisholm. We were very satisfied with the deal that was finally struck. We could see our way clear to retain the players. We knew we could see off Super League with the type of money we now had. But we didn't know at that point what WRC was offering. We'd taken the first step: getting the money. The next was to re-sign the players because their contracts ran out at the end of the World Cup.

•

The day after the World Cup final, we met the players and I told them we had secured the money and that we would be able to offer them salaries commensurate with the $150,000 per annum they'd been talking about. It was pretty clear to me then, although nobody said anything, that something was going on because they didn't all rush up and say, "We'll sign now." In hindsight, when we first talked to them, we should have tried to contract them subject to us getting the money. That's what WRC did. I didn't think anyone would sign a contract without any money, but the players did that with WRC. The promise of money was enough.

Francois Pienaar
Springbok captain in 1995.

I spoke to Fitzpatrick, Kearns and Carling and told them I was definitely going ahead with it [WRC], but I said it wasn't up to me, it was up to the guys. I was just the spokesman for the team. Then I was asked to become an agent and said I would. I'd already signed up the guys.

Geoff Levy

We signed the All Blacks in Wellington. I was picked up by Andy Haden and we drove to a motel where he'd arranged a big room for us. A chap named Derek Dallow, a solicitor for the players, was there.

Pro Rugby – The Quinn Tapes

They all sat down, all dressed in their full black blazers and trousers. Jonah Lomu was there, walking behind the rest of them with his earphones on. They sat down and looked bored – "What the hell are we doing here?"

So I gave them my story, my vision [for WRC]. A few heads lifted, then more. Eventually I opened up to questions and there were some very pointed questions from the coach [Laurie Mains] and various players. Fortunately we had the answers. We'd done a lot of research and were really with it. I saw Jonah taking off his headphones and thought, "Now we have their attention." We said that from there we wanted to go forward and negotiate contracts, but that they had to sign confidentiality agreements. To a man they did.

Jonah Lomu
was New Zealand rugby's superstar in 1995.

I was sceptical in lots of ways. We would have been giving up a fair bit of history with the All Blacks. A lot of people didn't know that I was the only one in that room who didn't sign on the dotted line. I was sitting down the back listening to my Walkman, but I took things in. I just didn't want to leave New Zealand. I had a lot of things I hadn't achieved and more I wanted to do in that black jersey. There was unfinished business. Sure, there was crazy money in it, but at the end of the day you have to be happy in what you do. I was glad everything was sorted out and we carried on for the All Blacks.

Geoff Levy

We discovered that the [All Black] players had been talking to News [Corp] and got very concerned. On the Friday before the Bledisloe Cup game in Sydney I spoke to some of the senior players in the team, about six of them. I wanted an assurance from them. After the Bledisloe Cup, they were going to a big dinner party and I was nervous that there was going to be a statement there like, "If anyone signs…" Now it was out [news of the WRC bid] everyone was talking about it. Their lawyers had gone to News to see if they could broker a better deal for the boys. So I said to these senior players that I wanted assurances. They said, "You've got our assurances." I said, "You have to sign a guarantee." And they said, "Look, we're giving you our word as All Blacks. If it's good enough for us, it should be good enough for you." I said, "Unfortunately, my background is that when you've written your word, it's good enough for me. Words not written on paper are not worth anything."

So they eventually agreed they would sign before the dinner. I left there feeling I'd take these guys' words. It was a very sincere discussion, very passionate.

We decided to take them to the house of Brian Power, who was chairman of the Packer Group organisation and Channel Nine, so they would see there was a genuine involvement with that organisation.

They came in off the bus, leaving some of their coaching staff on the bus. They went downstairs into a large room where they met with their lawyers. None of

Jonah Lomu

Legends of the All Blacks

Playing for Keep$

us went down. We stayed upstairs until we were asked to come down. Then they said, "Here are the contracts." They'd nearly all been signed. There were one or two who hadn't signed because they needed one or two clauses sorted out. There was one guy whose agent wanted a lot more money, so we had to reconsider that. He was an international star of high repute. Other than that, everyone signed, and they went off to the dinner.

•

Jonah's agents had asked for extra money and there were lots of negotiations. Whether he came in with us or not, you'll have to ask him because I'm still bound by a confidentiality clause.

Jonah Lomu

I just wasn't interested in negotiating with them [WRC]. The money they were offering was on the table, but I wanted to stay with the New Zealand Rugby Union and play rugby in New Zealand.

Louis Luyt

We initially didn't know we were fighting against Turnbull's WRC group. When we discovered how serious the situation was, that our players had signed up, Chisholm nearly blew a fuse at his home in Sydney. He jumped up and down like a jack in the box, telling us what we had to do, shouting and screaming, ranting and raving. I tried to get him to calm down and then I called Francois Pienaar and told him to get the players together at my home the following Sunday.

When I got there I said to the players, "Look, we'll match whatever you have been offered." They opted to stay [with the South African union, instead of joining WRC], much to the disgust of Sean Fitzpatrick and the rest of the New Zealanders and Australians. As soon as Francois Pienaar said yes [to what Luyt was offering], the deal [with WRC] was gone. At the time of the famous satellite link-up with Australia and New Zealand, Francois never appeared. He was committed to me by then, so Hennie le Roux appeared on the link up. I think that killed WRC.

I told the players they would be betraying their countries if they went somewhere else. At that time every youngster in South Africa was looking up to the Springboks, who were world champions. And here they were deserting their country. I said that we weren't willing to watch that and asked what it would take to make them stay. It didn't take much for them to decide. They asked me to give them a few minutes and half an hour later they came back. Francois Pienaar did all the talking and said they would stay. At that stage I had his guarantee, but nothing had been signed. Australia and New Zealand were very relieved when I phoned them eventually to say the Springboks had signed. The next day Australia's players started to sign too, and then the New Zealanders followed.

Jock Hobbs
former All Black captain who negotiated for the New Zealand union.

One of the most dramatic moments of the whole affair came in Sydney during the first week. There was to be a meeting held in the evening with the All Black lawyers. This was later in the day after we'd all met with Sam Chisholm. But the lawyers didn't turn up to that meeting and I didn't get a call from them until much later in the night. Then one of the lawyers apologised to me over the phone for not making the meeting and said he had to advise me he could no longer meet with me, or offer any further help. I asked him where we [the NZRFU] sat and he said, "Well, as we came to Sydney I think you had a finger in the window frame. Now it's a finger nail." He was talking about the All Black players.

•

In my first week working for the New Zealand Rugby Union [as rugby went professional] I met with the All Blacks and All Black lawyers, and worked on budgets and contracts, went to Australia and met with News

Pro Rugby - The Quinn Tapes

Jock Hobbs

Corp representatives. I was then able to report back to the union's council which held an emergency meeting at our hotel in Sydney. The enormity of what the union was facing was obvious to me and at that meeting I tried to communicate that by saying that I sincerely believed that this might well be the last meeting of any significance of the New Zealand Rugby Union council.

There were lots of issues – league, Super League, the WRC, Japan. Heading the list was WRC and I was given an extraordinarily wide brief: basically do what needs to be done.

The first thing to do was to meet with the players. We made a short presentation acknowledging that there may have been some mistakes in the past, that we were going to make a fresh beginning. They didn't want to see us for a week because it was building towards the Bledisloe Cup match in Sydney, so I asked the players that they not change the status quo before we could come back to them. I said I believed we would impress them with what we were going to offer them for the future. So that was a big part: just to try to hold the situation and not let it get any worse. Then we had meetings with the lawyers for the All Blacks to try to get more information. I went with two All Black lawyers to Sydney to meet Sam Chisholm from News Corp. That was a very exciting and entertaining meeting. The All Blacks had expressed concern about the real intentions of News Corp, so that's why the meeting was arranged. Sam Chisholm is a very direct man. He was pleasant, but if he disagreed with anything, you were made well aware of it. At the end of the meeting he made it very, very plain to me that News Corp were not impressed.

He said that as far as he was concerned the deal was struck. They had been told all the leading players in the Southern Hemisphere were in. He said they weren't putting up these hundreds of millions of dollars to watch anything less than the very best. They were not accustomed to being embarrassed as they felt they were on a world stage. He told us to get the mess sorted out very quickly, otherwise the money would be lifted off the table. He said he would sue, that he would send a ▶

Legends of the All Blacks

Playing for Keep$

barrage of lawyers from his organisation, that he would bonk the New Zealand Rugby Football Union so deep it would take us a long time, if ever, to get our head out of the swamp. So after that meeting, when I went back to New Zealand, there was a lot that needed to be done in a very short time and there was the feeling that the World Rugby Corporation intended to launch the following week.

It was a very high-powered, tense situation. I think it is difficult for people to understand how serious the situation was and the potential damage. For example there was a lawyer who was involved with several players. He doesn't live in Wellington and he did a very good job. During the heat of the battle, as it were, after a very long night of negotiations, he told me he was standing in the shower later in the morning and he heard a very sharp loud crack, and he dived to the bottom of the shower with the first thought that someone had fired a shot at him.

Now I know that must sound absolutely incredible to people not involved, but at the time we were talking about two very powerful international businessmen, hundreds of millions of dollars, tiers of people who could potentially earn enormous sums of money through success fees. There was a lot involved. It's big business, a big game.

Through the rest of the week I was busy redrafting the contracts, trying to make everything more understandable. I tried to establish a budget, set categories for players and put together all those sorts of essential requirements.

KQ: *How much did you get paid for your work on behalf of the New Zealand union?*

Nothing. Not a cent. Not a cent in kind – nothing.

•

Kensington Swan were the lawyers for the New Zealand Rugby Football Union, so we decided to base ourselves there. We took over a board room which had a speaker phone we could negotiate on, a couch which I spent a bit of time on because there wasn't much time for going home to sleep, whiteboard with strategies that would be debated. We called it the War Room. It wasn't a war in the true sense of that word but it was a race that had a lot on it, and if you got second there were no prizes.

Richie Guy

Those days when Jock Hobbs was barnstorming up and down the country were very tense. We didn't know the players had signed with WRC or that WRC had also signed a number of provincial players. Had WRC come up with the money in the finish, they actually had the players. That's really the reason we were able to get the players back.

Jock Hobbs did a tremendous job for us. He left his work and did it fulltime for several weeks. He was a recent All Black captain, he was quite well respected by the players – he was an ideal person to do the job and he did it very well.

However, the real turning point was that WRC didn't have any money. If they'd come up with the money by a given date, then we'd have lost the players, no question. The players – including Kronfeld and Wilson – fitted into the same category. They were either all going to stay or all going to go. The reason they didn't go was because there was no money.

That's as plain as the nose on my face. If the money had been there, they had signed the contracts and they would have gone. They were entitled to do that, to peddle their wares to the highest bidder. Obviously I wanted the game to stay under the control of the New Zealand Rugby Union and the All Blacks to stay as they were. It's a tremendous tradition, but if the players had gone there would be little we could do about it.

Peter FitzSimons
former Wallaby and now a leading Australian sports writer.

It seemed at one time as if there were going to be two competitions, the establishment competition and the rebel one run by Ross Turnbull. It became obvious the Springboks held the key. They were world champions and if there were two competitions, if you didn't have the Springboks, you were kiddin'. So most of the pressure came right on the forehead of Mr Francois Pienaar [Springbok captain]. He was the linchpin and he had Louis Luyt on one side saying, "You do this or I'll wear your balls for ear-rings." And on the other hand he had the Turnbull people saying, "Matey, your contract here. You signed it. We have the documentation that you are with us, so don't tell us you're not."

It all came to a head with the video hook-up when Phil Kearns fronted in Australia, Sean Fitzpatrick in New Zealand, but no Francois Pienaar in South Africa. The South Africans never committed and that meant WRC had pretty much fallen over.

Ross Turnbull

We were all going down to the studio [in South Africa] and Francois was with us, plus James Small, the winger. I could see a discernible difference in Francois' demeanour. From being the enormously powerful, impressive man I had first seen, I now saw a guy who was scared, really frightened. I knew something had got to him. He said he wouldn't be coming down [to the studio] with me, that he would go with someone else. I knew then that whatever forces were out there had got to him, and I felt very sad for him. Those forces turned out to be money. The money came from Louis Luyt, but not his personal money. He'd got money from somewhere, perhaps the South African Rugby Union or television.

When I first met Francois Pienaar, I thought he was one of the most outstanding men I'd met. But I felt sorry for Francois because he was just a young sportsman and was under a lot of unnatural, unusual pressure from forces that he could not contend with. He had to renege on a deal that we'd not only shaken hands on, but that he'd signed. That's a problem he's going to have to face for the rest of his life.

Francois Pienaar

WRC collapsed because the South African players decided as a whole to sign with the South African Rugby Football Union. At our meeting, I explained to the players about the sureties and the pitfalls, and said it was their decision and that we had to go with what the majority decided. Then the bulk of the team signed with the South African union.

Phil Kearns
was the Wallaby captain in 1995.

Nearly all the Aussies except Timmy Gavin and Jason Little had signed [for WRC]. Then came the video hook-up. When Francois didn't front, the feeling of the rest of us in Australia and New Zealand was, "We've been sold out." Then a little while later Jeff Wilson and Josh Kronfeld signed for the New Zealand union, so that was the first chink in New Zealand's armour.

Jock Hobbs

The significant day in terms of turning the situation was when we signed fifty or sixty of New Zealand's leading provincial players, and also two All Blacks, Jeff Wilson and Josh Kronfeld. They were all very important because they were WRC targets and had been grappling with the decision about which party to align themselves with. We got a breakthrough at about three or four o'clock one morning. We needed to complete all the contractual arrangements and the details and that same day get those contracts out to the players, then back to Wellington. We wanted to have a press conference to announce this breakthrough because it was important ▶

Legends of the All Blacks

Playing for Keep$

Josh Kronfeld
All Black flanker from 1995-99.

KQ: Did you have any second thoughts about your decision to break ranks?

There wasn't a lot of pressure. Once I'd made my decision, I was happy. It was the most comfortable I'd felt in a long time.

A number of them [fellow All Blacks] weren't happy, but there was never any real malice. Richard Loe gave me a whole lot of grief when I roomed with him the following year, but he wasn't being vindictive. He was just being Loey. It was more amusing than anything. I wasn't the saviour of New Zealand rugby. Jeff [Wilson] and I were just the ones who started the ball rolling.

other players around the country, who were considering their situations, realised this breakthrough had occurred. So this was a very big day, but typical of the whole exercise… very little time to do it and get it out.

The Otago group were met at the airport with their contracts and on the way to Wellington we went through the process of signing them, so that when they arrived at Wellington airport just before the press conference, they were complete. But even going to that press conference, calls were coming in from around the country with issues. It was just before that press conference that I was handed confirmation that Wilson and Kronfeld would commit themselves to the New Zealand union. I think Kronfeld and Wilson got good advice. It was significant that their Otago team-mates were all signing with the New Zealand union, so they came as part of that. The negotiations with the Otago squad were separate to the discussions with Wilson and Kronfeld, but I'm sure it had some influence.

The next day was very significant, too. The tables had turned. I received a call from the All Black camp that they wanted to meet with me, and that was significant.

The first week was spent on a lot of preparatory work, the contracts, budgets, going to Sydney, finding out the situation, setting up strategies. The second week was the presentations around the country. The third week was a heavy negotiation week with the provincial players. At the end of that week, after signing this tier, the very important players, the table turned. On the Friday of that third week, I had a call from the All Black camp asking for a meeting. In the fourth week, there were discussions with individual All Blacks about their contracts. Some of those meetings were quite dramatic and emotional. I can think of one player who had tears in his eyes. Some of the players felt the situation intensely. It was new territory for the New Zealand union and the players. Some of the players had four or five different offers, lots and lots of money,

Pro Rugby – The Quinn Tapes

Jeff Wilson

All Black winger from 1993-99.

My biggest family was the Otago rugby side, the guys who'd given me my opportunity to be an All Black. They'd made a decision to go with the New Zealand union. Josh and I talked about it at length and wanted to support them as much as we possibly could. A lot of people talked about Josh and I signing, but the people in Otago were the catalysts. Josh and I had grown up wanting to be All Blacks and to sacrifice that for a competition that might or might not be successful... Everyone was always going to love the All Blacks, so we got to the point where we didn't want to jeopardise that.

and had never had to deal with that situation before. So there was a lot of pressure on them, as which way to jump or go.

Sean Fitzpatrick

The players were trying to do what was best for rugby, and what happened has been the result of what the players and the union were trying to achieve. I'm pleased that it all turned out the way it did. The union made a huge turnaround. In my early years in the All Blacks, it was them and us. But in the end, we couldn't have got on better with the union. It was a wonderful relationship.

When Jeff and Josh made their decision, that forced some people's hands. It was their decision, what they wanted, and it was great. We had said at the beginning that there was no way there could be two competitions and when they did that, it was obviously over for the WRC guys.

Jock Hobbs

KQ: *When the battle with WRC was all over, were the players grateful?*

If they were, it was not evident, no.

KQ: *Has any prominent All Black ever thanked you for what has come out of it? It was said you saved the All Blacks.*

No, but they may not have liked that because it implied they were doing something wrong. Also, they were on a particular course and wanted to see it to its end, and it wasn't, so there may have been some disappointment and frustration about that as well from the players' point of view.

Legends of the All Blacks

Playing for Keep$

I was very surprised to learn of a memo sent around councillors which I hadn't received, essentially seeking support and a resolution that the New Zealand union would enter into an arrangement with WRC. I was not very happy about that at all. I don't know whether I had deliberately been left out of the loop, but I do know that in the normal course of events, I wouldn't have heard about it until after a decision had been made. After learning about it, I made it very plain that if it [the resolution to seek an arrangement with WRC] was passed, I would finish. I would have resigned; that was the only course open to me.

Richie Guy

The concept of combining with WRC never really appealed to me. We had a fair bit of control over the grounds in New Zealand, so we could possibly have struck a deal with WRC, but really they were an entrepreneur attempting to hijack the professional arm of the game, so there wasn't room for both parties in the contest.

•

KQ: How close was the News Corp deal to being pulled out from under the New Zealand union?

So long as we retained the top players, there wasn't any chance, because we had a binding contract. But one of the clauses in the contract was that we had to provide top quality players and if we hadn't been able to, that would have been a reason for News Corp to withdraw from the deal. The players were crucial to the whole question.

Ross Turnbull

In the end, we decided not to create undue pressure in world rugby, because we were all rugby people. Once the settlement between the Australian and New Zealand unions and WRC took place, that was the catalyst to cease what we were about, even though our contracts outside those two countries were still in place.

Sean Fitzpatrick

The one thing WRC did wrong was that they didn't guarantee the money.

Jock Hobbs

KQ: What impact did those turbulent weeks of negotiation have on you?

Well, I haven't gone to very many rugby matches since, though I've attended some for work reasons. The whole exercise was quite draining and you need time away to fill up the reservoir again. There had also been some disappointments through the exercise. Besides the election of the NZRFU board [Hobbs, a sitting councillor missed a seat on the streamlined board], there were some events I found difficult to understand on a personal level. That's drained the cup to reasonably empty, but I'm sure it's a temporary thing.

Laurie Mains
All Black coach from 1992-95.

KQ: What's your understanding of why WRC folded?

At the end of the day, it was Packer who pulled the pin because of the arrangements he had made with Murdoch. I don't think any one person could possibly say they had a significant hand in it, other than Packer and Murdoch, though Louis Luyt was a huge deterrent to the Packer organisation – he was a very strong player. I had a ring from the WRC people the day before it collapsed and was told a deal had been reached between Murdoch and Packer. It was something to do with racing, and therefore Packer was withdrawing from this exercise. The Packer people didn't pull out because of signings with the New Zealand union or what was going on in South Africa. It was purely over Murdoch and Packer reaching a deal.

There was talk in New Zealand about Jeff Wilson

Pro Rugby – The Quinn Tapes

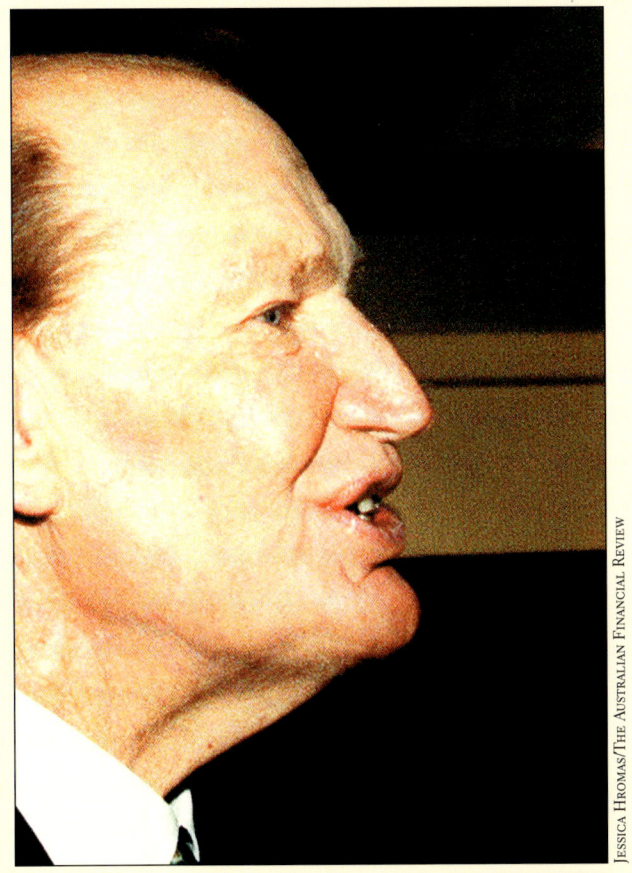 

The big players in the pro game – Kerry Packer (left) and Rupert Murdoch, who controlled the fate of world rugby.

and Josh Kronfeld signing with the New Zealand union and all that, but that wasn't significant. The deal that Packer and Murdoch did turned everything around.

Phil Gifford
New Zealand journalist.

If there was one person treated really badly in the wake of the whole professional issue, it was Jock Hobbs. They should have been erecting a statue of him in front of the new Wellington Stadium. Instead they wiped him out and kept dumping on the guy. If he doesn't feel bitter, he must be an extraordinarily saint-like person.

Jock Hobbs

A very powerful man, and a powerful international company, had committed a considerable amount of money – hundreds of millions of dollars over a 10-year period. This was a very, very big deal for rugby and it was there to fund professional rugby. Alongside that you had the league/Super League situation, which involved another big international player. So at the very highest level, there were big deals and lots and lots of money. So that's what was at stake at the highest level.

For me, apart from the threat of possible consequences from the highest level if we were not successful, I was more interested in the potential ▶

203

Legends of the All Blacks

Playing for Keep$

damage that might be caused to our game. This was a game owned by New Zealanders, not by a corporation based in Sydney, which was then possibly going to sell off some franchises back here and scatter our best players all around the world. This was a game for New Zealanders, run by New Zealanders.

Geoff Levy

KQ: Why won't anyone confirm the real reason the battle [between WRC and the various national rugby bodies] was stopped was because of the negotiation at the very highest level, between Kerry Packer and Rupert Murdoch?

You've got to ask those people and their organisations what occurred. It's hearsay for me to state what happened in a hotel room in London. Certainly we noticed a lot of deals afterwards between the two groups. Whether they were related or not, you have to ask them… I did get a call saying, "Let's make peace. Let's do it in a way that we preserve the boys, get the best deals for them."

Ross Turnbull

The battle with WRC and the Rugby Unions was stopped by powers bigger than rugby people. People make these decisions in a business environment. It is very interesting to learn how world sport is controlled by a few groups. Murdoch, of course, John Malone from TCI, Andy Brilliant from ESPN, Ted Turner from Time Warner… and, to an extent Kerry Packer. Those guys make the decisions as to what is going to happen, where and when. I have absolutely no doubt that Kerry Packer and Rupert Murdoch, in whatever fashion it may have happened, had a significant influence in what happened in rugby league and rugby union.

I've heard it said that Jock Hobbs saved New Zealand rugby. I'm sure Jock did a terrific job for New Zealand rugby, but for someone to say more than that is ridiculous. It was played in a world much bigger than me in South Africa, or Jock Hobbs in New Zealand or Simon Poidevin in Australia. There were forces outside that decided what happened with the game of rugby.

Geoff Levy

Even after some of the Springboks wavered, we could have gone ahead. We had more than five hundred players signed, four of the top Super 12 teams in New Zealand, plus all the All Blacks. Whether Jock Hobbs and the union had signed up one or two provinces wasn't really a factor. I don't think it is right to say Jock Hobbs saved the game. We would have gone ahead had I not been asked to make the peace and had the financial backing remained. But we didn't want anything that was half-hearted. It had to be unanimous. The boys had to really want it.

KQ: There is a story that Josh Kronfeld and Jeff Wilson in fact signed twice, for WRC and for the New Zealand union. Is that true?

Josh and Jeff were certainly part of that All Black squad. I don't want to name names, but there were some people who signed two contracts.

Ross Turnbull

When I was in South Africa, it was passed on to me that Josh Kronfeld and Jeff Wilson had signed with the New Zealand Rugby Union. I said, "That's ridiculous. Both of those players have signed with WRC." They did so immediately after the Bledisloe Cup match in Sydney.

Geoff Levy

In my view, WRC was the catalyst to professionalism. Without it, there would have been a slow evolution, rather than a revolution.

The All Black captain [Sean Fitzpatrick] was someone I gained enormous respect for. Here was a guy who cared about the whole group and he was as close to a great leader as I've met. He would never negotiate one on one, which we tried to do. We wanted to deal with each player and their manager separately, but he always wanted it as a team. He always put the team first. There was only one person outside the team, who had his own price. The rest of them were one group. The captain would not let some poor old prop get a lousy payment just because he wasn't going to be able to go to rugby league. He was always an absolute gentleman, true to his word. Never once was Sean two-faced throughout the whole process. At all times he was straightforward, upfront, very impressive.

Geoff Levy – key negotiator for WRC.

Alan Jones
Wallaby coach from 1984-87.

Rupert Murdoch laughed. We sold rugby – Super 12 and Tri-Nations – to Rupert for ten years for the amount of money you could get for the game in one year now. Rupert's a good businessman, so good on him. He's laughing all the way to the bank. Our mob were wet behind the ears.

Ross Turnbull

Rupert Murdoch got a fabulous deal because it's not a ten-year contract, but a fifteen-year contract. He has a five-year option. It was a great deal for Murdoch, but not a great deal for rugby, which sold itself very cheaply. The deal should have been worth an extra couple of hundred million dollars on top.

Louis Luyt

Top players in South Africa earn 1.8 million rand [per year]. That's like dollars because it's so much cheaper here. It's like saying they are earning $1.8 million.

They're better paid than league players now and it seems the money's just going up and up. How we are going to keep up with the demands, I don't know, because it's going down the line as well now. It was a horrendous experience to turn professional overnight. We wanted to do it in an orderly way, but it was almost a disaster for us because we paid out virtually everything we got from News Corp the first year just to keep our players. It was a terrible drain on the funds.

The future is very up in the air because the News Corp contract is for $555 million over 10 years. They will not be able to negotiate anything like near it again, let alone more, nowhere near. It's too expensive.

Legends of the All Blacks

Playing for Keep$

Richie Guy

Even by today's standards, it's still a very good deal. A number of people have said that we should never have done a ten-year deal because you don't know what's going to happen in five years. Well four years are up and I'm still happy with the quantum of the deal. Obviously when the deal is renegotiated towards the conclusion of the contract, more money will be required, but that's life.

Ross Turnbull

In Australia they are paying ninety-five per cent of the television money to the players, a spectacularly silly decision.

David Kirk
All Black captain from 1986-87.

It pains me to say this, but I don't think New Zealand people love the All Blacks as much now as they used to. The relationship has evolved. I think you can date it from the transition to professional rugby. Something went out of the transaction between the New Zealand public and the players when money came into it. It may well be that current All Blacks are just as dedicated to the joy of rugby and to winning for their team-mates and for New Zealand as previous players, but inevitably when you add another dimension – getting paid – if people watch a bad game or watch a player who doesn't seem to be giving his all, instead of saying, "He's no good. He should be dropped," they say, "He's getting paid a lot of money. Why isn't he performing?" The financial question inevitably undermines that sense of the players doing it because they love the game, and the public loving our players doing it because they love the game and love doing it for New Zealand.

The whole corporate image has cut down that personal relationship between the New Zealand public and the players.

Andy Dalton

The money aside, I'd like to think we played in a professional era and I'm sure there's nothing they do now in terms of playing that we didn't do then. We were under more work pressure – we had to hold down a job, train five times a week and Sundays – so it was a huge commitment in our lives. I don't think any of us had the golf handicaps they have now.

If I was given the opportunity they have now, I'd jump at it and hold it with both hands and you wouldn't shake me for a long time. I don't want to sound like an old crone, but I sometimes wonder if the players now realise what has gone on before them and just how very fortunate they are to be in this position.

The Players

In Their Own Words

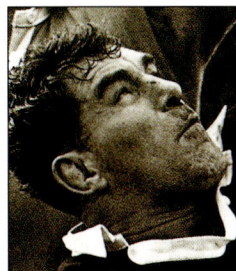

The players who have represented the All Blacks this century have very much reflected New Zealand society. They have been of mainly European, Pacific Island and Maori extraction. They have been thin and thick-set, dark and pale, tall and short, serious and humorous. Some have endured at the top for a decade; others had test careers of precisely one match. Some were flamboyant and colourful; others were dour and grim. In short, except for the fact that they have been better at rugby, the All Blacks have not really been any different from the rest of New Zealand. Perhaps that's one reason why New Zealanders have empathised with them, been thrilled by them, felt sad with them and been so happy to bask in their reflected glory.

During the course of the dozens of interviews completed in researching this book, and the accompanying television documentary, Keith Quinn unearthed many gems about All Blacks through the years. Perhaps it was a memory of a great piece of rugby or of a particular piece of bravery. Maybe it was a summary of a great player or a much-loved team-mate or family member.

Here are some of those jewels of observation…

George Nepia – one of New Zealand's early rugby legends.

Legends of the All Blacks

Ron Palenski
New Zealand journalist.

My theory about the name the All Blacks is that it's purely evolutionary. We know the hoary old theory about J A Buttery, the *Daily Mail* correspondent, being so enthralled with the New Zealand team's play that he wrote that they played "like all backs" and that a printer subsequently inserted an "l" thinking the writer was mistaken. But there's no evidence to back that up.

On the *Rimutaka* on the way to Britain in 1905, the team was constantly referred to by manager George Dixon in his diary as "The Blacks", whether they were inspecting the engine room, or going to dinner. It's only a small step from that to the All Blacks.

Kiwi Rowlands
George Nepia's daughter.

Dad loved so many of his team-mates from that 1924 tour. He always had a soft spot for Cyril Brownlie, and Bert Cooke and Bill Irvine and McGregor… a lot of them. He used to meet Ian Harvey at Ian Harvey's hotel in Wellington and there they'd go upstairs, arm in arm, to a sitting room and they'd reminisce, sometimes in tears. One chap that dad really loved was Quentin Donald from Wairarapa. Quentin had a lot of money. When he went away in 1924, he was to be married on his return. His father gave him a lot of money to buy a collection of silver while he was away. They were his father's gift to the bride. Quentin took a fatherly interest in dad because he was so young. He had such a lot of money, he used to say: "How are you, Hori?" and he'd slip something into dad's pocket. They all called him Hori. The term is abused today, but they meant in a nice way.

•

It was very hard for us when my father went to play rugby league in Britain. My mother refused to leave us. Her mother, who had helped bring us up, was quite old and she didn't want to be away from her. So it was very difficult for my father and mother to be separated for so long. I slept with our mother and she used to cry herself to sleep many a night, hugging me so much sometimes that it hurt.

Kevin Skinner
Prop who made his test debut in South Africa in 1949.

Johnny Simpson was special to me. He helped me in South Africa, in my first year in the All Blacks with front row techniques and encouraged me. Ray Dalton was another terrific bloke in Africa. He was on the selection panel and maybe could have got a test or two at my expense, but he didn't. He must have been itching to put himself in, but he didn't. That's the sort of person he was.

Bob Scott had his greatest season in South Africa in 1949. He really showed what a fullback could do, with the ball in hand and running. He played what is now called "the modern game". He was a great athlete. He just couldn't put his kicks over and I think poor old Bob still has regrets about that to this day.

•

Fred Allen
All Black captain from 1946-49.

Deep down I'm a fairly sensitive person and like everyone I take defeats very much to heart. That whitewash in South Africa [in 1949] was just too much. I thought I was still playing pretty good football, but I couldn't handle the results and on the boat home I decided I'd had enough. I made the announcement that I was retiring. We had a ceremony on board the ship. Ron Elvidge held the boot on the deck and I kicked it over the side of the boat.

That was really the finish of my playing career. I was 29 and I suppose I could have gone on and played against the Lions in 1950. I would have if we'd won in South Africa, but not after what happened over there.

It's true I was a New Zealand boxing champion, but that was early on, before I got into top rugby, a carry-over from my school days, really. I didn't think it had a lot of bearing on my rugby, and would have preferred it wasn't mentioned. But later on in my career the boxing got dredged up by you media fellows with nothing better to do.

Don Clarke
All Black fullback from 1956-64. He was often the heaviest player in the New Zealand team.

I can recall as an eleven-year-old playing third grade rugby in the Morrinsville sub-union competition. That's totally stupid. I had to do that to get rugby, because I wasn't allowed to play rugby in primary school. I was too heavy. In those days, if you were too big… well, bad luck Charlie. I played netball with the girls' team. When you think back, what a way to prepare for an All Black future!

JJ Stewart
New Zealand Colts team coach, 1955.

Colin Meads was in the Colts team I took to Ceylon, as it was. He was a nice country boy, a top guy. He was only 19 or 20 at the time, and was a very pleasant boy, but shy on the field. I remember saying to him, "For God's sake, you won't be any good until you score a try. You keep letting the ball go. You have to go for the line a bit yourself." He just needed confidence. He scored his first try in the game at Perth on the way over and he never looked back.

John Gainsford
Springbok centre in the 1960s.

Colin Meads was the greatest rugby player I played against. He was a character as a player. Everything about him was magnificent and I loved him as a man, still do, even if he did remove my front teeth at Newlands in the second test in 1960. Meads had an aura and respect about him, but also a wonderful sense of humour. After we played the first test in 1965, we went down to play King Country and the combined provinces. He tackled me during the game and grabbed hold of me and squeezed me where it hurts a little bit. He said he'd been trying to get me for a couple of days and gave me a little tug where it hurts. At the end of the game, which they won, I went up to him and told him I hadn't been able to repay him during the game, but that I was going to give him something that nobody could send me off the field for. I grabbed a handful of mud and rubbed it into his face as hard as I could!

Colin Meads
All Black forward from 1957-71.

Stan [Meads] was a great athlete. He always struggled for physique and weight, like I did early in my career. But Stan could give me about 10 yards over the length of a football field. He was one of the fastest All Black forwards around, yet he was spring-heeled as a leaper. He was all those things Colin Meads wasn't.

Stan Meads

But he was unfortunate early in his career because he had a tremendous amount of injuries. In those days a cartilage operation meant you were out for a season, and he had three operations like that. I suppose being family, he was great to lock with. He always made me work like hell to keep up my side. Even though he wasn't big, he was a great pusher in scrums.

Stan and I never played King Country trials on the same team. We were always against each other. One time when I played against Stan, we were winning and at one stage I yanked him back as he was charging through. I gave him a tug, then I chased him onto the ball, went down on him. Bang! He hit me, and we had a little set-to.

So the next day, there's not too much talk over the breakfast table. Then mum lined us up and gave us a speech. She said if that sort of thing happened again, she'd march onto the field and lead us off by our collars.

Mum was a great rugby follower, but always stayed at home. She saw us play only one test. We got her up to Auckland once. During the test, Stan got skittled. He was actually knocked out. I said to him, "Mum's watching this, you know. That's why she doesn't come to rugby. She's scared we're going to get hurt. You've got to get up." So we carried Stan through the next couple of scrums and he was on his way again.

Here I was, this shy kid from the King Country. I recall after being picked in the All Blacks – all of King Country would have said I'd be out on the booze – I was in bed by ten at night. All the senior players had gone somewhere, but was I was in a state of shock. There was a medical on the Sunday morning and I was down for breakfast at about seven, the only one there.

Three of the great stalwarts of New Zealand rugby – Jack Sullivan, Tom Morrison and Cuth Hogg – were there. They saw me in the corner by myself and invited me over to sit with them. They warned me never to talk to Terry McLean, who I didn't know at all. I often wondered what Terry McLean thought of me in the early years because if he said "Good morning", I'd just grunt. That was sad because I got to know Terry later in

Colin Meads contests lineout ball with long-time French rival Benoit Dauga.

life and he was a fine old gentleman and a very good conversationalist.

I had no idea what the All Blacks were about. My first room-mate was Morrie Dixon. Well, of all people to room with! He had me on a string. I was running here, doing this, getting the morning tea, afternoon tea. The things that fellow got me to do were amazing. I suppose I was broken in at the deep end.

The silver fern was always something to aim for. Before I played my first game for New Zealand, I was terribly scared of getting hurt. After being selected I had to play a club game and I reckon I spent most of the time on the wing. I was hiding. I didn't want to be involved in anything.

Our first game on the tour of Australia [in 1957] was

at Woollongong. I remember being in the dressing room saying to Whineray, who was also having his first game for New Zealand, "I'm scared to get up. I'm going to trip over and fall. I've got to get out on that field and play in this jersey before I can say I'm an All Black." I had a feeling of tremendous pride when I put on that All Black jersey.

•

The French [in 1961] started the peeling off the back of the lineout, what we now call the Willie Away. They used to do it in twos and threes. Then it got to Auckland, where Wilson Whineray did it brilliantly, and it came to be named after him, a tribute to a great player. But when other teams picked up on it, it wasn't always best to be first. In Wilson's day it was, but when everyone latched onto it and the first man was put down, it was often better to be the second man. When young fellows would come along, they always wanted to do the Willie Away and I was pretty keen to let them be first because they got crunched and the second guy got the plum, if there was such a thing.

John Gainsford
Springbok centre from 1960-67.

Kel Tremain was not just a very good player, he was a great player. We played the New Zealanders in 1960, but got to know some of them better when they spent a month in South Africa in 1964 as part of our jubilee celebrations. The South African forwards teamed up with the overseas backs and the South African backs with the overseas forwards, so we were actually playing with great All Black forwards like Colin Meads and Kel Tremain. Kel was a classic player, solid and strong, a hard grafter, but also a man who could move the ball and had fantastic hands.

In 1960 we had a terrific flanker named Martin Pelser. In the lineouts, Meads and Tremain used to hold their opposite numbers when they were jumping, and somehow they would get away with it. They had never heard of Pelser. So during the first test, it was Tremain's turn to hold, which he did. Pelser gave him such a wallop that I think Tremain reviewed the situation and decided holding wasn't such a good idea. Meads had seen this and also decided it wasn't such a good idea. But next time it was his turn to hold, he did. Then he quickly ducked around to the back of the scrum and there he ran straight into Pelser. Well that was the end of holding against South Africa while Martin Pelser was playing!

Des Connor
All Black halfback from 1961-64.

Everywhere you went on the field, Don Clarke wanted the ball from you. He kept yelling, "To me, to me." He either wanted to have a drop at goal or he wanted to kick it as far as he could down field. You had to ignore him to a certain extent because we were trying to expand the approach of the backline.

Once we were playing against Queensland at the Exhibition Ground. We had a scrum on the 25, attacking their line. Clarkey was standing on halfway, calling for the ball. I thought, "All right, you smart so and so, here you go." So I fired the ball back to him and he shaped to kick it off his right foot. But Jules Guerassimoff ran at him to charge down the ball. Clarkey did a complete turn and dropped-kicked if off his left foot through the bloody goal-posts.

It was one of the most amazing things I've seen. It ranks up there with John Eales jumping up in front of the goal-post and knocking back the ball. It was an incredible feat. But that's the sort of guy Clarkey was. He was a great player.

Legends of the All Blacks

Brian Lochore
who first played for New Zealand in 1963.

The All Black trial at Athletic Park in 1963 was one of the most embarrassing days of my life. There was a man in the stand who had an enormous voice. He'd wait until everything was quiet and then he would let go this booming, "C'mon Lochore!" It would echo around Athletic Park. It was extremely embarrassing. I tried to find out who it was for a whole twelve months before I found out. He was a Masterton person, not someone I knew particularly well. He probably tried to avoid me after that because he knew I wasn't particularly happy about it. I suppose you could say he drew attention to me during the trial, but I would like to think that I got in on my merits.

•

My entry into test football was somewhat fortuitous. It was on the tour of Britain in 1963-64. Waka Nathan broke his jaw and I ended up playing the test against England, but I didn't know I was playing until 10 o'clock in the morning. I was rooming with Keith Nelson, who'd trained in Waka's position, or trained with the test team during the week, and it was assumed by everybody he would play if Waka wasn't fit.

I decided I'd go and have a game of squash with a friend in London the morning of the test, just to try to keep up my fitness. I was about to get into the lift to go to play squash when Wilson Whineray walked past and asked me where I was going. I told him I was off for a game of squash. He said, "I don't think you should go. I think you should go back to your room. We might need you." So I was really quite puzzled and went back to my room. Keith was on the phone to his parents. They'd heard the rumour he might be playing and he was saying if Waka couldn't play, he thought he'd be in.

When he got off the phone, he asked me why I was back and I told him that I'd been told to stay there and didn't know what was going on. About two minutes later Frank Kilby, our manager, phoned. He asked for me and said I was playing in the afternoon. I told him I had a bit of the flu and he said I'd rise above it and put the phone down. So that was my preparation for the first test. It wasn't what you'd call the ideal build-up, though it went pretty well for me.

They told Keith at fairly much the same time as they told me. It was lucky both of us were in that same room because we could see that neither of us knew what was going on. Keith and I have remained friends. There was never any animosity or suggestion of behind-the-scenes activity because we knew where each of us was at that particular time. That was probably fortunate.

Don Clarke

Ian meant a lot to me as a brother. He was a wonderful player and his passing was a shock to us in the family. He was highly thought of as a person and a rugby player. He went from the front row, where he might not have been the biggest player but was always strong, to No 8 from where he captained the All Blacks in 1955 against the Australians, then back to the front row against the mighty Springboks the following year. After that he played in the front row almost all the way through his career. He packed down against players like Koch, Bekker and Shehadie and company – big, strong men. Ian was never done over. I saw him get home after a tough game and his tiredness and muscle soreness was very evident. He was an unbelievable tackler. I never saw him beaten by anyone when he lined up a tackle. He had a great pair of hands and was a real student of the game. He loved rugby and went on to become President of the New Zealand Rugby Union. Then he was asked to be on the judicial panel. I recall him saying one day, "If I can clean up this game so it's played as I expect it should be, without dirt or fuss, I'll have done what I have set out to do." He had a life commitment to rugby.

My father was a blacksmith and Ian was always on the light side as a prop. They used to put us on the scales so Ian always carried lead-weighted shin pads in his gear bag. When we were asked to weigh in, he would put on the shin pads and cover them with his socks. He'd weight in half a stone heavier than he really was.

•

The Players – The Quinn Tapes

Brothers and All Black team-mates, Don (left) and Ian Clarke.

When I was place-kicking, I dug a round hole that the ball sat in perfectly. I used to try to hit the ball plus or minus about half an inch below the centre of the ball. There's where I believe you get the greatest velocity at the point of impact. If you catch the ball too low it spins too fast; if you catch it too high, you top it and it won't lift into the air. Timing is vital. It's impossible to kick a ball perfectly every time, but the more time you spend at it and the more concentration you put into your kicking, the better you'll get. I never stopped practising and thinking about my kicking, whether it was punting, drop kicking or place kicking.

Earle Kirton
was an All Black first five-eighth from 1963-70.

When I first got in the All Blacks, for the tour of Britain in 1963-64, I was called "Unconscious" because they reckoned I was basically away with the fairies. I'd go into dream mode and was terribly vague. There was a suggestion that it be changed to "Just Conscious" because they reckoned I got a bit better towards the end of the tour. In 1967 Pinetree [Colin Meads] made a solemn declaration to the rest of the team that they would drop the "Un" bit and call me "Concho", which was a far nicer term. So to this day I'm Concho Kirton.

Fergie McCormick
All Black fullback from 1965-71.

With Mick [Williment] being a Wellingtonian and me from Christchurch, there was a fair bit of rivalry. We used to play in All Black trials against each other. In those days the All Black trials used to be quite extended – they'd go on for a week or two. I can't say I was over-friendly towards Mick, what with him trying to get my spot and me trying to get his. With the New Zealand union having its headquarters in Wellington, I got the impression they always felt Mick should be in the test team – you know, here's this fellow from Canterbury who used to play a bit over the top at times. But that's the way it is. There's always someone lurking, trying to get your position. Mick and I eventually became great buddies after all those years playing against each other.

Legends of the All Blacks

Gareth Edwards
Welsh and British Isles halfback from 1967-78.

Growing up as a schoolboy, I read about Colin Meads, heard a bit about him on radio and caught the odd glimpse on television. I was led to believe he was seven feet five, twenty-five stone, and had an eye in the middle of his head. Though when I met him he wasn't that big, he was still a man of immense proportions. I will never forget his prowess as a player. And I'll never forget the moment in Australia a couple of years ago when we were celebrating some occasion or another and Colin was singing Elvis Presley songs. I never thought I'd see the day when the mighty Pinetree Meads was singing Elvis Presley songs. I looked at him and wondered why I had ever felt concerned about him. But then, it was seeing somebody in a completely different light.

Marilyn MacRae
wife of All Black Ian MacRae, who represented New Zealand from 1963-70.

It was Ian's delayed reaction to hearing about his All Black selection that fascinated me. We were at home, sitting around the kitchen table when the team was announced. It got to "I R MacRae" and I was all ready to scream and shout when Ian said, "Shhh, listen to the rest of the team." Then he quietly got up and said, "Okay, I'd better go out and shout for the boys now." He walked outside and as he got halfway across the street he leapt in the air yelling, "Yipppeeee!" That's the first time I'd seen him excited.

Earle Kirton
played with Chris Laidlaw for the University club in Dunedin, for Otago and New Zealand.

He could put up with my vagueness and I could put up with his repartee and the fact that he was so casual. He was one of the great halfbacks of all-time, though he never quite gets the kudos. He could kick, but didn't run much. He was very effective at going around the scrum and catching the other scrumhalf, maybe six or seven times in a test, which is basically the end of the ball-game. He was very self-analytical and only Meads was as hard on himself. If he got caught more than twice you couldn't speak to him. He would cut away into the night and we wouldn't see him till morning. In fact, "Cutaway" became one of his nicknames. He pursued excellence.

His passing was incredible and made Gareth Edwards change his style of passing. But Gareth's pass was never as fast as Laidlaw's. Chris' reaction time was instinctive. The leading All Black forwards of the day always wanted Laidlaw ahead of Sid Going because they knew they'd get a lot more ball and they'd be able to go wider. And whereas Sid was such a brilliant runner he'd score tries himself, when Laidlaw played, there was more happening for the flankers.

Fergie McCormick

I was under the stand at Athletic Park when the 1967 [All Black] team was announced. One of the men on the panel told me I'd made the side, but I was still sceptical. Mick [Williment] was the incumbent fullback and I knew I'd have to be well over the top to shift Mick and get the trip to Britain. We were allowed to take 30 players and it was almost certain Mick would get in. The story goes that they named too many players in the side, but I didn't know that at the time. I heard my name called out and then they read out Phil Clarke and I thought, "Who's this other fullback, Phil Clarke?" It turned out he was a winger. So that's how I came to be named the only fullback in the team. It was most certainly a big shock.

Fergie McCormick

The Players – The Quinn Tapes

The story of Jazz Muller

Brian Muller, known to everyone in rugby as Jazz, played for the All Blacks from 1967-71. He was a very big man for his times and became famous for trimming his hedge with a lawn mover. Since his All Black days he has become a recluse and is virtually never seen in or around rugby. But he retains fond memories of his days in the All Blacks and his home at Eltham contains many mementoes of those times.

KQ: What did being an All Black mean to you?
It's good while you're there, but when you've finished, that's the name of the game. Better to be a has-been than a never-was. It did give me a nickname. I was just an ordinary person, so being an All Black, it really meant something to me.

Keith Quinn (left) and Jazz Muller.

Earle Kirton
played for New Zealand with Ken Gray from 1963-69.

I think Ken Gray was the greatest forward we've produced. Colin Meads was a wonderful runner and a wonderful player in space, quick and versatile, and he normally gets the accolade of being the great forward. But Ken beat him in a way. Ken could play lock, on either side of the scrum or the front row. He was versatile. He could scrum like no-one else, but he loved to move the ball and run with it.

Graham Williams
was an All Black flanker from 1967-68.

One of the reasons I admired Ken Gray was that he did so much more for the young guys in the team. In that era it was hard to be accepted by the senior players. My background in rugby was the team atmosphere, but on some occasions in the All Blacks it was pretty hard to break into the A team, because it was a sort of senior club within the team.

By 1967 there were a lot of senior players who'd been in the team for quite a period and it was very, very hard to break into that old school. Waka Nathan would always talk to me, and I have a ton of admiration for him. But a guy like Kelvin Tremain, who was an awesome footballer, would possibly look at me and think, "Hang on, he's after my position, so I'm not going to give him too much assistance." As a young player I found that aspect very unsatisfying.

Brian Lochore
All Black captain in South Africa in 1970.

Bryan Williams was an amazing player in South Africa in 1970. I only ever saw him play once like that back in New Zealand. He was always a good All Black, but he was an amazing All Black in South Africa. Whether he was playing at centre or on the wing, he did everything so well – he'd beat guys with pace, or swerve, or just go straight through them. His form on that tour was really fantastic.

Legends of the All Blacks

Sid Going
All Black halfback in South Africa in 1970.

There's no doubt, 1970 was Bryan Williams' year. He was on fire. Those hard grounds over in South Africa really suited his running style. He had the stepping ability to get through and the pace and skills, and thrived on it. Bryan played some tremendous football.

In one game we ran the short side and it seemed to me he was blocked or marked, so I put through a little kick on attack and it went out just a couple of metres from the corner. The spectators all clapped and thought it was a wonderful kick. But Beegee said to me, "Give it to me in the hand," and it was a lesson to me. If I'd given it to him, he might have scored. His attitude was that if he got the ball, even if there were two players in front of him, he might get past. After that the first option was always to give the ball to him, rather than to try to put it in behind.

Kit Fawcett
was the All Black fullback in 1976 and was noted for his unique approach to life.

I got picked for the All Black trial in 1974 as an 18-year-old. I had been in Dunedin but had not played for Otago, so didn't have a uniform. My air tickets arrived by mail and I turned up at the hotel. They said, "Who are you?" They asked me where my blazer was. I was wearing a bright red pair of striped leather shoes, and a pink pair of trousers and quite a bright shirt. I think I was wearing a cap, and of course I had long hair. They didn't know if I was an artist or what, but they certainly got a shock when I turned up!

Andy Leslie
All Black captain from 1974-76.

KQ: Andy Leslie first played an All Black trial in 1967. By 1974 many rugby followers – and Leslie himself – felt his chance of representing New Zealand had gone. Then he was not only selected in the All Black team to tour Australia, but was named captain. He explains his thoughts in the lead-up to his selection:

I thought it had passed me by. In 1973 when I wasn't selected for the trials, I thought, "Well, that's gone." I was picked for a Barbarians team to Fiji and I thought that was a great way to finish – to go over there and play with Colin Meads, Fergie McCormick, Ian Kirkpatrick and these guys. Then our Petone club was invited to go to South Africa in 1974 and I thought what a super way to finish your career – with all your team-mates. I wrote a letter to Lesley [his wife] from South Africa, saying I'd never go away without her again and that this was the last trip I'd be on. Fortunately the chap who posted the letter sent it surface mail and Lesley received it when I was in Australia representing New Zealand!

JJ Stewart
All Black coach 1974-76.

One of the reasons we didn't take Sid Going to Australia in 1974 was that we wanted to play an expansive game. He was a great player, one of the greatest in the history of the game, and a great personality. He was too good and I knew that on a tour of Australia, Sid and the loose forwards would win the games, but that we wouldn't develop players who should be developing. We had some great players – Bruce and Duncan Robertson, Doug Bruce, and a few others.

Kit Fawcett
All Black fullback in South Africa in 1976.

Laurie Mains was everything I wasn't, or I'm everything he's not. He was a traditional fullback. Even back in Dunedin, I was playing fullback for Varsity A and running and getting headlines and kicking goals and tackling and making tries. Laurie was staying back, safety-first. I was probably a rash under Laurie's skin, the way I played. In South Africa [in 1976], he got shoved into the background. I don't think the selectors did their job picking the right fullbacks before we went. Greg Rowlands should have been the No 1 and I should have been his understudy.

Andy Irvine
was the great Scottish fullback of the 1970s.

Grant Batty was a real little firebrand, a niggly so and so on the park, but an absolutely great bloke off it. If ever there was a Jeckyl and Hyde character, it was him.

Ian Kirkpatrick
All Black loose forward from 1967-77.

I was a little disappointed when I was dropped in 1977, but not shattered. I intended going on the tour of France and then calling it quits, so they beat me by one tour. People have talked about me being let down by the way I was dropped, without being spoken to privately, but to be honest it didn't worry me too much. It would have still been really disappointing if someone had rung me and said I wasn't in the team. In those days you heard that sort of news on the radio. It wasn't a big deal.

Andy Dalton
All Black hooker from 1977-85.

The back seat of the bus is the spoke of the wheel of the All Blacks. The senior players sitting there make the rules; what they say goes. I've a vivid memory of being summoned down to the back seat in 1977 by Bryan Williams, Bruce Robertson, Andy Haden and Brad Johnstone and being made to stand in front of them. Bryan Williams, who was senior counsel, asked me what it meant to me to be an All Black. I had to state what my feelings were for the jersey, and to do it to people who were icons of the game and who, except for Bruce Robertson, a Counties team-mate, I didn't know. That was something I'll never forget; it had quite an influence on me.

Grant Batty – 'a real little firebrand.'

Legends of the All Blacks

The Baby Blacks

David Kirk
captained the Baby Blacks in 1986. They were so called because most of them were newcomers to test football.

My involvement with the Baby Blacks and winning the World Cup were the pinnacles of my rugby career. I have a soft spot for the Baby Blacks. It was a team of people who had never played for the All Blacks and were thrust in against a successful French team. We felt an obligation to do our best for the All Blacks, notwithstanding the fact that at the beginning of the season, few of them could have expected to play for New Zealand. Some of them would have known they were not likely to have long All Black careers, but they set out to deliver for the All Blacks.

When the team got together in Christchurch, players were introducing themselves to each other. They knew each others' names from the newspapers, but had not met. Normally All Blacks have played each other at trials and been on tours together and it's just two or three players being filtered in. Here we had players turning up and saying, "Hi, I'm so and so. I play in this position and I'm looking forward to Saturday."

It was an easy team to lead. No motivation was needed. What they required was self-confidence and cohesion, a pattern. I don't think Sean Fitzpatrick would have gone backwards in a scrum so often in an All Black jersey as that day. Because our scrum was so weak, we had to play the game fast and loose.

I had a sense of trepidation waiting for the kick-off, but was really proud to be there. There'd been a lot of support in the media and you could tell New Zealanders really wanted the team to do well. We started pretty well and Joe [Stanley] knocked over a few guys in the midfield and it started to build. Frano Botica's a confident player and ran with the ball. John Kirwan was always talking and contributing and charging about, and we started to have a sense of, "We can do this." We were never in charge, just running around doing all we could to win. It was bootstraps stretched to breaking point the whole time. But once Mike Brewer scored his try we really did believe we were going to win.

When I look back now at the television coverage of me leaving the field that day, I can sense the joy bursting out. There was a huge feeling of satisfaction and joy in that team.

Sean Fitzpatrick
made his test debut with the Baby Blacks.

When we arrived in Christchurch before the test against France, I was told I was rooming with Joe Leota, so I walked into my room and said, "Hi Joe, I'm Sean Fitzpatrick." He asked me where I played and that sort of thing. Then we went to lunch and Andy Earl came to our table. Joe said to Andy, "Hello Andy, this is… um." He'd forgotten my name! It was that sort of team. We were very green.

France had an amazing scrum and for the whole game we got smashed back in every scrum. It was a baptism of fire. We got through on sheer enthusiasm and enjoyment.

Mike Brewer scores the Baby Blacks' only try against France.

David Kirk

A great example of All Black toughness and doing it for your team-mates occurred on the tour of France late in 1986. The first game was in Strasbourg and we were training at a ground which had only a fairly old run-down scrum machine with those industrial strength springs that you push back on. I was playing, so I was putting the ball into the scrum and all the non-players were standing on the scrum machine to stop it sliding.

Mark Shaw was a reserve and he was standing on the machine looking down at the front. I would put the ball in and the scrum would hit. Well, this time as the scrum hit there was a funny sort of strangled squeal which I thought was a bit odd. As I was about to put the ball in, I'd say, "Coming, coming, coming!" and the pressure would go on and on and on. Then the ball would go in. The scrum really pushed and slammed the springs in. Then it would be, "Hold, hold, hold!" and I could hear this "ooohh, ooohh, ooohh" in the background. When I decided to call "break" the scrum broke and then there was an "Aaaggghhhh!!!" and we turned around and saw Mark Shaw holding his hands. His knuckles were totally bruised and scraped and scuffed. His fingers had been caught between the spring and the backboard. Everyone asked him why he didn't yell out so we could have taken the pressure off the scrum. He said, "Oh, the boys had a good hit on and I didn't want to ruin that scrum."

Wayne Shelford
All Black No 8 from 1985-90.

That second test against France in 1986 was a tough test. I went off twenty minutes into the second half. I'd had three or four teeth kicked out. I'd been knocked out by Jean-Pierre Garuet. And then I got kicked in the goolies by Daniel Dubroca. It hurt at the time, but it was just like another bruise. I mean any time you get kicked down there, it's going to hurt. At the time I

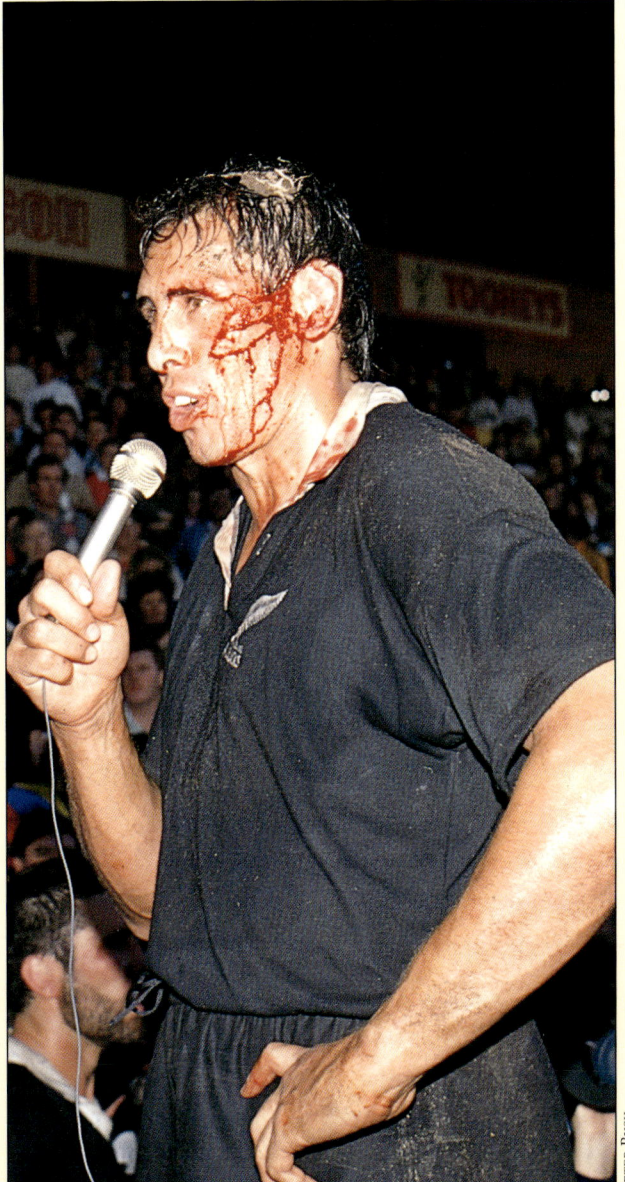

Buck Shelford – warrior captain.

didn't realise what had actually happened. But after the game, when I was getting changed, I saw my testicle was hanging out, probably a good six or seven inches below the scrotum. So that was pretty nasty and a lot of the boys cringed at the sight of it. But the doctors sewed it back up pretty quickly and I just got on with it. Now when I go to speak at rugby clubs, it becomes a bit of a story and people have a laugh at it.

Legends of the All Blacks

Gary Whetton
played for the All Blacks from 1981-91.

AJ [Whetton's twin brother Alan] and I spent a lot of time together, training and during games. I was very lucky to have a twin brother, and even luckier to play with him for the All Blacks. It was a very unusual situation. I was always at a loss when I was taking the field and AJ wasn't behind me. Every time I ran onto the field, he'd run beside me or behind me and hold onto my jersey. In the changing room, we'd always be together. We'd have a little word we'd say to each other, grab each other's jersey and away we'd go. There was definitely some telepathic communication there. If one of us was injured, the other could feel it straight away. I could feel when AJ was injured without even knowing it was him. I'd run up to him and say, "What's the problem?" And he'd say, "My face has been cut open," or "I've done my hamstring." When AJ wasn't on the field, I never played as well. He was an inspiration.

Clive Norling
Welsh test referee.

During the second New Zealand-Argentina test at Wellington in 1989, Sean Fitzpatrick came out of a scrum and asked me to sort out an Argentinian player who, he said, was biting him. I turned to look at the Argentinian, who didn't have a tooth in his head. So I turned back to Fitzy and said, "We've got a problem here. I can't penalise him for biting, but I'll penalise him for sucking you the next time he does it."

Gary Whetton

KQ: Can you tell us about the circumstances when you were dropped from the All Blacks?

It happened very quickly. We arrived back after the 1991 World Cup and they named a new All Black coach, and selection panel – Laurie Mains, Earle Kirton and Peter Thorburn. It was a surprise to me and I didn't know what it meant. I trained through the summer. The All Black selectors had been talking to the players, but they hadn't talked to me, though I was the incumbent captain. Then they named four trial teams and reserves and after they named them the only current All Blacks missing were AJ and GW Whetton. That was a hard pill to swallow. No communication. They ended our careers and it wasn't done on form. It was done more as a vendetta, or a personality issue.

I knew Laurie Mains. He was a very focused man. He had his opinions and could pick who he wanted. They could have given AJ and me a trial to gauge our form, but I think they were afraid we would show up and they would have to pick us. We were only thirty-two. I felt sorry for my brother because I think it was more my side that brought his career to an end. The Whettons went out as a job lot. If you look at the results of the All Blacks over the next couple of years, they lacked a bit of direction.

Laurie Mains could have phoned me and said, "This is how I see it, Gary. This is where the All Blacks have

Gary Whetton – sudden end to All Black captaincy.

gone wrong. I don't need you as captain." I would have accepted that. We could have discussed it, the pros and cons. Was there an opportunity for a trial? Could I fit into his team? In that way you can get over it and you can talk about it with your wife and family. But to be cut down all of a sudden… that was hard to take.

Will Carling
England's most successful test captain.

I know it sounds crazy, but the colour of the All Black uniform helps build up the aura they have. Men in black – sinister. They come over, they don't smile, they play, they win, they go home.

Frank Bunce epitomises the All Blacks to me. He was one of the greatest centres I played against. When we played that World Cup semi-final [in 1995], we went down the right and made a break and put Tony Underwood away. I got hit as hard as I've ever been hit in my life, and I lay on the ground and was in a lot of pain. I thought, "You've got to get up." And I got up and walked. There was a lineout. I knew who had hit me and eventually I looked over at Frank and he was looking straight at me. He just winked. That summed him up. He was going to be at you the whole game. He was never dirty, but he would hit you as hard as he could every single time and he expected you to do the same to him. If you didn't, you lost. That's really what it was all about.

Bill McLaren
Scottish television commentator.

I thought Zinzan Brooke was the best loose forward I've ever seen. He was so astute and clever and strong. He was tactically sound, he was rough. He had everything.

Gavin Hastings

What I learned from Grant Fox while I was playing club rugby in Auckland in 1987 made me the player I became. He trained at one hundred per cent. Like all the really good All Blacks, he was composed in everything he did, and that was simply because he trained so intensely.

Gavin Hastings
played for Scotland from 1986-95.

Many people have asked me what it was like facing up to the haka. The first time, I thought, "What the hell's going on here?" Half the Maori guys' eyeballs were popping out. I remember facing Inga Tuigamala one day and his eyes were popping out and I fixed my eyes on him. There was no way I was going to blink. Then at the end he jumped up, and when he came back down, he winked at me and we both laughed. If that's what the haka meant to him, it was good enough for me as well. I think it's just a show for the punters who go along.

Inga Tuigamala doing the haka – a nod and a wink.

Legends of the All Blacks

Phil Kearns
Australia's hooker since 1989.

For a start Sean Fitzpatrick had absolutely no respect for me as a young player, and nor should he have had, because I hadn't done anything. As we played against each other more, and got to know each other a little bit, there was some mutual respect. On the field it remained as competitive and combative as ever, but off it a more mellow relationship developed, and I was sad to see him go.

Francois Pienaar

I enjoyed Sean Fitzpatrick as a player and a person. His gamesmanship was never dirty. It was niggling and unsettled the opposition. He was a great leader. He knew what to do in test matches.

Jonah Lomu
In 1994 Jonah Lomu became New Zealand's youngest test player.

I remember an under-16 tournament in Te Kuiti. Everybody kept talking about "Pinetree" and "Pinetree Country". They said, "Jonah, you're going to be playing against Pinetree's son." Finally I said, "Who's this Pinetree?" The room just went quiet. I suppose that was the start of my initiation into the All Blacks and All Black traditions. I had a crash course in history.

KQ: Jonah, you've gone on to become a rugby superstar. What has the price of fame been?

I've lost my privacy, more than anything else. I don't have much time to myself. I'm constantly hounded and wanted by people. One time I went through a drive-thru at McDonald's and the next thing I knew, someone four cars ahead had run back and asked me for an autograph. The next minute, I had everyone else hopping out of their cars. That's just one example. It comes with the territory and I've adapted to it and I have no regrets or any problems with it. The great thing about New Zealanders is that they keep you on a level plane and keep your feet on the ground.

You know, when a guy comes from south Auckland, like I did, what's happened to me is like a dream. The difference is I've made my dream a reality.

David Campese
Australian David Campese is test rugby's most capped player with 102 appearances.

I respect the haka, but every individual's different. I've never been a person to stand there and watch it because it intimidated me a bit. I did my own thing while they were doing the haka. I got letters from New Zealanders saying how dare I not respect it, but I didn't have to stand there. We decided if a player wanted to stand there and eyeball them, great, but if you wanted to do something else, it was up to the individual.

Wayne Shelford

When I got into the All Blacks in 1985, a lot of players didn't want to do the haka overseas and had never done it in New Zealand. They asked Hika Reid to sort it out. I watched Hika taking a session and said, "If you're not going to do this properly, don't do it at all, because all you're doing is embarrassing the Maori community." So we went to a team vote and decided to do it properly.

From that time, in Argentina in 1985, the team started doing it correctly and with more passion. The stance became more correct and so did the hand movements. In 1987 we did it in New Zealand for the first time. We had the likes of John Gallagher and Gary Whetton getting down and doing it correctly and knowing more about it. It is a war dance, a war chant and it's got to be done with pride. At the end of the day, guys like Gallagher and Terry Wright loved doing it because it made them feel so powerful and it was just that last edge before starting to play the game. A lot of teams over the years became very scared of the haka. We used it as an intimidatory sort of force and it did work.

World Cup

Going for Gold

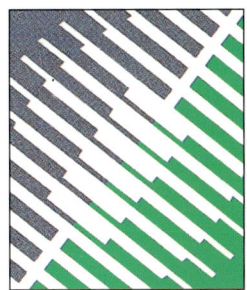

Since 1987 world rugby has revolved increasingly around the World Cup. Whereas previously tours and major series would be anticipated and planned for years ahead, now the focus is firmly on the World Cup. Many New Zealanders feel the All Blacks should win every World Cup as of right, but it hasn't worked out that way. After a sensational triumph at home in the first World Cup, the All Blacks had to settle for third and second in the next two tournaments.

David Kirk with the greatest prize in rugby.

Legends of the All Blacks

Captain Kirk's Rugby Starship

1987
(May 22–June 20)

Pool matches
- v Italy — won 70-6 — Auckland
- v Fiji — won 74-13 — Christchurch
- v Argentina — won 46-15 — Wellington

Quarter-final
- v Scotland — won 30-3 — Christchurch

Semi-final
- v Wales — won 49-6 — Brisbane

Final
- v France — won 29-9 — Auckland

Jock Hobbs
captained New Zealand in 1986, but was ruled out of the 1987 World Cup through injury.

I dearly hoped to play in the 1987 World Cup. For me there was a double blow – having to stop playing, and also being so close to the World Cup. But you suffer lots of disappointments. We all do, in all areas of life. It was painful, but you get on.

At the end of 1986, after the tour of France [when Hobbs had captained the All Blacks], programmes were issued for training over the summer period in preparation for the 1987 World Cup. I carried out those programmes, and was part of a television campaign organised before the World Cup. I had moved to Wellington and my first game for them was against Horowhenua. My next game was at Athletic Park, against Auckland. I took a very big hit. I was very sick, and didn't seem to be recovering, or if I was, it was very slow. I had been on a final warning from a neurosurgeon before that. Checks were made and still there was no improvement. I spoke with Brian Lochore, who I respected enormously. After that discussion, and taking into account the advice I'd been given and how I was feeling, I decided to stop. It was a very difficult decision, but I can see it was the right one for me.

Of course I may not have even been selected. That's just conjecture now. But when I made the decision, it was very painful. Playing for the All Blacks is quite a special thing and tends to dominate your life. You organise your life around it and become used to the tours, the games, representing your country, making the appearances that you do because you are an All Black. When that suddenly stops, when you haven't had time to prepare for the transition, it's difficult. It took me a bit of time to get reorganised and refocused, to set some new goals and get going again.

For a part of the World Cup I went overseas. I needed a holiday and thought it best to get away. I can recall sitting on a very small plane between islands in Rarotonga and an obviously rugby-mad pilot switched on the final commentary over the intercom, so I heard the game anyway!

Jock Hobbs follows the play against Argentina, 1985.

World Cup – The Quinn Tapes

Andy Dalton
was captain of the New Zealand team for the 1987 World Cup, but through injury was unable to take the field.

Probably 1987 was just a year too long for me. But I was determined not to go out on a crook note and 1985 and '86 were dark patches. I was thrilled after the trial at Whangarei to be given the opportunity to lead the team. Then I got just a little too keen to catch JK [John Kirwan] in a game of touch and twinged my hamstring. I tried to play the first game when I should have sat it out. I pushed the hamstring too hard and damaged it quite badly and that ruled me out, though I did get named in the reserves for the last few games. It was still a thrill to be involved with the side and I'd like to think I had a part to play in its success.

In the final, old Fitzy [Sean Fitzpatrick, who replaced Dalton as hooker in the test side] pulled a couple of injuries on me. I'll never forgive him for that because I got excited that I was going to get a run before the end. I should have known better – there was no way he was going to do that, and I wouldn't have either in his position.

When Kirky [David Kirk] was named as captain, there was still some underlying feeling regarding the Cavaliers tour. I did my best to break that down. Kirky was relatively inexperienced at that level. He struggled earlier on, but grew as the series went on. I'd like to think I played a supporting role.

After the final, there was a feeling that I had missed an opportunity, which was frustrating. I was feeling sorry for myself, though quite happy. I intended sitting it out in the changing room, but Brian Lochore took me out the front. Then David pulled me over, which was quite a gesture. It was an emotional time.

David Kirk
was on-field captain during the 1987 World Cup.

I just wanted to be part of the World Cup team in 1987. I had no particular wish to be the captain. There were a lot of Aucklanders in the squad, and I knew what they could do. I was a fairly senior player by then and was there to make a major leadership contribution. Andy [Dalton] got injured in the first training run and was always dodgy after that. We thought he'd come right, but he didn't train and finally he came in to try out his hamstring when we were at the Pukekohe Basin.

He went for a few minutes of the team run, then just stood and pulled up and said he couldn't do it. Brian Lochore was right there and just said to me, "You're captaining the team on Saturday." It was as simple as that. It was an obvious decision because I was leading the backs, as it were. From then on it really was full steam ahead.

Gary Whetton
All Black lock from 1981-91.

It was a step into the unknown. Was it going to be a success? Was it going to capture the public's imagination? There was a clean-out of the old brigade in 1986 after the Cavaliers tour. There were new selectors and a new, young team. It was a very exciting time. We were training and being coached a different way. We had exciting young players. And we were playing the game differently. We went from an All Black team that used to win by three or six points, with a few kicks here and there, to a team winning by thirty or forty points, trouncing teams. We really didn't know why, but we were just enjoying it.

Legends of the All Blacks

Captain Kirk's Rugby Starship

Wayne Shelford
All Black No 8 from 1985-90.

Going into the 1987 World Cup, we were just an ordinary side. We'd lost a series and drawn one and were struggling along. But a young brigade of All Blacks came in, players like myself, McDowell, Alan Whetton, and a few others, and we resolved to make it a bloody good All Black side. Then after the team was named, it was all laid out in black and white by Brian Lochore, John Hart and Alex Wyllie, and we knuckled down and did the work. Our game was based on being fit and fast and we caught the rest of the world wanting because of the speed we played the game.

David Kirk

No-one will forget John Kirwan's try against Italy. I caught the kick-off and passed it to Foxy, who kicked it out up at halfway. We won the lineout and knew we were going to run. A nice long pass went to Kirwan, who took it running, a long way out. Normally he would have been much closer. He just ran and ran and kept on running. I didn't really follow him because I simply thought, "He's going to do it." I felt as if support wasn't needed, though I notice from the television replay that Michael Jones was right there, though. It was an extraordinary try. I was absolutely gob-smacked.

•

I remember a beautiful moment in the game against Fiji. From a lineout we moved the ball to midfield where Joe Stanley took the ball straight and looked inside on his hip, and there was Michael Jones at full speed, like a gazelle. He took the ball and accelerated through the gap and had so much speed he totally outran the cover. Craig Green, who was running straight up the wing ran him into position with the fullback and put away the try in the corner. That was a brilliant try in its cleanness and its athleticism.

•

Right at the end of the game against Argentina, they had a penalty on about the halfway line and Hugo Porta took the ball and kicked a very high up-and-under. I happened to be in the wrong place at the wrong time. It should have been a No 8 catching it. But anyway the ball came down right on the 22 and I was underneath it waiting for it. The Argentinian openside flanker made

John Kirwan on his way to glory against Italy in the World Cup opener.

World Cup – The Quinn Tapes

up his mind that he was going to arrive the same time as the ball, but he got his calculation wrong and arrived just before the ball. He hit me very high and basically knocked me out for a few seconds. We got the penalty, of course, and I had just enough wits about me to tell Grant Fox to kick it out. I wanted the game to end; I didn't want Foxy to tap it and run because I would have had to wobble after him. Anyway Gary Whetton and John Drake did me a great favour by ushering me into the changing rooms where the door was shut. I recovered and said I was okay, and I was. But under today's rules – and the rules of the day, too – if it had been known that I'd been knocked unconscious, I would have been stood down for three weeks.

David Kirk

The Scotland quarter-final worried me. I was more stressed about losing before the Scotland game than either the semi-final or final. Scotland had played very well when they'd drawn with France, and were the best of the Home Nations teams. Losing in the quarter-finals would have been a total failure and we had to win. We were always ahead, mainly through Grant Fox penalties, but couldn't quite break them for a long time.

Gary Whetton

The feeling for the final was hugely different to what it had been in my test debut at Eden Park in 1981 [against the Springboks]. We were in the same hotel, but there were no police. It was a very relaxed, happy team. The public had taken to us and the encouragement we had was unbelievable. Faxes, posters from schools, telegrams, phone calls.

Wayne Shelford

I remember two tries in the final and thinking, "We've got this baby." It was a tough game of football. The French aren't easy to play and they'd beaten us in the previous test. We wanted France in the final. We watched France play Australia in the semi-final and when Blanco scored that try in the last minute to put them in the final, we thought, "Yes! Payback time!"

David Kirk

We were very tense before the final. It was a historic moment. We 15 players alone in all of rugby history had the opportunity to be the best in the world. We had one opportunity in our lives to be world champions. Also, in the context of the whole All Black tradition and history and in the context of the 26 players in the squad, only 15 of whom could take the field, there was this sense of wanting to prove ourselves for our country. It was: don't wake up tomorrow morning having missed this opportunity. You're definitely good enough, this team is good enough, we've played well enough, don't let it slip.

Andy Dalton made a contribution, and Wayne Shelford and a lot of players did [in the dressing-room before the game]. It was a test match to be won. We got a bonus with Michael Jones' try and Grant Fox's sliced dropped goal. The first half was quite a slow one, and I wasn't happy at halftime. At the break I talked about not only the joy of winning, but about the grind of winning test matches. It was about hard work and cutting down errors, about playing for position and taking opportunities by being on attack. I said that as we ground them down the opportunities would emerge. I remember distinctly saying, "Work, work, work. That's what we have to do in the second half. If we work and do the basics, we're going to be world champions."

Just into the second half, I conceded a penalty which would have got them back to 12-9 if they'd kicked it, and they were playing with a slight breeze. It was the only ▶

Legends of the All Blacks

Captain Kirk's Rugby Starship

French skipper Daniel Dubroca tries to contain Michael Jones in the '87 World Cup final.

moment of the final where I thought, "This could be close; it could go down to the wire." But they missed the kick and we went back down on attack, kicked a couple of penalties and then came my try. That was the moment, the feeling that we were going to be champions. For me it's not the final whistle I remember, it's the moment when we scored the try and knew we'd done it. The rest – John Kirwan's try – was the icing.

The feeling afterwards was of satisfaction. There was joy we'd won, but it was the sense of satisfaction at proving we were as good as we knew we were, that we were the best, we hadn't let ourselves down. It was the sense that the burden had been lifted, because there was a real rising expectation in New Zealand that we would win. We had to win, and had lots of support. So it was "Whew! we didn't let anyone down." I was really looking forward to getting off the field and walking up the stairs and completing the circle, as it were. There was a great sense of anticipation about actually getting our hands on the cup, getting our medals and facing the crowd.

KQ: And you made the gesture to call in Andy Dalton to share the moment.

That was totally on the spur of the moment. Andy

World Cup – The Quinn Tapes

had been very humble and had made a significant contribution to the success of that team. I looked around and saw him again humbly shrinking away from the team because I think he felt strongly that as he hadn't been able to play, he hadn't really been as much a part of the team as he would have wanted to be. But I knew his contribution in helping prepare the team throughout was significant and I remember grabbing his jacket and pulling him over. He was so modest, he looked as if he didn't want to be there, but I wanted to publicly express the team's appreciation for his contribution.

Kirk: 'I wanted to express the team's appreciation for his (Dalton) contribution.'

I felt very much we had won not only for the current squad, but for all those other All Blacks who would have loved to have been world champions. They could play in the best team that won the test series against the other best teams in the world, but they could never say, "We've won the World Cup. We're world champions." That was a privilege that we got and were very grateful for.

Wayne Shelford

In 1991 and 1995, the All Black teams to the World Cup had more preparation and more money behind them than we did in 1987, yet we were the team that pulled it off. I don't think our personnel was any better, but we did it, and we did it with panache and integrity.

David Kirk

I enjoyed the recognition side of that year. It got a bit overwhelming towards the end, to be honest. I was looking forward to leaving New Zealand at the end of 1987 to study overseas. I don't really understand what Danyon Loader has gone through as an athlete, but I can sense in him his desire to get away from it all, and I think I had some of that towards the end. But it would be wrong if I said I didn't enjoy the exposure and the success.

Brian Lochore

was the New Zealand coach for the 1987 World Cup.

Coaching the All Blacks to win the 1987 World Cup was a great thrill. It was the first World Cup and none of us had gone down that road before. No international player had played six internationals in a month, so a lot of planning went into it. I was ably assisted by John Hart and Alex Wyllie and we really got on well together. We all wanted to play the same style and selected the players to do it.

The thrill of winning wasn't as great for me as captaining New Zealand to a test series victory, or even just playing, because you can't get out on the field and do it yourself. It was more satisfying than thrilling. We picked on form, the players performed to their potential and in the end we were better prepared than any other team there.

Legends of the All Blacks

Our Cup Runneth Out

1991
(October 3–November 2)

Pool matches
- v England   won 18-12   London
- v USA   won 46-6   Gloucester
- v Italy   won 31-21   Leicester

Quarter-final
- v Canada   won 29-13   Lille

Semi-final
- v Australia   lost 6-16   Dublin

Third place play-off
- v Scotland   won 13-6   Cardiff

Alex Wyllie
was co-coach of the New Zealand team for the 1991 World Cup.

You need to look at the background to our disappointing semi-final loss to Australia. The New Zealand Rugby Union took it upon themselves to bring in two coaches of equal standing. It didn't work. That was obvious. I thought that at the end I could still turn around and say, "Well, the forwards played pretty well that day. They won the ball. We attacked enough. We didn't finish off." One of the problems with the co-coach situation is that it becomes a matter of who has the right to say what he wants. When you have one guy in charge, you know what you're dealing with. But with co-coaches the whole business is confused.

It was forced upon me. But it was only one of many issues. No-one's ever answered the question of why Mike Brewer had to go and have a medical. He was told not to worry about taking the special mould that he had and then he was told he had to do some jumping exercises. He said, "Look, if I do that, I'm going to blow it." Now I know that some other players had their ankles strapped and everything else as well, on every training run. We went to the next World Cup when some of the players couldn't even play the first game. Why was Mike Brewer made to stay behind and yet he turned around and played two and a half of the three NPC games that followed? To me, Mike Brewer was forced out. He was put through a medical he should not have had. It was the first time that we hadn't had the coaches and management along. It was done behind our backs. Then Mike comes back and says, "I'm sorry, I failed the medical." I said, "What do you mean failed?"

I think Eddie Tonks [Rugby Union chairman] had a lot to do with it, but he will deny it. We rang him up and he just said straight out that if Mike had failed the test he couldn't go. Yet Mike Brewer played from then to the end of the season without problems. It was obvious that Michael Jones wasn't going to be able to play in a couple of games because they were on a Sunday. If Mike was needed for only one thing, it was to play in those two games. And the fact was he was a great leader, great with the team, great in organisation… but he wasn't wanted.

KQ: Did the addition of John Hart as co-coach help or hinder New Zealand at the World Cup in 1991?

You could ask the players, but a lot of them have said to me that it split the team. And John Sturgeon [the team manager] has been on record as saying that we – myself and John Sturgeon – should have carried on. I'll never forget one day during the World Cup when I walked into the team room and one player said, "Hey, have a look down the street here to see what's going on." There was a group of players going away with a certain part of the management to have their own meal and it left these other guys and me. I didn't know what was happening either. I wouldn't say it was a north-south split exactly. It might have been northern, but it was pretty obvious what was happening.

KQ: What sort of stress were you under?

Well, what it did was undermine me. No-one can operate properly when they're being undermined. But it was coming from different angles, so obviously it told

World Cup – The Quinn Tapes

Keith Quinn interviews John Hart and Alex Wyllie during the ill-fated '91 World Cup campaign.

on me. It also didn't help some of the players because they didn't know where they stood – whether it was this direction or that direction.

It hurt me. When Mike Brewer was ruled out, I went to Sturgeon. I said, "Forget me. I'm out. I'm finished." He said, "Well, if you do that, I'll go too." I said, "There's no need for you to go." Sturgeon told me not to quit. He said I'd be letting down the players. So I thought about it that night and decided to carry on for the sake of the team, because of what it would do and the pressure it would probably put on certain players when they were over at the World Cup. Looking back now, it might have been better the other way around. It might have been better if I'd pulled out. At least there'd have been one controller going in one direction.

Eddie Tonks
was chairman of the New Zealand Rugby Union in 1991.

KQ: Why was the decision made to appoint a co-coach for the 1991 World Cup?

There had been some unrest from the team with the coaching set up. Grizz didn't get on with a lot of the players at that time. There were certain issues the players committee took exception to – certain behavioural situations that they didn't like and had expressed concern to the council, and that we felt we should do something about. But it was very late in the day from the World Cup point of view, and we didn't want to take a major decision, like getting rid of someone, because that would have been worse for us.

It wasn't the most platonic relationship between Harty and Grizz and in hindsight I know dashed well that the co-coach set-up didn't work. They actually had almost identical points of view, but there was a temperament difference. That's what caused the conflict. But at the time we thought it was in the best interests of the All Blacks. I was certainly one of the people behind the decision. I was the chairman and had to lead the way. But I wasn't the only decision-maker. It was a decision of council, after discussion with Alex, I might add. ▶

Legends of the All Blacks

Our Cup Runneth Out

As a group of selectors, with Lane Penn included, there was no problem. It was the coaching aspect, off the field, that caused concern. Maybe it would have been wiser to do what they do now, with the chief coach, whether it was Alex or John, picking his own people to work with him.

John Hart
was appointed co-coach of the All Blacks for the 1991 World Cup.

The All Blacks didn't have a tremendously successful year in 1991 and the New Zealand union decided that they wanted me to go to the World Cup with Alex as an assistant. I didn't think that would work and said that if I was going to go, I had to have some authority, or I wouldn't be able to do anything. That's when they came up with the co-coaching concept. It wasn't in Alex's interest or mine and I don't think it worked. It wasn't a meeting of minds.

The union were doing their best to turn the boat around, but the boat was taking in water at the time and it was too late. I should not have agreed to go. It was the wrong decision for the team, and certainly for my future.

It was ludicrous. Sharing authority was never going to work, and it made things difficult for the players and the coaches. I didn't enjoy it. It was my loneliest time in rugby and I couldn't wait to get home.

Alex didn't really want me there and I don't blame him. Having said that, I think Alex had struggled in 1991. Maybe today I understand more why. The pressures coaching All Black sides are immense. The public expectation is so great. It's a difficult role and he handled some of it well and some of it not so well. You could say the same of me.

I've always had a soft spot for Alex Wyllie. It's a disappointment to me that we never had a relationship. Other people, with their own agendas, have made it more difficult than Alex and I have. I took Alex for what he was: a genuine rugby man, a great performer, a very good coach in his day. We got on well in the lead-up to the 1987 World Cup. That worked really well.

KQ: Alex Wyllie is very critical of Eddie Tonks' role in the matter.

Eddie was concerned about the way the All Blacks were going. He was chairman of the Rugby Union and it was his responsibility to take action. It's fair to say Eddie and Alex didn't really get on, but Eddie was doing what he was thought was right at the time.

Gary Whetton
All Black captain at the 1991 World Cup.

We were struggling. We weren't a happy team. We'd had an arduous tour of Argentina that we didn't need, then lost the first test in Australia. Questions were being asked of the management, the players, the captain. What's needed here? Where are we? John Hart was brought in before the second test against Australia, which we won 6-3. I suppose that cemented John's position to go to the World Cup. But if left me as the captain in two camps, because while there's always been respect for John Hart and Alex Wyllie, they were two different people and different leaders. So that made it hard.

I'd had a lot to do with both of them. I knew John from the early days. He was a friend. Alex had been the coach the last three or four years and I knew him very well. Within the team they didn't socialise a lot together. So I had to be careful if I was socialising with one and not the other.

We got things going. There were a lot of differences of opinion as regards selections, and how to play it. It wasn't easy being in the middle. Sometimes when we wanted to get certain opinions across from one to the other, it might have been done through me so it wasn't coming directly. It wasn't done in front of the team, which was very good, but they were two direct, opinionated guys. They were great coaches, but working together wasn't the best way of doing it.

World Cup – The Quinn Tapes

Alex Wyllie

Perhaps the reason we didn't win the World Cup in 1991 was the same as why Australia didn't do any good in 1995. Maybe we should have brought through more players so they would be ready for 1991. But there was a bit of a split in the camp in the end – there'd been doubt put in there.

If we go back to the French tour [in 1990], things were said during that tour about the way we were playing, and they were totally wrong. I'd said before we went on that tour that I was going to give everyone the opportunity to play in the early games, and we lost a couple. But in the end it's the tests that count, and we were experimenting with some players. Then we got to the tests and played as well against the French as we ever had. We completely dominated them in the first test and won well. I didn't think due credit was given to the team or the management. There was some behind-the-scenes work going on about certain things, and that's come out since. It was a shame. The game didn't need that sort of carrying on. ▶

Grant Fox

was the New Zealand first five-eighth at the 1991 World Cup.

We went there in 1991 with high hopes of defending the title we'd won four years earlier, so it was a huge disappointment. We can talk about John and Alex not being compatible, but the bottom line is that we were the guys who ran onto the field and we didn't do the job. Some of the more established players hadn't done as much work as they should have and were mentally struggling a bit. Perhaps we thought that the same old game plan that had been successful for a long period would get us through. It's a natural human instinct to look around for peripheral factors to blame, but when you're dispassionate about it you have to realise it was we players who didn't perform. The preparation that the Australians in particular had put into it was like what we'd done in 1987 and they got a jump on everybody. Their off game was against Ireland, but they were good enough to get through that.

John Hart does the talking at the press conference following New Zealand's semi-final exit. Also pictured are manager John Sturgeon (left), Alex Wyllie and captain Gary Whetton.

Legends of the All Blacks

Our Cup Runneth Out

John Eales
was a member of the 1991 Australian World Cup team.

A lot of the great local support for us came from the fact that we had played Ireland in Dublin the week before and had won a very close tussle. A lot of Irish people were saying that because we beat Ireland by one point in the quarter-final, that if we went on to win the World Cup, they could rightly claim that they came second in the World Cup. It's typically Irish logic, but it was great for us to have that support. It was very noticeable when we played the All Blacks.

David Campese
Australian winger and star of the 1991 World Cup.

Coming to Dublin, it was obvious we were playing pretty well and the All Blacks were having a few problems. We knew the way the All Blacks played and that they'd come out at a hundred miles an hour. But we countered that with a try when I ran the blind on the angle and had JK [John Kirwan] in two minds because there were two players outside me. Bob Dwyer had always told me to run straight, but I got the ball, saw JK coming at me and ran where I thought it would be the best angle. I had the pace on the angle and that's hard to defend against. Their defenders – JK, Sean Fitzpatrick, Foxy, Gary Whetton – they were running backwards and that made it look easy. But it was really more instinctive. That try, and later on the overhead pass to Tim Horan for another try – they helped.

Bob Dwyer
Wallaby coach at the 1991 World Cup.

I thought one of the great errors New Zealand made was that all they did was look to John Kirwan to win the game for them. They didn't look for opportunities to set up Kirwan, so we were able to defend against him easily. Generally speaking, we had three defenders every time JK got the ball. If they'd worked a bit harder to give him a one-on-one opportunity… well, he was a pretty fair player himself.

Nick Farr-Jones
Wallaby captain at the 1991 World Cup.

A major reason why we won the World Cup semi-final was our 6-3 defeat by the All Blacks in Auckland a couple of months earlier. We were so annoyed at having lost when we were the better team. I remember saying to the guys after Auckland that they had to remember the despair and the disappointment of that day and carry it through to the World Cup. The resolve that built in the Australian team before the World Cup semi-final was unbelievable. I'd never been in a team that prepared and focused for a match like we did.

We played mistake-free rugby in the first half, then there were a couple of fantastic tries, with Campo breaking all the rules and no-one putting a hand on him. I was really proud to be the Aussie captain that day because the guys were magnificent. But really, it all went back to that loss in Auckland.

Gary Whetton

KQ: Why did New Zealand go out in the World Cup semi-finals?

There were lots of factors. We had a lot of injury problems. We didn't play well in certain games. The forwards played very well against the Australians when we got knocked out, but we had a lot of problems in the backline. Foxy had a major injury and in hindsight

World Cup – The Quinn Tapes

A sign of things to come – David Campese works some magic on John Kirwan during the second test of the 1991 Bledisloe Cup series in Auckland. The Wallabies lost this match, but reversed the result in the one that counted at Dublin.

perhaps he shouldn't have played. We had players out of position at fullback. The selections could have been a little different.

Maybe the lack of unity in selectors and management did reflect on the team. It wasn't the same cohesive team as in years gone by. But that happens when things aren't going well and you start to lose.

Sean Fitzpatrick
played in the first three World Cups.

We had the players to win in 1991, but our attitude was wrong. Maybe as world champions we thought we were better than we were. If the players had done the mental and physical work, we were by far the best team there. The disharmony between Alex Wyllie and John Hart has been well-documented, but there were a lot of other factors that caused problems.

John Hart

We hadn't played well even against the United States and Italy. Still, we could have beaten Australia if we'd taken the opportunities. The team was shattered afterwards. There was a lot of disappointment, a lot of tears. But Australia deserved to win on the day, and to win the World Cup.

Legends of the All Blacks

Our Cup Runneth Out

Grant Fox

was the All Black first five-eighth and a senior member of the team during the 1991 World Cup.

I hope New Zealand never tries a co-coaching system again, as we had at the 1991 World Cup. It didn't work then because of the different personalities of Alex Wyllie and John Hart. I feel you need to have a head coach and an assistant. You can't have co-responsibility. It was a mistake putting John and Alex together.

The decision the New Zealand Rugby Union needed to make was to tell Grizz they were supporting him and were going with him, or that they were sacking him and putting in John. Putting in the two together was a halfway house, a cop-out. If we'd had one or the other, we might have been in better shape.

Grant Fox

Alex Wyllie

Before the third place play-off in 1991, I got the team together and told them we mustn't let ourselves down. I thought we played damn well and that the team showed real guts that day. Afterwards a lot of the players stayed behind in Britain – we came back home in dribs and drabs, and that's probably a bit like the way the team had been during the whole World Cup.

•

In the end, when you look at the 1991 World Cup, we got beaten only once. England, who actually made the final, were beaten twice.

Bob Dwyer

A year before the World Cup final, I rang Nick Farr-Jones and some of the players and told them to get a bottle of champagne out and have a drink. I said that if we did things right twelve months from the day, we might just go out and win the World Cup.

World Cup – The Quinn Tapes

THE POISONED CHALICE?

1995
(May 27–June 24)

Pool matches
- v Ireland — won 43-19 — Johannesburg
- v Wales — won 34-9 — Johannesburg
- v Japan — won 145-17 — Bloemfontein

Quarter-final
- v Scotland — won 48-30 — Pretoria

Semi-final
- v England — won 45-29 — Cape Town

Final
- v South Africa — lost 12-15 — Johannesburg

Ian McIntosh
coached the 1994 Springbok team to New Zealand.

I thought 1994 was the start of a great All Black side. They beat us in the series in New Zealand and they went to the World Cup the next year and played the best rugby there. However, they made the same mistake in the final of the World Cup that they had against us in 1994. They played a little too deep and we were able to cut off their backs. The All Black forwards took it up really well and chucked it back so deep to their backs that it gave us the chance to cut them off. That's what stopped us from getting beaten by more in 1994, and that's one thing that enabled South Africa to win the World Cup final.

Francois Pienaar
captained the 1994 Springbok team to New Zealand and then led South Africa through the 1995 World Cup campaign.

We came away from the 1994 tour with a lot of experience and confident [South Africa lost the first two tests against New Zealand and drew the third].

Laurie Mains
coached the New Zealand team at the 1995 World Cup.

KQ: Did the style of rugby you played through the 1995 World Cup have its origins in the exciting comeback the All Blacks made in the second half of the final test against Australia in 1994?

No, though many people have alluded to that. It's true that the players did open up the ball a lot more in that second half and give the outsides more opportunity and turned it over quickly at second phase, almost as if they were constipated in the first half. That had been caused by officious refereeing and the fact that we had really been set back on our rockers in the first minute [when Jason Little scored a try].

Sean Fitzpatrick
captained New Zealand at the 1995 World Cup.

In hindsight, our second half performance in the third test against Australia in 1994 was the turning point for the team, my captaincy and for Laurie. We were 18 points down at halftime. Nothing was really said. We just said we needed to go out there and enjoy ourselves. That was very foreign to the All Blacks because we weren't meant to enjoy ourselves; ▶

Legends of the All Blacks

The Poisoned Chalice?

we were meant to win. So in the second half we enjoyed ourselves and played a great brand of rugby. Maybe we could have won it but for a George Gregan tackle on Jeff Wilson. We took a lot from the game into 1995.

It was very unlike Laurie to be so passionate and let the guys do what they were best at, which was playing footy. Early in his All Black coaching career he was very much a dictatorial coach, but he finally decided that day to let the players do what they thought was best. When we got down to planning for the World Cup, what we had achieved in that second half became the starting point for us to focus on as a game plan for 1995. It was the blueprint of what we were going to take forward into the World Cup.

We had a camp at Queenstown at the end of 1994 and set a few targets there. Over summer we trained as hard as we'd ever trained and worked hard on turning over a quick ball. We had a whole day on rucks in terms of getting quick ball to let the backs go.

Then some key players came into the picture – Kronfeld, Mehrtens, Lomu. Before the World Cup we played Canada at Eden Park and that was the start of something pretty special. We proved we were capable of putting away teams by big scores.

Laurie Mains

At the end of our last training camp, Brian Lochore and I had a talk to Jonah and said that if we were selecting two trials teams to play for World Cup places, we couldn't put him in because he wouldn't be fit enough to play the style of rugby we wanted. Jonah had trouble training on his own and Sean Fitzpatrick came

Laurie Mains runs one of his famous pre-World Cup training runs.

to me and said that he, Olo Brown and Eric Rush would be prepared to alternate and do extra training with Jonah. Their normal training times were six in the morning, but they were prepared at lunchtimes to alternate and go running with him. That's what the All Black culture is all about. Jonah was going to be one of the factors that gave us the edge at the World Cup if we could get what we wanted because the style of game we were developing was going to ideally suit him.

So slowly but surely we got Jonah fitter. By the time of the North-South game in Dunedin he was fair firing. Jonah was called late to join us for the Harlequins game at Hamilton as part of our preparations. Eric Rush had an injury and had to cry off, and Jonah arrived in Hamilton a little bit down because he'd only been with what was effectively the B team to play Canada. I walked from the motel to the training ground with Jonah and said to him, "Now listen, Jonah, you've got to get in there and make your presence felt. Make these guys respect you. Take it to them. Don't hold anything back. Get stuck into them." Well, we were doing an exercise where we had four forwards out holding tackle bags and players were running into them feeding the ball to another player coming back diagonally. I'll never forget Jonah hitting Paul Henderson like a ton of bricks. Paul left the ground, did a couple of somersaults backwards and naturally everybody just erupted. Ten minutes later we were doing another move and had Richard Loe holding the bags and Jonah coming in from the blindside wing. He hit Richard Loe and lifted his feet half a metre off the ground. He was really coming into himself.

At the World Cup, Jonah was impressive against Wales and Ireland, very impressive against Scotland and sensational against England. We were utilising his strengths, giving him the space to move in and he was using it.

Jonah Lomu
was the outstanding player at the 1995 World Cup.

When I arrived in South Africa, no-one had a clue who I was, which was really good. I enjoyed that. It wasn't until we hit the quarter-finals and semi-finals that things started to move. In the end I couldn't even go shopping. That's what my life has been since. The World Cup was the turning point in my life.

Sean Fitzpatrick

We went to South Africa rated about No 5 in the world, and I was quite happy about that. But I was quietly confident that we had a team capable of getting through and winning it. At training people were in awe of us and the style of rugby we were trying to play, that quick ruck ball, hitting rucks in numbers, having locks standing in the backline running like outsides.

I remember at the meeting we had before we played Ireland at Ellis Park, asking Andrew Mehrtens what he wanted out of the tournament and he said he just wanted to have a good time. That's the theme we took into it, that we enjoyed everything we did, training and playing.

Gavin Hastings
Scotland's captain at the 1995 World Cup.

Jonah Lomu got the ball in the opening minute and he ran through Craig Joiner, then my brother Scott had a shot at him. Then I lined him up and he trampled all over me and two seconds later he touched down. I thought, "My God, we haven't managed to sort him out at all."

Sean Fitzpatrick

We were very concerned about the size of the England pack [for the semi-final] and thought they would definitely nullify us at lineout time. But we thought that if we sped up the game, maybe with some quick lineouts, and put pressure on them, especially at scrum time, that would help. They'd been a bit of a bogey team for us and it was funny playing at Cape Town, which is very much an English-based sort of city. They had a huge amount of support. We had real doubts about whether we'd be good enough to beat them. They were Five Nations champions.

So we decided to play a very expansive game, get Jonah involved early. We'd said before the game that if we won the toss we'd definitely take the kick-off no matter which way the wind was blowing and we'd call "Mahurangi", the call for Jonah out left. I won the toss and Will Carling asked me what I was going to do. I said I'd tell him when we got out there, though I knew perfectly well what we were going to do. So back in the changing room we said to Jonah we'd won the ▶

Legends of the All Blacks

The Poisoned Chalice?

Jonah Lomu against England, 1995 – has there ever been a greater individual performance in test rugby?

World Cup – The Quinn Tapes

Will Carling
England's captain at the 1995 World Cup.

We watched Lomu on video and analysed him. We thought, "Yeah, he's a big guy, he's fast," and everything else, but we felt we could deal with him. When I saw him on the pitch, it was completely different. I said he was a freak, and I meant it as a compliment. I've never seen anything like him in rugby. He was awesome during the World Cup. His fitness, his power – the way he ran over Mike Catt and all sorts of people. They scored three tries in about ten minutes in the semi-final and it was the most incredible start to a game I've ever experienced because of the pace and power with which they played. They were on fire; after twenty minutes the game was over.

Keith Quinn interviews Will Carling for the television series.

toss and would be kicking off. He was sort of bouncing his head all over with the headphones on. I'm still not sure whether he got the message, but I can remember standing in that dressing room thinking that this team was one I wanted to be involved in because it had the best players in the world. For the first time since I'd been All Black captain, I felt totally confident we had a team capable of beating the opposition convincingly. I knew we were going to have a good game.

It turned out to be amazing. Everything just gelled so well; the lineouts went well, every pass seemed to stick, Zinny had that drop kick. It was one of those games when everything went off. Jonah put on a really special performance to score four tries. It was a game where he was given space and people hadn't quite realised his potential. He's impossible to stop when he's got ten yards on you.

I spoke to Will after the game. We thought he had played quite well and scored a couple of tries. But he was just in awe. He said no team in the world would ever have beaten the All Blacks that day and maybe he was right, especially in that first half. I didn't think England were particularly unhappy – they realised they were beaten by a better team and that they really hadn't played all that badly.

Laurie Mains

Jonah Lomu was sensational against England. Right from the start when he ran over the top of Mike Catt and he stepped out of Tony Underwood's tackle. Underwood had made a fatal mistake before that game. Earlier in the tournament, when Jonah had done so ▶

Legends of the All Blacks

The Poisoned Chalice?

well against Ireland and Wales, he'd commented to the paper that Jonah hadn't played anybody yet. I reminded Jonah of this a couple of times in the build-up to the game. Jonah just opened up on them. His footwork, his pace, his power, were just sensational.

Jonah Lomu

Before the England game, the guys were all telling me not to hold anything back, to get out there and have a go. They said, "It doesn't matter where you get the ball, just have a go and we'll follow you." I was glad I had Frank [Bunce] inside me. He kept saying to me, "Catch the ball and run, that's all you have to do. Catch the ball and run," and that's what I did. I wanted to play for a full eighty minutes and I did.

Francois Pienaar

We were shocked at the way New Zealand demolished England. One guy stood out. All week after that there was talk about Jonah Lomu – how to stop him, because he had run over the Irish, the Scots and the English. We had played the bulk of the All Blacks in 1994, but he was the unknown factor.

Kitch [Christie, the Springbok coach] came up with a totally different game plan for the final. It left us a bit unsettled and we had to restructure it before the game. I sat the side down on the Thursday night and went through the whole World Cup, what it meant to South Africa, and what we'd learned in New Zealand in 1994.

We knew we were a much better side than we had been the year before, more cohesive, more experienced. The one thing that came out of the meeting was that we needed to be street-wise in the final. We came up with a defensive strategy for Lomu. We stuck James Small right out wide on the wing, to force Lomu to come back inside where the cross-defence could take care of him.

We knew the game was going to be close, so our focus was on discipline, controlled aggression and not to get too overawed by this big fellow on the wing who'd been so phenomenal in the World Cup.

Sean Fitzpatrick

I was always confident we could beat the Springboks in the World Cup final. But when I look back on it now, there were some things we should have done differently. We got a bit caught up in the hype of the World Cup. Being based where we were made it difficult for the guys in terms of the atmosphere and the pressure they were under. We were in Sandton and it was sheer pressure. At the start of the tournament, Louis Luyt told me all he wanted was for the All Blacks to play the Springboks in the final and for the next five weeks they looked after us like kings. But in the last week it was very much a them and us situation. We should have moved out of the city and gone to a game reserve and regrouped and refocused for the last week.

The Lomu factor had an effect, too. The attention Jonah was getting and the effect on the team. It added to the pressure.

KQ: Could you explain the background to the illnesses some of the All Blacks suffered before the final?

We were under extreme pressure all that final week. We'd go into the restaurant of a hotel and you'd have every Afrikaner there telling us how we were going to get beaten on Saturday. It was just getting a bit much, so on the Thursday we decided we'd have lunch in a separate restaurant. Unfortunately that night 16 of the 21 guys [in the team for the final] were sick with food poisoning. I think it was just one of those things, that we ate or drank something that was off. I don't think we were nobbled. Only two of the guys were still quite sick on Saturday, but it did hinder our build-up. Personally I wasn't too badly affected at all. I think the food poisoning had an underlying effect on the team. We couldn't train very well on the Friday.

Laurie Mains

We've heard lots of theories – a bug in the lettuce, English bookmakers... It came down to the tea and coffee being contaminated. The four or five players who didn't get sick came in late and ordered fresh tea and coffee.

Brian Lochore
All Black campaign manager at the 1995 World Cup.

Our team should have won in 1995. They were robbed, not by any particular person, but by circumstances. There's no way you can play to your full potential when two-thirds of the side have had food poisoning the day before. I think they did an absolutely amazing job to front up not only for 80 minutes, but the extra 20 on top. It was the most difficult 48 hours I've spent in rugby, and probably the most disappointing, because for Laurie and the players there was nothing you could do.

We had some difficult decisions when we found we had the problem. We could tell everyone we had food poisoning and the South Africans would have had a psychological advantage over us. Until then they were worried about us and I think that was a good way to have them. Or we could tell no-one and just go out there and give it our best shot. If we then won, we were heroes. If we lost, we were going to sound like whingers. So we chose not to tell anyone, which was actually very difficult.

Colin Meads
All Black manager at the 1995 World Cup.

Colin Meads

Laurie always had a fear that something was going to go wrong. He was that sort of person. But everything went brilliantly until lunchtime Thursday. After that the players started getting crook. Mehrts [Andrew Mehrtens] was first, then there were four or five, then more and more. By Thursday night I was sitting in the house bar waiting to see who'd be next. We had Richard Loe sick in the garden. It was a circus. I went to bed about eleven thirty and by one in the morning I was ill. I collapsed on the floor while trying to ring the doctor. The next day I couldn't even get up to go for a walk around the ground with the players.

We had a short meeting and decided not to tell anyone we were crook. In hindsight, that was the wrong thing. We should have said we had a terrible virus or whatever it was and pulled the pin – postponed the final. I was the manager and felt I did the wrong thing. We shouldn't have played that day. We should at least have let the world know we weren't well, rather than try to hide it.

KQ: Did it make a difference to the result in the final?

One will never know. Some of them were getting over it, but Jeff Wilson and Craig Dowd weren't well at all. I'd like to think it would have made a huge difference, but with everything that happened afterwards – the tragic dinner that night, the trip home, the professionalism issue – it was a traumatic time for New Zealand rugby, and the illness got put on the back-burner. I felt sorry for Laurie. He's come out and "Suzie" [the fictitious name for the woman Mains ▶

Legends of the All Blacks

The Poisoned Chalice?

named in his book] has got the blame for it all. No-one believed him. That's where I feel I let the team down as manager. I should have made it public.

KQ: Do you think the team was deliberately poisoned?

I would like to think not, but one has suspicions. For so many in a fit, healthy bunch to go down. We'd been in the country seven or eight weeks and never had more than one player at a time crook, nothing more than a sore throat. So one has to have doubts about the reasons.

Francois Pienaar

When the All Blacks lined up for their haka, Jonah was opposite James Small. This was going to be the contest – James against Jonah. You could see Jonah was very focused and he moved closer and closer to James as the haka progressed. James stood there, staring him right in the face. Then Kobus Weiss moved right in front of James and said to Jonah, "You've got to run over me before you can get to James." This was the epitome of our team spirit. I had to pull the guys back – the other players were moving forward. I said to them this was just an invitation to take up the challenge, that the battle started in a couple of minutes. You could see neither team would give an inch. That's how the game started and finished – with that same intensity in every player's face.

Laurie Mains

We were a yard slower getting to rucks. We made mistakes in the backs we hadn't made the whole tournament. That could have been because South Africa had a better defence than anything we stuck. I'm not prepared to say that if the players had not been sick we could have won – that is unknown. All I know is that we weren't even close to one hundred per cent when we took the field that day, and that some of the players had to come off and were vomiting on the field, that sort of thing. It's hard to play rugby under those conditions.

KQ: Were the players deliberately poisoned?

We believe there is a strong possibility they were. We know the World Cup committee and the hotel chain ran an investigation and that they identified a lady who worked in the kitchen and was paid to slip something into the tea and coffee. That's as far as it has gone.

KQ: And Suzie?

Yes, well it's a little bit unfortunate that that name was put in there because that wasn't a name given to me. We were just told it was a black woman.

Sean Fitzpatrick

KQ: What are your memories of the final?

It was an amazing feeling that day before the final going to the ground and knowing that within 24 hours there would be a capacity crowd there. Then on the Saturday it was unreal. Even though we lost the final, just to be involved in the whole occasion with the Mandela factor, and the plane flying over and on the way to the ground the sheer intimidation of the South African people whacking our bus – the excitement of the whole occasion. I remember arriving at the ground and our bus was getting bashed. In the distance we could see the Australian test team waiting to clap us as we got off the bus, wishing us the best of luck, which was quite neat. Then going onto the ground with Mandela walking down wearing Pienaar's jersey. I looked over to the South African team and there were tears coming down their cheeks. The boost they got from Mandela was unbelievable. He's a special sort of

World Cup – The Quinn Tapes

man and what he did for the World Cup profile was amazing. Even though I am a New Zealander, I can see what a big thing it was for South Africa as a nation when they won the World Cup.

The Springboks played like men possessed. In 1995 we were definitely the fittest team at the World Cup, but in the final they worked us out pretty well. They got inside our heads. Maybe in the final we might have done things differently if we'd thought about it more clearly beforehand.

I asked the referee after fulltime, "What's the story after extra time?" And he said we'd win because South Africa had had two players sent off in previous games. I hoped it wouldn't get to that. When they got that drop kick over it was like, "Okay, we can still win this. We just need to get down the other end." Unfortunately we ended up down our end. I can still remember when someone knocked the ball on in a final scrum and the ref said, "Fulltime." I looked at the Springboks and they were waving their arms in the air and I was thinking, "This can't be happening." But it did. Obviously it was very disappointing, but life goes on. It was character-building.

The guys were pretty disappointed afterwards. We thought we definitely had the best team to win the World Cup. Maybe we were a bit young, a bit naive and very disappointed. Some of the guys were very unhappy. We'd come so far and fallen over at the last hurdle, put a huge amount of effort into it and then maybe not played the final the way we knew we could.

Louis Luyt and Nelson Mandela during the playing of the South African national anthem.

In saying that, the South Africans worked us out pretty well and shut us down.

I look back now and think that maybe we weren't the strongest team at the World Cup. We were the fittest, but maybe we weren't strong enough. In 1996, we were the strongest and fittest team, and that showed in our performance. But in the World Cup final, we were exposed by the South Africans in terms of our sheer strength.

Maybe we played the best brand of rugby at the World Cup, and were the best entertainers, but the nice ▶

245

Legends of the All Blacks

The Poisoned Chalice?

guys don't always come first. The Africans shut us down and when they did that we didn't have any other options up our sleeve to say, "Hey, how can we get past these guys?"

Francois Pienaar

We had never thought about going into extra time, didn't even talk about it. I tore my calf muscle just before the whistle for fulltime and played those extra minutes with a torn calf muscle without even realising it. The emotion kept you going. Playing at home was a great advantage, the singing, the emotion. It must have had an effect on the New Zealand side.

KQ: What about Joel Stransky's last drop goal?

Funnily enough, when we played a couple of lead-up games to the World Cup, a mock Springbok side played Western Province. In the last minute Stransky hit a drop goal for us to win the game and the press later criticised us, saying we couldn't even beat Western Province properly without a drop goal. I said at the time that it showed that when the chips were down Joel Stransky could turn a game.

KQ: What are your memories of the post-match presentations?

I was standing there and all the people were singing, flags were waving and I was about to receive the World Cup. I was asked how it felt to receive the cup in front of sixty thousand people. But it wasn't sixty thousand people. In the six weeks of the World Cup, South Africa had changed tremendously – the power of sport. So I said it was forty-three million people, not sixty thousand. It was an instinctive comment, but it summed up the feeling.

Whenever we'd trained or left our hotel, there had been guys running next to the bus shouting, "I'm a Boko Boko" which is the affectionate name the black supporters gave the Springboks. So you couldn't say it was just those select few who played or the privileged

World Cup triumph for Francois Pienaar.

World Cup – The Quinn Tapes

ones who had tickets for the game. It was the whole of South Africa.

John Hart

We didn't win in 1995 because we didn't have a game plan to beat the South Africans. We'd played spectacular rugby in the quarters and semis and tried to play the same style in the final. The South Africans had it worked out. Our game plan was so much about Jonah, but their defence read that. We didn't vary it. We froze a little in the final, believing we had the game to win it without giving the opposition enough credit.

But there was only a bit of paint in it. A drop goal going over and we'd won it and we would be saying what a wonderful World Cup it was. The All Blacks performed really well at the 1995 World Cup. They played some great rugby.

Josh Kronfeld

All Black flanker at the 1995 World Cup.

When the game finished and we'd lost, there was just this pure emptiness. There was nothing left in the tank. You come off the field and you're vacant, can't speak to people. It was a bizarre sort of feeling.

I'm unwilling to subscribe to the feelings that we were nobbled. I can't believe any country would stoop to that level, no matter what the occasion. There are a lot of bugs you can have in food. Everyone gets sick at some time in their career from something they eat. It was just unfortunate that a number of our team got sick and it affected us hugely.

Jonah Lomu

A lot of people hold grudges [about the final]. There's speculation about food poisoning, but to me that's just trying to make an excuse. South Africa won the World Cup fair and square. There was eighty minutes, then extra time, and they won it. We've got another shot at it this year, so let's try to correct it this time.

Louis Luyt

was the South African Rugby Football Union president in 1995. He gave a much-criticised speech at the official dinner after the World Cup final and upset many of the New Zealand team.

They didn't walk out because of my speech. That's nonsense. The Springboks were two hours late for the dinner. I was very unhappy about it and so were the New Zealanders. Colin Meads came to me and nearly punched me. The South Africans were rude. Colin said to me that if they'd won the World Cup, they'd have been there at seven o'clock. I said, "But you didn't win it." He nearly punched me for that. The New Zealanders were fed up with everything by then.

In my speech I tried to make a joke. I said, as Danie Craven used to say, that nobody could call themselves world champions unless they'd beaten South Africa. I said in 1987 if we had been there, we'd have won it. In 1991 Australia won it alright. They beat us comfortably the next year, so they should have known I was joking in my speech. I said that **with** us, not **after** us, we were the best two sides in the world. I stressed that I wanted to bracket them together as the best two sides in the world. I still felt the most complete side at the time was New Zealand.

But by then the New Zealanders were just looking for an excuse to walk out. They were annoyed with having to wait for the World Cup champions. Mike Brewer came and said something to me and I told him he was just a bad loser. He was, because he turned on his heels and walked away. ▶

Legends of the All Blacks

The Poisoned Chalice?

The presentation of the gold watch at the dinner after the World Cup was a stupid thing to do. I didn't give away the gold watch. I was asked to present a watch to the best referee while making my speech. I didn't make the decision and I should have refused to do it, but stupidly agreed to. People thought I gave him the watch. I didn't. The referees decided that I should give it to him.

Sean Fitzpatrick

Too much was made of the dinner incident. That was Louis Luyt having a bit of fun. He was elated; it was everything he ever wanted, for South Africa to be world rugby champions and in their home country. The Springboks were very humble at the dinner. They were great. I think some of our guys were bitterly disappointed at their performance – the way we'd played.

Brian Lochore

We were staggered when we came back to New Zealand with the reception the players got. They deserved it, too. None of the players wanted to go to the Aotea Centre, but people insisted there were a lot of supporters who wanted to show their appreciation, so we talked hard to the players and got them there. I'm pleased they went and I'm sure when they saw the reception that they were pleased too. They realised that they hadn't let down New Zealand. They'd given it their best shot under the circumstances.

Fred Allen
is New Zealand's most successful All Black coach.

If I was preparing an All Black team now, I'd emphasise position, learning not to drop balls, passing correctly, body position, using your eyes and hands. I'd want them to be dedicated for 80 minutes non-stop. If they can't get to that state, move them out and put the next bloke in.

I'd also emphasise the All Black tradition. Look how far it goes back and what it means even to young Islanders. They all want to be All Blacks. It made you so proud to pull on that jersey. You were about ten feet tall. We have a lot of top footballers in New Zealand now. There's so much depth, but it needs fine tuning. Above all, we have to make sure our ball-handling is 100 per cent, because if you give away possession, it's hard to get it back. Rugby's still a very simple game. Players must stick to the basics and do them well.

Sean Fitzpatrick

John [Hart] and the coaching staff need a game plan that's different from any other team. And the plan needs to be known by the whole team. They need to know exactly what they're trying to do. The team needs to be as fit and strong as they've ever been and the players need to be totally committed. They have to forget about all the promotion and media stuff and be totally focused for one year.

Sean Fitzpatrick with John Hart – 'We need to be totally focused.'